Machine Learning with Swift

Artificial Intelligence for iOS

Alexander Sosnovshchenko

BIRMINGHAM - MUMBAI

Machine Learning with Swift

Copyright © 2018 Packt Publishing

All rights reserved. No part of this book may be reproduced, stored in a retrieval system, or transmitted in any form or by any means, without the prior written permission of the publisher, except in the case of brief quotations embedded in critical articles or reviews.

Every effort has been made in the preparation of this book to ensure the accuracy of the information presented. However, the information contained in this book is sold without warranty, either express or implied. Neither the author, nor Packt Publishing or its dealers and distributors, will be held liable for any damages caused or alleged to have been caused directly or indirectly by this book.

Packt Publishing has endeavored to provide trademark information about all of the companies and products mentioned in this book by the appropriate use of capitals. However, Packt Publishing cannot guarantee the accuracy of this information.

Commissioning Editor: Veena Pagare
Acquisition Editor: Vinay Argekar
Content Development Editor: Mayur Pawanikar
Technical Editor: Dinesh Pawar
Copy Editor: Vikrant Phadkay, Safis Editing
Project Coordinator: Nidhi Joshi
Proofreader: Safis Editing
Indexer: Pratik Shirodkar
Graphics: Tania Dutta
Production Coordinator: Arvindkumar Gupta

First published: February 2018

Production reference: 1270218

Published by Packt Publishing Ltd.
Livery Place
35 Livery Street
Birmingham
B3 2PB, UK.

ISBN 978-1-78712-151-5

www.packtpub.com

mapt.io

Mapt is an online digital library that gives you full access to over 5,000 books and videos, as well as industry leading tools to help you plan your personal development and advance your career. For more information, please visit our website.

Why subscribe?

- Spend less time learning and more time coding with practical eBooks and Videos from over 4,000 industry professionals

- Improve your learning with Skill Plans built especially for you

- Get a free eBook or video every month

- Mapt is fully searchable

- Copy and paste, print, and bookmark content

PacktPub.com

Did you know that Packt offers eBook versions of every book published, with PDF and ePub files available? You can upgrade to the eBook version at www.PacktPub.com and as a print book customer, you are entitled to a discount on the eBook copy. Get in touch with us at service@packtpub.com for more details.

At www.PacktPub.com, you can also read a collection of free technical articles, sign up for a range of free newsletters, and receive exclusive discounts and offers on Packt books and eBooks.

Contributors

About the author

Alexander Sosnovshchenko has been working as an iOS software engineer since 2012. Later he made his foray into data science, from the first experiments with mobile machine learning in 2014, to complex deep learning solutions for detecting anomalies in video surveillance data. He lives in Lviv, Ukraine, and has a wife and a daughter.

Thanks to Dmitrii Vorona for moral support, invaluable advice, and code reviews; Nikolay Sosnovshchenko and Oksana Matskovich for the help with pictures of creatures and androids; David Kopec and Matthijs Hollemans for their open source projects; Mr. Jojo Moolayil for his efforts and expertise as a contributing author and reviewer; and my family for being supportive and patient.

About the reviewers

Jojo Moolayil is an artificial intelligence, deep learning, and machine learning professional with over 5 years of experience and is the author of *Smarter Decisions – The Intersection of Internet of Things and Decision Science*. He works with GE and lives in Bengaluru, India. He has also been a technical reviewer about various books in machine learning, deep learning, and business analytics with Apress and Packt.

> *I would like to thank my family, friends, and mentors.*

Cecil Costa, also known as Eduardo Campos in Latin American countries, is a Euro-Brazilian freelance developer who has been learning about computers since he got his first PC in 1990. Learning is his passion, and so is teaching; this is why he works as a trainer. He has organized both on-site and online courses for companies. He is also the author of a few Swift books.

> *I'd like to thank Maximilian Ambergis for creating the delete key; it has been very useful for me!*

Packt is searching for authors like you

If you're interested in becoming an author for Packt, please visit authors.packtpub.com and apply today. We have worked with thousands of developers and tech professionals, just like you, to help them share their insight with the global tech community. You can make a general application, apply for a specific hot topic that we are recruiting an author for, or submit your own idea.

Table of Contents

Preface

Machine learning, as a field, promises to bring increasing intelligence to software by helping us learn and analyze information efficiently and discover certain things that humans cannot. We'll start by developing lasting intuition about the fundamental machine learning concepts in the first section. We'll explore various supervised and unsupervised learning techniques in the second section. Then, the third section, will walk you through deep learning techniques with the help of common real-world cases.

In the last section, we'll dive into hardcore topics such as model compression and GPU acceleration, and provide some recommendations to avoid common mistakes during machine learning application development. By the end of the book, you'll be able to develop intelligent applications written in Swift that can learn for themselves.

Who this book is for

This book is for iOS developers who wish to create intelligent iOS applications, and data science professionals who are interested in performing machine learning using Swift. Familiarity with some basic Swift programming is all you need to get started with this book.

What this book covers

Chapter 1, *Getting Started with Machine Learning*, teaches the main concepts of machine learning.

Chapter 2, *Classification – Decision Tree Learning*, builds our first machine learning application.

Chapter 3, *K-Nearest Neighbors Classifier*, continues exploring classification algorithms, and we learn about instance-based learning algorithms.

Chapter 4, *K-Means Clustering*, continues with instance-based algorithms, this time focusing on an unsupervised clustering task.

Chapter 5, *Association Rule Learning*, explores unsupervised learning more deeply.

Chapter 6, *Linear Regression and Gradient Descent*, returns to supervised learning, but this time we switch our attention from non-parametric models, such as KNN and k-means, to parametric linear models.

Chapter 7, *Linear Classifier and Logistic Regression*, continues by building different, more complex models on top of linear regression: polynomial regression, regularized regression, and logistic regression.

Chapter 8, *Neural Networks*, implements our first neural network.

Chapter 9, *Convolutional Neural Networks*, continues NNs, but this time we focus on convolutional NNs, which are especially popular in the computer vision domain.

Chapter 10, *Natural Language Processing*, explores the amazing world of human natural language. We're also going to use neural networks to build several chatbots with different personalities.

Chapter 11, *Machine Learning Libraries*, overviews existing iOS-compatible libraries for machine learning.

Chapter 12, *Optimizing Neural Networks for Mobile Devices*, talks about deep neural network deployment on mobile platforms.

Chapter 13, *Best Practices*, discusses a machine learning app's life cycle, common problems in AI projects, and how to solve them.

To get the most out of this book

You will need the following software to be able to smoothly sail through this book:

- Homebrew 1.3.8 +
- Python 2.7.x
- pip 9.0.1+
- Virtualenv 15.1.0+
- IPython 5.4.1+
- Jupyter 1.0.0+
- SciPy 0.19.1+
- NumPy 1.13.3+
- Pandas 0.20.2+
- Matplotlib 2.0.2+
- Graphviz 0.8.2+

- pydotplus 2.0.2+
- scikit-learn 0.18.1+
- coremltools 0.6.3+
- Ruby (default macOS version)
- Xcode 9.2+
- Keras 2.0.6+ with TensorFlow 1.1.0+ backend
- keras-vis 0.4.1+
- NumPy 1.13.3+
- NLTK 3.2.4+
- Gensim 2.1.0+

OS required:

- macOS High Sierra 10.13.3+
- iOS 11+ or simulator

Download the example code files

You can download the example code files for this book from your account at www.packtpub.com. If you purchased this book elsewhere, you can visit www.packtpub.com/support and register to have the files emailed directly to you.

You can download the code files by following these steps:

1. Log in or register at www.packtpub.com.
2. Select the **SUPPORT** tab.
3. Click on **Code Downloads & Errata**.
4. Enter the name of the book in the **Search** box and follow the onscreen instructions.

Once the file is downloaded, please make sure that you unzip or extract the folder using the latest version of:

- WinRAR/7-Zip for Windows
- Zipeg/iZip/UnRarX for Mac
- 7-Zip/PeaZip for Linux

The code bundle for the book is also hosted on GitHub at `https://github.com/PacktPublishing/Machine-Learning-with-Swift`. In case there's an update to the code, it will be updated on the existing GitHub repository. The author has also hosted the code bundle on his GitHub repository at: `https://github.com/alexsosn/SwiftMLBook`.

We also have other code bundles from our rich catalog of books and videos available at `https://github.com/PacktPublishing/`. Check them out!

Download the color images

We also provide a PDF file that has color images of the screenshots/diagrams used in this book. You can download it here: `https://www.packtpub.com/sites/default/files/downloads/MachineLearningwithSwift_ColorImages.pdf`.

Conventions used

There are a number of text conventions used throughout this book.

`CodeInText`: Indicates code words in text, database table names, folder names, filenames, file extensions, pathnames, dummy URLs, user input, and Twitter handles. Here is an example: "The library we are using for datasets loading and manipulation is `pandas`."

A block of code is set as follows:

```
let bundle = Bundle.main
let assetPath = bundle.url(forResource: "DecisionTree",
withExtension:"mlmodelc")
```

When we wish to draw your attention to a particular part of a code block, the relevant lines or items are set in bold:

```
let metricsSKLRandomForest = evaluateAccuracy(yVecTest: groundTruth,
predictions: predictionsSKLRandomForest)
print(metricsSKLRandomForest)
```

Any command-line input or output is written as follows:

```
> pip install -U numpy scipy matplotlib ipython jupyter scikit-learn
pydotplus coremltools
```

Bold: Indicates a new term, an important word, or words that you see onscreen. For example, words in menus or dialog boxes appear in the text like this. Here is an example: "In the interface, the user selects the type of motion he wants to record, and presses the **Record** button."

Warnings or important notes appear like this.

Tips and tricks appear like this.

Get in touch

Feedback from our readers is always welcome.

General feedback: Email feedback@packtpub.com and mention the book title in the subject of your message. If you have questions about any aspect of this book, please email us at questions@packtpub.com.

Errata: Although we have taken every care to ensure the accuracy of our content, mistakes do happen. If you have found a mistake in this book, we would be grateful if you would report this to us. Please visit www.packtpub.com/submit-errata, selecting your book, clicking on the Errata Submission Form link, and entering the details.

Piracy: If you come across any illegal copies of our works in any form on the Internet, we would be grateful if you would provide us with the location address or website name. Please contact us at copyright@packtpub.com with a link to the material.

If you are interested in becoming an author: If there is a topic that you have expertise in and you are interested in either writing or contributing to a book, please visit authors.packtpub.com.

Reviews

Please leave a review. Once you have read and used this book, why not leave a review on the site that you purchased it from? Potential readers can then see and use your unbiased opinion to make purchase decisions, we at Packt can understand what you think about our products, and our authors can see your feedback on their book. Thank you!

For more information about Packt, please visit `packtpub.com`.

1
Getting Started with Machine Learning

We live in exciting times. **Artificial intelligence (AI)** and **Machine Learning (ML)** went from obscure mathematical and science fiction topics to become a part of mass culture. Google, Facebook, Microsoft, and others competed to become the first to give the world general AI. In November 2015, Google open sourced its ML framework with TensorFlow, which is suitable for running on supercomputers as well as smartphones, and since then has won a broad community. Shortly afterwards, other big companies followed the example. The best iOS app of 2016 (Apple Choice), viral photo editor Prisma owes its success entirely to a particular kind of ML algorithm: **convolutional neural network (CNN)**. These systems were invented back in the nineties but became popular only in the noughties. Mobile devices only gained enough computational power to run them in 2014/2015. In fact, artificial neural networks became so important for practical applications that in iOS 10 Apple added native support for them in the metal and accelerate frameworks. Apple also opened Siri to third-party developers and introduced GameplayKit, a framework to add AI capabilities to your computer games. In iOS 11, Apple introduced Core ML, a framework for running pre-trained models on vendors' devices, and Vision framework for common computer vision tasks.

The best time to start learning about ML was 10 years ago. The next best time is right now.

In this chapter, we will cover the following topics:

- Understanding what AI and ML is
- Fundamental concepts of ML : model, dataset, and learning
- Types of ML tasks
- ML project life cycle
- General purpose ML versus mobile ML

What is AI?

"What I cannot create, I do not understand."

– Richard Feynman

AI is a field of knowledge about building intelligent machines, whatever meaning you assign to the word *intelligence*. There are two different AI notions among researchers: strong AI and weak AI.

Strong AI, or **artificial general intelligence** (**AGI**), is a machine that is fully capable of imitating human-level intelligence, including consciousness, feelings, and mind. Presumably, it should be able to apply successfully its intelligence to any tasks. This type of AI is like a horizon—we always see it as a goal but we are still not there, despite all our struggles. The significant role here plays the **AI effect**: the things that were yesterday considered a feature of strong AI are today accepted as granted and trivial. In the sixties, people believed that playing board games like chess was a characteristic of strong AI. Today, we have programs that outperform the best human chess players, but we are still far from strong AI. Our iPhones are probably an AI from the eighties perspective: you can talk to them, and they can answer your questions and deliver information on any topic in just seconds. So, keeping strong AI as a distant goal, researchers focused on things at hand and called them **weak AI**: systems that have some features of intelligence, and can be applied to some narrow tasks. Among those tasks are automated reasoning, planning, creativity, communication with humans, a perception of its surrounding world, robotics, and emotions simulation. We will touch some of these tasks in this book, but mostly we will focus on ML because this domain of AI has found a lot of practical applications on mobile platforms in the recent years.

The motivation behind ML

Let's start with an analogy. There are two ways of learning an unfamiliar language:

- Learning the language rules by heart, using textbooks, dictionaries, and so on. That's how college students usually do it.
- Observing live language: by communicating with native speakers, reading books, and watching movies. That's how children do it.

In both cases, you build in your mind the language model, or, as some prefer to say, develop a sense of language.

In the first case, you are trying to build a logical system based on rules. In this case, you will encounter many problems: the exceptions to the rule, different dialects, borrowing from other languages, idioms, and lots more. Someone else, not you, derived and described for you the rules and structure of the language.

In the second case, you derive the same rules from the available data. You may not even be aware of the existence of these rules, but gradually adjust yourself to the hidden structure and understand the laws. You use your special brain cells called **mirror neurons**, trying to mimic native speakers. This ability is honed by millions of years of evolution. After some time, when facing the wrong word usage, you just feel that something is wrong but you can't tell immediately what exactly.

In any case, the next step is to apply the resulting language model in the real world. Results may differ. In the first case, you will experience difficulty every time you find the missing hyphen or comma, but may be able to get a job as a proofreader at a publishing house. In the second case, everything will depend on the quality, diversity, and amount of the data on which you were trained. Just imagine a person in the center of New York who studied English through Shakespeare. Would he be able to have a normal conversation with people around him?

Now we'll put the computer in place of the person in our example. Two approaches, in this case, represent the two programming techniques. The first one corresponds to writing ad hoc algorithms consisting of conditions, cycles, and so on, by which a programmer expresses rules and structures. The second one represents ML , in which case the computer itself identifies the underlying structure and rules based on the available data.

The analogy is deeper than it seems at first glance. For many tasks, building the algorithms directly is impossibly hard because of the variability in the real world. It may require the work of experts in the domain, who must describe all rules and edge cases explicitly. Resulting models can be fragile and rigid. On the other hand, this same task can be solved by allowing computers to figure out the rules on their own from a reasonable amount of data. An example of such a task is face recognition. It's virtually impossible to formalize face recognition in terms of conventional imperative algorithms and data structures. Only recently, the task was successfully solved with the help of ML .

What is ML ?

ML is a subdomain of AI that has demonstrated significant progress over the last decade, and remains a hot research topic. It is a branch of knowledge concerned with building algorithms that can learn from data and improve themselves with regards to the tasks they perform. ML allows computers to deduce the algorithm for some task or to extract hidden patterns from data. ML is known by several different names in different research communities: predictive analytics, data mining, statistical learning, pattern recognition, and so on. One can argue that these terms have some subtle differences, but essentially, they all overlap to the extent that you can use the terminology interchangeably.

 Abbreviation ML may refer to many things outside of the AI domain; for example, there is a functional programming language of this name. Nevertheless, the abbreviation is widely used in the names of libraries and conferences as referring to ML . Throughout this book, we also use it in this way.

ML is already everywhere around us. Search engines, targeted ads, face and voice recognition, recommender systems, spam filtration, self-driven cars, fraud detection in bank systems, credit scoring, automated video captioning, and machine translation—all these things are impossible to imagine without ML these days.

Over recent years, ML has owed its success to several factors:

- The abundance of data in different forms (big data)
- Accessible computational power and specialized hardware (clouds and GPUs)
- The rise of open source and open access
- Algorithmic advances

Any ML system includes three essential components: data, model, and task. The data is something you provide as an input to your model. A model is a type of mathematical function or computer program that performs the task. For instance, your emails are data, the spam filter is a model, and telling spam apart from non-spam is a task. The *learning* in ML stands for a process of adjusting your model to the data so that the model becomes better at its task. The obvious consequences of this setup is expressed in the piece of wisdom well-known among statisticians, *"Your model is only as good as your data"*.

Applications of ML

There are many domains where ML is an indispensable ingredient, some of them are robotics, bioinformatics, and recommender systems. While nothing prevents you from writing bioinformatic software in Swift for macOS or Linux, we will restrict our practical examples in this book to more mobile-friendly domains. The apparent reason for this is that currently, iOS remains the primary target platform for most of the programmers who use Swift on a day-to-day basis.

For the sake of convenience, we'll roughly divide all ML applications of interest for mobile developers into three plus one areas, according to the datatypes they deal with most commonly:

- Digital signal processing (sensor data, audio)
- Computer vision (images, video)
- Natural language processing (texts, speech)
- Other applications and datatypes

Digital signal processing (DSP)

This category includes tasks where input data types are signals, time series, and audio. The sources of the data are sensors, HealthKit, microphone, wearable devices (for example, Apple Watch, or brain-computer interfaces), and IoT devices. Examples of ML problems here include:

- Motion sensor data classification for activity recognition
- Speech recognition and synthesis
- Music recognition and synthesis
- Biological signals (ECG, EEG, and hand tremor) analysis

We will build a motion recognition app in Chapter 3, *K-Nearest Neighbors Classifier*.

 Strictly speaking, image processing is also a subdomain of DSP but let's not be too meticulous here.

Computer vision

Everything related to images and videos falls into this category. We will develop some computer vision apps in Chapter 9, *Convolutional Neural Networks*. Examples of computer vision tasks are:

- **Optical character recognition** (OCR) and handwritten input
- Face detection and recognition
- Image and video captioning
- Image segmentation
- 3D-scene reconstruction
- Generative art (artistic style transfer, Deep Dream, and so on)

Natural language processing (NLP)

NLP is a branch of knowledge at the intersection of linguistics, computer science, and statistics. We'll talk about most common NLP techniques in Chapter 10, *Natural Language Processing*. Applications of NLP include the following:

- Automated translation, spelling, grammar, and style correction
- Sentiment analysis
- Spam detection/filtering
- Document categorization
- Chatbots and question answering systems

Other applications of ML

You can come up with many more applications that are hard to categorize. ML can be done on virtually any data if you have enough of it. Some peculiar data types are:

- Spatial data: GPS location (Chapter 4, *K-Means Clustering*), coordinates of UI objects and touches
- Tree-like structures: hierarchy of folders and files
- Network-like data: occurrences of people together in your photos, or hyperlinks between web pages
- Application logs and user in-app activity data (Chapter 5, *Association Rule Learning*)
- System data: free space disk, battery level, and similar
- Survey results

Using ML to build smarter iOS applications

As we know from press reports, Apple uses ML for fraud detection, and to mine useful data from beta testing reports; however, these are not examples visible on our mobile devices. Your iPhone itself has a handful of ML models built into its operating system, and some native apps helping to perform a wide range of tasks. Some use cases are well known and prominent while others are inconspicuous. The most obvious examples are Siri speech recognition, natural language understanding, and voice generation. Camera app uses face detection for focusing and Photos app uses face recognition to group photos with the same person into one album. Presenting the new iOS 10 in June 2016, Craig Federighi mentioned its predictive keyboard, which uses an LSTM algorithm (a type of recurrent neural network) to suggest the next word from the context, and also how Photos uses deep learning to recognize objects and classify scenes. iOS itself uses ML to extend battery life, provide contextual suggestions, match profiles from social networks and mail with the records in Contacts, and to choose between internet connection options. On Apple Watch, ML models are employed to recognize user motion activity types and handwritten input.

Prior to iOS 10, Apple provided some ML APIs like speech or movement recognition, but only as black boxes, without the possibility to tune the models or to reuse them for other purposes. If you wanted to do something slightly different, like detect the type of motion (which is not predefined by Apple), you had to build your own models from scratch. In iOS 10, CNN building blocks were added in the two frameworks at once: as a part of Metal API, and as a sublibrary of an Accelerate framework. Also, the first actual ML algorithm was introduced to iOS SDK: the decision tree learner in the GameplayKit.

ML capabilities continued to expand with the release of iOS 11. At the WWDC 2017, Apple presented the Core ML framework. It includes API for running pre-trained models and is accompanied by tools for converting models trained with some popular ML frameworks to Apple's own format. Still, for now it doesn't provide the possibility of training models on a device, so your models can't be changed or updated in runtime.

Looking in the App Store for the terms *artificial intelligence, deep learning, ML* , and similar, you'll find a lot of applications, some of them quite successful. Here are several examples:

- Google Translate is doing speech recognition and synthesis, OCR, handwriting recognition, and automated translation; some of this is done offline, and some online.
- Duolingo validates pronunciation, recommends optimal study materials, and employs Chatbots for language study.
- Prisma, Artisto, and others turn photos into paintings using a neural artistic style transfer algorithm. Snapchat and Fabby use image segmentation, object tracking, and other computer vision techniques to enhance selfies. There are also applications for coloring black and white photos automatically.
- Snapchat's video selfie filters use ML for real-time face tracking and modification.
- Aipoly Vision helps blind people, saying aloud what it sees through the camera.
- Several calorie counter apps recognize food through a camera. There are also similar apps to identify dog breeds, trees and trademarks.
- Tens of AI personal assistants and Chatbots, with different capabilities from cow disease diagnostics, to matchmaking and stock trading.
- Predictive keyboards, spellcheckers, and auto correction, for instance, SwiftKey.
- Games that learn from their users and games with evolving characters/units.
- There are also news, mail, and other apps that adapt to users' habits and preferences using ML .
- Brain-computer interfaces and fitness wearables with the help of ML recognize different user conditions like concentration, sleep phases, and so on. At least some of their supplementary mobile apps do ML .
- Medical diagnostic and monitoring through mobile health applications. For example, OneRing monitors Parkinson's disease using the data from a wearable device.

All these applications are built upon the extensive data collection and processing. Even if the application itself is not collecting the data, the model it uses was trained on some usually big dataset. In the following section, we will discuss all things related to data in ML applications.

Getting to know your data

For many years, researchers argued about what is more important: data or algorithms. But now, it looks like the importance of data over algorithms is generally accepted among ML specialists. In most cases, we can assume that the one who has better data usually beats those with more advanced algorithms. Garbage in, garbage out—this rule holds true in ML more than anywhere else. To succeed in this domain, one need not only have data, but also needs to know his data and know what to do with it.

ML datasets are usually composed from individual observations, called samples, cases, or data points. In the simplest case, each sample has several features.

Features

When we are talking about features in the context of ML , what we mean is some characteristic property of the object or phenomenon we are investigating.

 Other names for the same concept you'll see in some publications are explanatory variable, independent variable, and predictor.

Features are used to distinguish objects from each other and to measure the similarity between them.

For instance:

- If the objects of our interest are books, features could be a title, page count, author's name, a year of publication, genre, and so on
- If the objects of interest are images, features could be intensities of each pixel
- If the objects are blog posts, features could be language, length, or presence of some terms

It's useful to imagine your data as a spreadsheet table. In this case, each sample (data point) would be a row, and each feature would be a column. For example, Table 1.1 shows a tiny dataset of books consisting of four samples where each has eight features.

Table 1.1: an example of a ML dataset (dummy books):

Title	Author's name	Pages	Year	Genre	Average readers review score	Publisher	In stock
Learn ML in 21 Days	Machine Learner	354	2018	Sci-Fi	3.9	Untitled United	False
101 Tips to Survive an Asteroid Impact	Enrique Drills	124	2021	Self-help	4.7	Vacuum Books	True
Sleeping on the Keyboard	Jessica's Cat	458	2014	Non-fiction	3.5	JhGJgh Inc.	True
Quantum Screwdriver: Heritage	Yessenia Purnima	1550	2018	Sci-Fi	4.2	Vacuum Books	True

Types of features

In the books example, you can see several types of features:

- **Categorical or unordered**: Title, author, genre, publisher. They are similar to enumeration without raw values in Swift, but with one difference: they have levels instead of cases. Important: you can't order them or say that one is bigger than another.
- **Binary**: The presence or absence of something, just true or false. In our case, the *In stock* feature.
- **Real numbers**: Page count, year, average reader's review score. These can be represented as float or double.

There are others, but these are by far the most common.

The most common ML algorithms require the dataset to consist of a number of samples, where each sample is represented by a vector of real numbers (feature vector), and all samples have the same number of features. The simplest (but not the best) way of translating categorical features into real numbers is by replacing them with numerical codes (Table 1.2).

Table 1.2: dummy books dataset after simple preprocessing:

Title	Author's name	Pages	Year	Genre	Average readers review score	Publisher	In stock
0.0	0.0	354.0	2018.0	0.0	3.9	0.0	0.0
1.0	1.0	124.0	2021.0	1.0	4.7	1.0	1.0
2.0	2.0	458.0	2014.0	2.0	3.5	2.0	1.0
3.0	3.0	1550.0	2018.0	0.0	4.2	1.0	1.0

This is an example of how your dataset may look before you feed it into your ML algorithm. Later, we will discuss the nuts and bolts of data preprocessing for specific applications.

Choosing a good set of features

For ML purposes, it's necessary to choose a reasonable set of features, not too many and not too few:

- If you have too few features, this information may be not sufficient for your model to achieve the required quality. In this case, you want to construct new ones from existing features, or extract more features from the raw data.
- If you have too many features you want to select only the most informative and discriminative, because the more features you have the more complex your computations become.

How do you tell which features are most important? Sometimes common sense helps. For example, if you are building a model that recommends books for you, the genre and average rating of the book are perhaps more important features than the number of pages and year of publication. But what if your features are just pixels of a picture and you're building a face recognition system? For a black and white image of size 1024 x 768, we'd get 786,432 features. Which pixels are most important? In this case, you have to apply some algorithms to extract meaningful features. For example, in computer vision, edges, corners, and blobs are more informative features then raw pixels, so there are plenty of algorithms to extract them (*Figure 1.1*). By passing your image through some filters, you can get rid of unimportant information and reduce the number of features significantly; from hundreds of thousands to hundreds, or even tens. The techniques that helps to select the most important subset of features is known as **feature selection**, while the **feature extraction** techniques result in the creation of new features:

Figure 1.1: Edge detection is a common feature extraction technique in computer vision. You can still recognize the object on the right image, despite it containing significantly less information than the left one.

Feature extraction, selection, and combining is a kind of the art which is known as **feature engineering**. This requires not only hacking and statistical skills but also domain knowledge. We will see some feature engineering techniques while working on practical applications in the following chapters. We also will step into the exciting world of **deep learning**: a technique that gives a computer the ability to extract high-level abstract features from the low-level features.

The number of features you have for each sample (or length of feature vector) is usually referred to as the **dimensionality** of the problem. Many problems are high-dimensional, with hundreds or even thousands of features. Even worse, some of those problems are sparse; that is, for each data point, most of the features are zero or missed. This is a common situation in recommender systems. For instance, imagine yourself building the dataset of movie ratings: the rows are movies and columns are users, and in each cell, you have a rating given by the user of the movie. The majority of the cells in the table will remain empty, as most of the users will never have watched most of the movies. The opposite situation is called **dense,** which is when most values are in place. Many problems in natural language processing and bioinformatics are high-dimensional, sparse, or both.

Feature selection and extraction help to decrease the number of features without significant loss of information, so we also call them **dimensionality reduction algorithms**.

Getting the dataset

Datasets can be obtained from different sources. The ones important for us are:

- Classical datasets such as Iris (botanical measurements of flowers composed by R. Fisher in 1936), MNIST (60,000 handwritten digits published in 1998), Titanic (personal information of Titanic passengers from Encyclopedia Titanica and other sources), and others. Many classical datasets are available as part of Python and R ML packages. They represent some classical types of ML tasks and are useful for demonstrations of algorithms. Meanwhile, there is no similar library for Swift. Implementation of such a library would be straightforward and is a low-hanging fruit for anyone who wants to get some stars on GitHub.
- Open and commercial dataset repositories. Many institutions release their data for everyone's needs under different licenses. You can use such data for training production models or while collecting your own dataset.

    Some public dataset repositories include:

    - The UCI ML repository: https://archive.ics.uci.edu/ml/datasets.html

    - Kaggle datasets: https://www.kaggle.com/datasets

    - data.world, a social network for dataset sharing: https://data.world

To find more, visit the list of repositories at KDnuggets: `http://www.kdnuggets.com/datasets/index.html`. Alternatively, you'll find a list of datasets at Wikipedia: `https://en.wikipedia.org/wiki/List_of_datasets_for_machine_learning_research`.

- **Data collection (acquisition)** is required if no existing data can help you to solve your problem. This approach can be costly both in resources and time if you have to collect the data ad hoc; however, in many cases, you have data as a byproduct of some other process, and you can compose your dataset by extracting useful information from the data. For example, text corpuses can be composed by crawling Wikipedia or news sites. iOS automatically collects some useful data. HealthKit is a unified database of users' health measurements. Core Motion allows getting historical data on user's motion activities. The ResearchKit framework provides standardized routines to assess the user's health conditions. The CareKit framework standardizes the polls. Also, in some cases, useful information can be obtained from app log mining.
    - In many cases, to collect data is not enough, as raw data doesn't suit many ML tasks well. So, the next step after data collection is data labeling. For example, you have collected dataset of images, so now you have to attach a label to each of them: to which category does this image belong? This can be done manually (often at expense), automatically (sometimes impossible), or semi-automatically. Manual labeling can be scaled by means of crowdsourcing platforms, like Amazon Mechanical Turk.
- Random **data generation** can be useful for a quick check of your ideas or in combination with the TDD approach. Also, sometimes adding some controlled randomness to your real data can improve the results of learning. This approach is known as **data augmentation**. For instance, this approach was taken to build an optical character recognition feature in the Google Translate mobile app. To train their model, they needed a lot of real-world photos with letters in different languages, which they didn't have. The engineering team bypassed this problem by creating a large dataset of letters with artificial reflections, smudges, and all kinds of corruptions on them. This improved the recognition quality significantly.
- **Real-time data sources**, such as inertial sensors, GPS, camera, microphone, elevation sensor, proximity sensor, touch screen, force touch, and Apple Watch sensors can be used to collect a standalone dataset or to train a model on the fly.

Real-time data sources are especially important for the special class of ML models called **online ML** , which allows models to embed new data. A good example of such a situation is spam filtering, where the model should dynamically adapt to the new data. It's the opposite of batch learning, when the whole training dataset should be available from the very beginning.

Data preprocessing

The useful information in the data is usually referred to as a **signal**. On the other hand, the pieces of data that represent errors of different kinds and irrelevant data are known as **noise**. Errors can occur in the data during measurements, information transmission, or due to human errors. The goal of data cleansing procedures is to increase the signal/noise ratio. During this stage, you will usually transform all data to one format, delete entries with missed values, and check suspicious outliers (they can be both noise and signal). It is widely believed among ML engineers, that the data preprocessing stage usually consumes 90% of the time allocated for the ML project. Then, algorithm tweaking consumes another 90% of time. This statement is a joke only partially (about 10% of it). In Chapter 13, *Best Practices*, we are going to discuss common problems with the data and how to fix them.

Choosing a model

Let's say you've defined a task and you have a dataset. What's next? Now you need to choose a model and train it on the dataset to perform that task.

The model is the central concept in ML . ML is basically a science of building models of the real world using data. The term *model* refers to the phenomenon being modeled, while *map* refers to the real territory. Depending on the situation, it can play a role of good approximation, an outdated description (in a swiftly changing environment), or even self-fulfilled prophecy (if the model affects the modeled object). *"All models are wrong, but some are useful"* is a well-known proverb in statistics.

Types of ML algorithms

ML models/algorithms are often divided into three groups depending on the type of input:

- Supervised learning
- Unsupervised learning
- Reinforcement learning

This division is rather vague because some algorithms fall into two of these groups while others do not fall into any. There are also some middle states, such as semi-supervised learning.

Algorithms in these three groups can perform different tasks, and hence can be divided into subgroups according to the output of the model. *Table 1.3* shows the most common ML tasks and their classification.

Supervised learning

Supervised learning is arguably the most common and easy-to-understand type of ML . All supervised learning algorithms have one prerequisite in common: you should have a labeled dataset to train them. Here, a dataset is a set of samples, plus an expected output (label) for each sample. These labels play the role of supervisor during the training.

In different publications, you'll see different synonyms for labels, including dependent variable, predicted variable, and explained variable.

The goal of supervised learning is to get a function that for every given input returns a desired output. In the most simplified version, a supervised learning process consists of two phases: training and inference. During the first phase, you train the model using your labeled dataset. On the second phase, you use your model to do something useful, like make predictions. For instance, given a set of labeled images (dataset), a neural network (model) can be trained to predict (inference) correct labels for previously unseen images.

Using supervised learning, you will usually solve one of two problems: classification or regression. The difference is in the type of labels: categorical in the first case and real numbers in the second.

To classify means simply to assign one of the labels from a predefined set. Binary classification is a special kind of classification, when you have only two labels (positive and negative). An example of a classification task is to assign *spam/not-spam* labels to letters. We will train our first classifier in the next chapter, and throughout this book we will apply different classifiers for many real-world tasks.

Regression is the task of assigning a real number to a given case. For example, predicting a salary given employee characteristics. We will discuss regression in Chapter 6, *Linear Regression and Gradient Descent* and Chapter 7, *Linear Classifier and Logistic Regression*, in more detail.

If the task is to sort objects in some order (output a permutation, speaking combinatorial), and labels are not really real numbers but rather an order of objects, ranking learning is at hand. You see ranking algorithms in action when you open the Siri suggestions menu on iOS. Each app placed in the list there is done so according to its relevance for you.

If labels are complicated objects, like graphs or trees, neither classification nor regression will be of use. Structured prediction algorithms are the type of algorithms to tackle those problems. Parsing English sentences into syntactic trees is an example of this kind of task.

Ranking and structured learning are beyond the scope of this book because their use cases are not as common as classification or regression, but at least now you know what to Google search for when you need to.

Unsupervised learning

In unsupervised learning, you don't have the labels for the cases in your dataset. Types of tasks to solve with unsupervised learning are: clustering, anomaly detection, dimensionality reduction, and association rule learning.

Sometimes you don't have the labels for your data points but you still want to group them in some meaningful way. You may or may not know the exact number of groups. This is the setting where clustering algorithms are used. The most obvious example is clustering users into some groups, like students, parents, gamers, and so on. The important detail here is that a group's meaning is not predefined from the very beginning; you name it only after you've finished grouping your samples. Clustering also can be useful to extract additional features from the data as a preliminary step for supervised learning. We will discuss clustering in Chapter 4, *K-Means Clustering*.

Outlier/anomaly detection algorithms are used when the goal is to find some anomalous patterns in the data, weird data points. This can be especially useful for automated fraud or intrusion detection. Outlier analysis is also an important detail of data cleansing.

Dimensionality reduction is a way to distill data to the most informative and, at the same time, compact representation of it. The goal is to reduce a number of features without losing important information. It can be used as a preprocessing step before supervised learning or data visualization.

Association rule learning looks for repeated patterns of user behavior and peculiar co-occurrences of items. An example from retail practice: if a customer buys milk, isn't it more probable that he will also buy cereal? If yes, then perhaps it's better to move shelves, with the cereals closer to the shelf with the milk. Having rules like this, owners of businesses can make informed decisions and adapt their services to customers' needs. In the context of software development, this can empower anticipatory design—when the app seemingly knows what you want to do next and provides suggestions accordingly. In `Chapter 5`, *Association Rule Learning* we will implement a priori one of the most well-known rule learning algorithms:

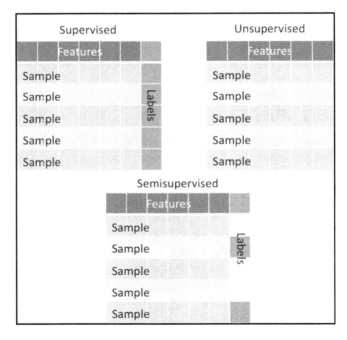

Figure 1.2: Datasets for three types of learning: supervised, unsupervised, and semi-supervised

Labeling data manually is usually a costly thing, especially if special qualification is required. Semi-supervised learning can help when only some of your samples are labeled and others are not (see the following diagram). It is a hybrid of supervised and unsupervised learning. At first, it looks for unlabeled instances, similar to the labeled ones in an unsupervised manner, and includes them in the training dataset. After this, the algorithm can be trained on this expanded dataset in a typical supervised manner.

Reinforcement learning

Reinforcement learning is special in the sense that it doesn't require a dataset (see the following diagram). Instead, it involves an agent who takes actions, changing the state of the environment. After each step, it gets a reward or punishment, depending on the state and previous actions. The goal is to obtain a maximum cumulative reward. It can be used to teach the computer to play video games or drive a car. If you think about it, reinforcement learning is the way our pets train us humans: by rewarding our actions with tail-wagging, or punishing with scratched furniture.

One of the central topics in reinforcement learning is the exploration-exploitation dilemma—how to find a good balance between exploring new options and using what is already known:

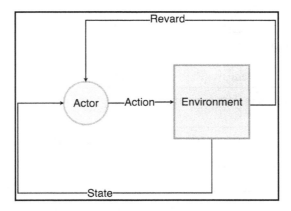

Figure 1.3: Reinforcement learning process

Table 1.3: ML tasks:

Task	Output type	Problem example	Algorithms
Supervised learning			
Regression	Real numbers	Predict house prices, given its characteristics	Linear regression and polynomial regression
Classification	Categorical	Spam/not-spam classification	KNN, Naïve Bayes, logistic regression, decision trees, random forest, and SVM
Ranking	Natural number (ordinal variable)	Sort search results per relevance	Ordinal regression
Structured prediction	Structures: trees, graphs, and so on	Part-of-speech tagging	Recurrent neural networks, and conditional random field
Unsupervised learning			
Clustering	Groups of objects	Build a tree of living organisms	Hierarchical clustering, k-means, and GMM
Dimensionality reduction	Compact representation of given features	Find most important components in brain activity	PCA, t-SNE, and LDA
Outlier/anomaly detection	Objects that are out of pattern	Fraud detection	Local outlier factor
Association rule learning	Set of rules	Smart house intrusion detection	A priori
Reinforcement learning			
Control learning	Policy with maximum expected return	Learn to play a video game	Q-learning

Mathematical optimization – how learning works

The magic behind the learning process is delivered by the branch of mathematics called **mathematical optimization**. Sometimes it's also somewhat misleading being referred to as mathematical programming; the term coined long before widespread computer programming and is not directly related to it. Optimization is the science of choosing the best option among available alternatives; for example, choosing the best ML model.

Mathematically speaking, ML models are functions. You as an engineer chose the function family depending on your preferences: linear models, trees, neural networks, support vector machines, and so on. Learning is a process of picking from the family the function which serves your goals the best. This notion of the best model is often defined by another function, the **loss function**. It estimates a goodness of the model according to some criteria; for instance, how good the model fits the data, how complex it is, and so on. You can think of the loss function as a judge at a competition whose role is to assess the models. The objective of the learning is to find such a model that delivers a minimum to the loss function (minimize the loss), so the whole learning process is formalized in mathematical terms as a task of function minimization.

Function minimum can be found in two ways: analytically (calculus) or numerically (iterative methods). In ML , we often go for the numerical optimization because the loss functions get too complex for analytical solutions.

A nice interactive tutorial on numerical optimization can be found here: `http://www.benfrederickson.com/numerical-optimization/`.

From the programmer's point of view, learning is an iterative process of adjusting model parameters until the optimal solution is found. In practice, after a number of iterations, the algorithm stops improving because it is stuck in a local optimum or has reached the global optimum (see the following diagram). If the algorithm always finds the local or global optimum, we say that it *converges*. On the other hand, if you see your algorithm oscillating more and more and never approaching a useful result, it diverges:

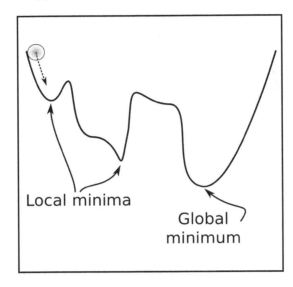

Figure 1.4: Learner represented as a ball on a complex surface: it's possible for him to fall in a local minimum and never reach the global one

Mobile versus server-side ML

Most Swift developers are writing their applications for iOS. Those among us who develop their Swift applications for macOS or server-side are in a lucky position regarding ML . They can use whatever libraries and tools they want, reckoning on powerful hardware and compatibility with interpretable languages. Most of the ML libraries and frameworks are developed with server-side (or at least powerful desktops) in mind. In this book, we talk mostly about iOS applications, and therefore most practical examples consider limitations of handheld devices.

But if mobile devices have limited capabilities, we can do all ML on the server-side, can't we? Why would anyone bother to do ML locally on mobile devices at all? There are at least three issues with client-server architecture:

- The client app will be fully functional only when it has an internet connection. This may not be a big problem in developed countries but this can limit your target audience significantly. Just imagine your translator app being non-functional during travel abroad.

- Additional time delay introduced by sending data to the server and getting a response. Who enjoys watching progress bars or, even worse, infinite spinners while your data is being uploaded, processed, and downloaded back again? What if you need those results immediately and without consuming your internet traffic? Client-server architecture makes it almost impossible for such applications of ML as real-time video and audio processing.

- Privacy concerns: any data you've uploaded to the internet is not yours anymore. In the age of total surveillance, how do you know that those funny selfies you've uploaded today to the cloud will not be used tomorrow to train face recognition, or for target-tracking algorithms for some interesting purposes, like killer drones? Many users don't like their personal information to be uploaded to some servers and possibly shared/sold/leaked to some third parties. Apple also argues for reducing data collection as much as possible.

Some of the applications can be OK (can't be great, though) with those limitations, but most developers want their apps to be responsive, secure, and useful all the time. This is something only on-device ML can deliver.

For me, the most important argument is that we *can* do ML without server-side. Hardware capabilities are increasing with each year and ML on mobile devices is a hot research field. Modern mobile devices are already powerful enough for many ML algorithms. Smartphones are the most personal and arguably the most important devices nowadays just because they are everywhere. Coding ML is fun and cool, so why should server-side developers have all the fun?

Additional bonuses that you get when implement ML on the mobile side are the free computation power (you are not paying for the electricity) and the unique marketing points (our app puts the power of AI inside of your pocket).

Understanding mobile platform limitations

Now, if I have persuaded you to use ML on mobile devices, you should be aware of some limitations:

- Computation complexity restriction. The more you load your CPU, the faster your battery will die. It's easy to transform your iPhone into a compact heater with the help of some ML algorithms.
- Some models take a long time to train. On the server, you can let your neural networks train for weeks; but on a mobile device, even minutes are too long. iOS applications can run and process some data in background mode if they have some good reasons, like playing music. Unfortunately, ML is not on the list of good reasons, so most probably, you will not be able to run it in background mode.
- Some models take a long time to run. You should think in terms of frames per second and good user experience.
- Memory restrictions. Some models grow during the training process, while others remain a fixed size.
- Model size restrictions. Some trained models can take hundreds of megabytes or even gigabytes. But who wants to download your application from the App Store if it is so huge?
- Locally stored data is mostly restricted to different types of users' personal data, meaning that you will not be able to aggregate the data of different users and perform large-scale ML on mobile devices.
- Many open source ML libraries are built on top of interpretable languages, like Python, R, and MATLAB, or on top of the JVM, which makes them incompatible with iOS.

Those are only the most obvious challenges. You'll see more as we start to develop real ML apps. But don't worry, there is a way to eat this elephant piece by piece. Efforts spent on it are paid off by a great user experience and users' love. Platform restrictions are not unique to mobile devices. Developers of autonomous devices (like drones), IoT developers, wearable device developers, and many others face the same problems and deal with them successfully.

Many of these problems can be addressed by training the models on powerful hardware, and then deploying them to mobile devices. You can also choose a compromise with two models: a smaller one on a device for offline work, and a large one on the server. For offline work you can choose models with fast inference, then compress and optimize them for parallel execution; for instance, on GPU. We'll talk more about this in `Chapter 12`, *Optimizing Neural Networks for Mobile Devices*.

Summary

In this chapter, we learned about the main concepts in ML .

We discussed different definitions and subdomains of artificial intelligence, including ML . ML is the science and practice of extracting knowledge from data. We also explained the motivation behind ML . We had a brief overview of its application domains: digital signal processing, computer vision, and natural language processing.

We learned about the two core concepts in ML : the data, and the model. Your model is only as good as your data. A typical ML dataset consists of samples; each sample consists of features. There are many types of features and many techniques to extract useful information from the features. These techniques are known as feature engineering. For supervised learning tasks, dataset also includes label for each of the samples. We provided an overview of data collection and preprocessing.

Finally, we learned about three types of common ML tasks: supervised, unsupervised, and reinforcement learning. In the next chapter, we're going to build our first ML application.

Bibliography

1. Good O. (July 29, 2015), *How Google Translate squeezes deep learning onto a phone*, retrieved from Google Research Blog: `https://research.googleblog.com/2015/07/how-google-translate-squeezes-deep.html`

2
Classification – Decision Tree Learning

In the previous chapter, we discussed different types of machine learning, including supervised classification tasks; in this chapter, we will build our first Swift application for this. We will discuss main components of machine learning development stack, and will also exercise in data generation, exploratory analysis, preprocessing, and models training and evaluation in Python. After this, we will transfer our model to Swift. We will also discuss a specific class of supervised learning algorithms—decision tree learning and its extension: random forest.

The following topics are waiting for us in this chapter:

- Machine learning software development stack
- Python toolbox for machine learning: IPython, SciPy, scikit-learn
- Dataset generation and exploratory analysis
- Data preprocessing
- Decision tree learning and random forest
- Assessing the model performance using different performance metrics
- Underfitting and overfitting
- Exporting scikit-learn models to Core ML format
- Deploying trained models to iOS

Machine learning toolbox

For many years, the programming language of choice for machine learning was one of the following: Python, R, MATLAB, C++. This is not due to some specific language features, but because of the infrastructure around it: libraries and tools. Swift is a relatively young programming language, and anyone who chooses it as a primary tool for machine learning development should start from the very basic building blocks, and build his own tools and libraries. Recently, Apple became more open to third-party Python machine learning tools: Core ML can work with some of them.

Here is a list of components that are needed for the successful machine learning research and development, and examples of popular libraries and tools of the type:

- **Linear algebra**: Machine learning developer needs data structures like vectors, matrices, and tensors with compact syntax and hardware-accelerated operations on them. Examples in other languages: NumPy, MATLAB, and R standard libraries, Torch.
- **Probability theory**: All kinds of random data generation: random numbers and collections of them; probability distributions; permutations; shuffling of collections, weighted sampling, and so on. Examples: NumPy, and R standard library.
- **Data input-output**: In machine learning, we are usually most interested in the parsing and saving data in the following formats: plain text, tabular files like CSV, databases like SQL, internet formats JSON, XML, HTML, and web scraping. There are also a lot of domain-specific formats.
- **Data wrangling**: Table-like data structures, data engineering tools: dataset cleaning, querying, splitting, merging, shuffling, and so on. Pandas, dplyr.
- **Data analysis/statistic**: Descriptive statistic, hypotheses testing and all kinds of statistical stuff. R standard library, and a lot of CRAN packages.
- **Visualization**: Statistical data visualization (not pie charts): graph visualization, histograms, mosaic plots, heat maps, dendrograms, 3D-surfaces, spatial and multidimensional data visualization, interactive visualization, Matplotlib, Seaborn, Bokeh, ggplot2, ggmap, Graphviz, D3.js.
- **Symbolic computations**: Automatic differentiation: SymPy, Theano, Autograd.
- **Machine learning packages**: Machine learning algorithms and solvers. Scikit-learn, Keras, XGBoost, E1071, and caret.
- **Interactive prototyping environment**: Jupyter, R studio, MATLAB, and iTorch.

This is not referring to domain-specific tools, like NLP, or computer vision libraries.

As for summer 2017, I'm not aware of Swift alternatives of comparable quality and functionality to any of the mentioned tools. Also, none of these popular libraries are directly compatible with Swift, meaning you can't call Keras from your iOS Swift code. All this means that Swift cannot be the primary tool for machine learning research and development. Killing Python is not on Swift's agenda so far; however, to a different degree, there are some compatible libraries and tools, which using a wide scope of machine learning problems can be addressed in your Swift applications. In the following chapters, we're building our own tools, or introducing third-party tools as we need them. We are talking about machine learning libraries specifically in Chapter 10, *Natural Language Processing*. Still, for anyone who wants to work with machine learning, it's more than advisable to know well at least one from this list: Python, R, and MATLAB.

Prototyping the first machine learning app

Usually, before implementing a machine learning application for mobile devices, you want to do a quick and dirty prototype just to check your ideas. This allows to save a lot of time when you realize that the model you initially thought works perfectly for your problem, in reality doesn't. The quickest way to do a prototype is to use Python or R tools listed in the previous section.

Python is a general-purpose programming language with rich infrastructure and vibrant community. Its syntax is similar in many ways to Swift's one. Throughout this book, we'll use it for prototyping, and Swift for actual development.

When you have tested your ideas and a model prototype works as you expect, you can start thinking about how to port it to an iOS. You have several options here:

Inference-only options:

- Check the Core ML, and a list of the Python libraries it supports. Maybe, you will be able to export your model in Core ML format, and run it on a device.
- Write the custom converter for your model if it is not supported by the Core ML.

Training and inference options:

- Write the algorithms from scratch. In this book, we are implementing a bunch of machine learning algorithms, so you'll see that it's not that hard. Still, this is the most time-consuming option, and the model's results may differ significantly.
- Check available iOS-compatible libraries (see chapter on `Chapter 11`, *Machine Learning Libraries*).

Tools

Here is a list of tools that we're using in the following tutorial:

- **Homebrew**: This is a package manager for macOS. Official site: `https://brew.sh/`.
- **Python**: This is a general-purpose programming language popular for machine learning and data science. Official site: `https://www.python.org/`.
- pip: This is a Python package manager. Unlike CocoaPods, it installs libraries globally, and not in a per-project manner.
- **Virtualenv**: This is a tool for creating separate Python environments with different Python versions and library sets.
- **IPython**: This is an interactive Python REPL for scientific computations.
- **Jupyter**: This is a web-GUI for IPython. Official site: `http://jupyter.org/`.
- **Graphviz**: This is an open source tool for graphs visualization. We're using it in this chapter to draw models' inner structures. Official site: `http://www.graphviz.org/`.

And, the Python packages are as follows:

- `scipy`: This is a Python-based ecosystem of open source software for mathematics, science, and engineering. Official site: `https://www.scipy.org/`.
- `numpy`: This is a numerical library.
- `matplotlib`: This is a popular plotting library.
- `pydotplus`: This is a library for tree visualization, a counterpart of Graphviz.
- `scikit-learn`: This is a popular machine learning library. Official site: `http://scikit-learn.org/`.
- `coremltools`: is an Apple package for saving scikit-learn models into Core ML format. Official site: `https://pypi.python.org/pypi/coremltools`.

Setting up a machine learning environment

There is a significant segmentation in the Python community due to an issue of back-compatibility between Python 2 and Python 3—many active projects still use Python 2.7 (released in 2010), while many new tools are not backward-compatible with it, because they are based on the Python 3.x. Some tools have both versions. macOS is shipped with legacy Python 2.7.10 (released in 2015) pre-installed, while an up-to-date version at the moment of writing this book is Python 3.6.1. We will use the system's default Python throughout this book, if the opposite is not mentioned explicitly. The primary reason for this is that Core ML tools are compatible only with Python 2.7.x.

The following steps assume that you don't have other Python versions installed (like Anaconda, or through a Homebrew), except the system's default one. If you have other Python distributions installed, you likely know how to install required packages and create virtual environments.

First, in the Terminal, go to the user's root:

```
> cd ~
```

On a Mac system, the user you use to log in by default has limited privileges by design for enhanced security measures. Using the sudo command allows you to perform tasks with additional privileges on a case-by-case basis. This process aids in simplifying the security features by avoiding accidentals actions.

pip is a Python package manager. Unlike the up-to-date version of Python, the system's one doesn't have it by default. Instead, it should have the old legacy package manager easy_install. Don't use it for anything except for pip installation; it will likely mess up your system. It requires sudo privileges to install things:

```
> sudo easy_install pip
```

If you have some version of pip preinstalled, you can upgrade it to the latest one with the following command:

```
> pip install --upgrade pip
```

Many third-party programs are using the system's Python version, so to not interfere with them, it's safer to create the separate Python environment and install all dependencies that we need into it. The Virtualenv is a tool for isolated Python environment creation. It is also missing from the macOS Python, while present by default in all recent distributions starting with Python 3.3 and later. After successful installation of pip, we can use it to install `virtualenv`:

```
> pip install -U virtualenv
```

The `-U` option tells pip to install the package for the current user only.

Never run `pip` with the `sudo`. Whenever you need the `sudo` to run it, you know that you're doing something wrong.

To create a virtual environment for the book, run:

```
> cd ~
> virtualenv swift-ml-book
```

This will create the `swift-ml-book` folder, and a separate copy of Python, pip, and other tools in it. To switch to this environment (activate the environment), run the following command:

```
> source swift-ml-book/bin/activate
```

Now `swift-ml-book` prepends all your commands in the Terminal, so you know on which environment you are now. When you want to deactivate the Python 3 environment, run:

```
> deactivate
```

Finally, we can install libraries; be sure that you've activated the environment:

```
> pip install -U numpy scipy matplotlib ipython jupyter scikit-learn
pydotplus coremltools
```

You should see a long output to the command line; downloading and installing all dependencies may take a while. Eventually, you should see the message `Successfully installed ...`, and a list of installed packages. It will be much longer than the one that we've provided pip with, because it includes a bunch of transient dependencies.

Most importantly, now you should have two new commands in your Terminal: `ipython`, and `jupyter notebook`. The first one runs interactive IPython REPL, and the second one runs a web-based GUI for IPython, where you can create notebooks—interactive documents, similar to Swift playgrounds.

Additionally, we should install Graphviz—an open source tool for graphs visualization. It can be downloaded from the official site, or installed using Homebrew:

```
> brew install graphviz
```

If you don't have Homebrew, install it. Installation instructions should look like the following, but you'd better check the official site (https://brew.sh/) for the exact command:

```
> ruby -e "$(curl -fsSL
https://raw.githubusercontent.com/Homebrew/install/master/install)"
```

IPython notebook crash course

Feel free to skip this section if you're familiar with the Python and Jupyter notebooks.

IPython notebook and its web-based GUI Jupyter are standard tools for data-driven machine learning development. Jupyter is also a handy tool for learning Python and its libraries. You can combine pieces of code with comments in markdown format. You can also execute pieces of code in place, chaining them one after another, and immediately seeing the results of computations. It also allows to embed interactive charts, tables, videos, and other multimedia objects inside the notebook. We will use Jupyter notebooks for writing quick prototypes of our models.

To create a new notebook, run in the Terminal:

```
> jupyter notebook
```

You will see output similar to this:

```
[I 10:51:23.269 NotebookApp] Serving notebooks from local directory: ...
[I 10:51:23.269 NotebookApp] 0 active kernels
[I 10:51:23.270 NotebookApp] The Jupyter Notebook is running at:
http://localhost:8888/?token=3c073db5636e366fd750e661cc597652025fdbf41162c1
25
[I 10:51:23.270 NotebookApp] Use Control-C to stop this server and shut
down all kernels (twice to skip confirmation).
```

Note those long URLs in the output:
http://localhost:8888/token=3c073db5636e366fd750e661cc597652025fdbf4116
2c125.

Copy and paste this address to your browser to open Jupyter.

With Python 3, Jupyter automatically opens a new tab in your default browser's window, with the address `http://localhost:8388/tree`.

Press the **New** button, and choose **Python 2** in a drop-down menu. This will open a new notebook in a new browser tab.

To stop IPython, you'll need to press *Ctrl + C* in the Terminal, and enter `y` when prompted. Don't forget to save your changes in the notebook before quitting.

Let's try something just to get the idea on how it works. In the top cell of the notebook, print `import this` and press *Shift + Enter*. You'll see `The Zen of Python`—a short list of rules every Python programmer should conform to. We will also try to conform to them. The extended version of Python-style guidelines is known as **PEP 8**, and can be found here: `python.org/dev/peps/pep-0008/`.

Type into the new cell:

```
a = 2**32
b = 64**(1/2.)
a = a+b
a
```

Then, press *Shift + Enter*. This calculates $2^{32} + \sqrt{64}$, and stores the results into variable a. Unfamiliar operator `**` is a power, a and b are variables (no `let` or `var`). Typecasting between integer 1 and float 2 happens implicitly. Python is weak-typed, so you can assign float value of variable b to an integer variable a. Jupyter outputs the value of a last line in the cell. Also, note that variables a and b are available now in the next cells.

 If you don't know Python, no worries—it's a relatively simple language. For a crash course on Python, please visit: `https://learnxinyminutes.com/docs/python/`.

To see how to add and format comments, place your cursor in the new cell, choose from the drop-down menu in the **Instruments** panel cell, type `Markdown`, and put some markdown snippet into the cell; for example, the following snippet is a simple text with MathJax-formatted formula and a picture:

```
# This is a sample text:
$$Formula = {Numerator over Denominator}$$
![]( https://imgs.xkcd.com/comics/conditional_risk.png)
> Sample text to demonstrate the few markdown feature available to easily
create documents. [Packt Hyperlink](http://packtpub.com/)
```

You'll get a nicely formatted MathJax formula, an image, and some formatted text. If you want to know more about markdown format, just Google for a markdown tutorial, or a cheat sheet.

You can also execute bash commands from the notebook; just prepend an exclamation mark to them:

```
In []:
! ls

Out[]:
The content of your work folder goes here...
```

Time to practice

In the following sections, we'll dive into machine learning practice, to get a feeling of what it looks like. Just like in a theater play, in machine learning you have a list of characters and a list of acts.

Two main characters are:

- Dataset
- Model

Three main acts are:

- Dataset preparation
- Model training
- Model evaluation

We'll go through all these acts, and by the end of the chapter we'll have our first trained model. First, we need to define a problem, and then we can start coding a prototype in Python. Our destination point is a working model in Swift. Don't take the problem itself too seriously, though, because as the first exercise, we're going to solve a fictional problem.

Machine learning for extra-terrestrial life explorers

Swift is undoubtedly the programming language of the future. In the nearest years, we're expecting to see Swift being employed to program-intelligent scout robots that will explore alien planets and life forms on them. These robots should be able to recognize and classify aliens they will encounter. Let's build a model to distinguish between two alien species using their characteristic features.

The biosphere of the distant planet consists mainly of two species: night predators rabbosauruses, and peaceful, herbivorous platyhogs (see the following diagram). Roboscouts are equipped with sensors to measure only three features of each individual: length (in meters), color, and fluffiness.

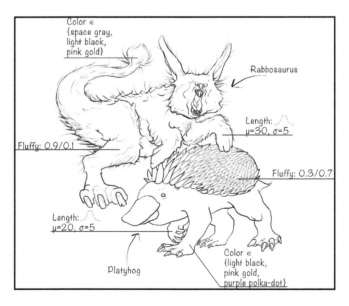

Figure 2.1: Objects of interest in our first machine learning task. Picture by Mykola Sosnovshchenko.

The full code of the Python part of this chapter can be found here: `ML_Intro.ipynb`.

Loading the dataset

Create and open a new IPython notebook. In the chapter's supplementary materials, you can see the file `extraterrestrials.csv`. Copy it to the same folder where you created your notebook. In the first cell of your notebook, execute the magical command:

```
In []:
%matplotlib inline
```

This is needed to see inline plots right in the notebook in the future.

The library we are using for datasets loading and manipulation is `pandas`. Let's import it, and load the `.csv` file:

```
In []:
import pandas as pd
df = pd.read_csv('extraterrestrials.csv', sep='t', encoding='utf-8',
index_col=0)
```

Object `df` is a data frame. This is a table-like data structured for efficient manipulations over the different data types. To see what's inside, execute:

```
In []:
df.head()
Out[]:
```

	Length	Color	Fluffy	Label
0	27.545139	Pink gold	True	Rabbosaurus
1	12.147357	Pink gold	False	Platyhog
2	23.454173	Light black	True	Rabbosaurus
3	29.956698	Pink gold	True	Rabbosaurus
4	34.884065	Light black	True	Rabbosaurus

This prints the first five rows of the table. The first three columns (length, color, and fluffy) are features, and the last one is the class label.

How many samples do we have in total? Run this code to find out:

```
In []:
len(df)
Out[]:
1000
```

Looks like the most samples in the beginning are rabbosauruses. Let's fetch five samples at random to see if it holds true in other parts of the dataset:

```
In []:
df.sample(5)
Out[]:
```

	Length	Color	Fluffy	Label
565	17.776481	Purple polka dot	False	Platyhog
491	19.475358	Light black	True	Rabbosaurus
230	15.453365	Purple polka dot	False	Platyhog
511	17.408234	Purple polka dot	True	Platyhog
875	24.105315	Light black	True	Rabbosaurus

Well, this isn't helpful, as it would be too tedious to analyze the table content in this way. We need some more advanced tools to perform descriptive statistics computations and data visualization.

Exploratory data analysis

First, we want to see how many individuals of each class we have. This is important, because if the class distribution is very imbalanced (like 1 to 100, for example), we will have problems training our classification models. You can get data frame columns via the dot notation. For example, df.label will return you the label column as a new data frame. The data frame class has all kinds of useful methods for calculating the summary statistics. The value_counts() method returns the counts of each element type in the data frame:

```
In []:
df.label.value_counts()
```

```
Out[]:
platyhog        520
rabbosaurus     480
Name: label, dtype: int64
```

The class distribution looks okay for our purposes. Now let's explore the features.

We need to group our data by classes, and calculate feature statistics separately to see the difference between the creature classes. This can be done using the `groupby()` method. It takes the label of the column by which you want to group your data:

```
In []:
grouped = df.groupby('label')
```

The grouped data frame has all the same methods and column labels as the original data frame. Let's see the descriptive statistics of a length feature:

```
In []:
grouped.length.describe()
Out[]:
```

Label	Count	Mean	Std.	Min.	25%	50%	75%	Max.
Platyhog	520.0	19.894876	4.653044	4.164723	16.646311	20.168655	22.850191	32.779472
Rabbosaurus	480.0	29.984387	5.072308	16.027639	26.721621	29.956092	33.826660	47.857896

What can we learn from this table? Platyhogs have a length with the mean of about 20 meters, and standard deviation of about 5. Rabbosauruses on average are 30 meters long, with a standard deviation of 5. The smallest platyhog is about 4 meters long, and the largest rabbosaurus is about 48 meters long. That's a lot, but less than the biggest Earth life forms (see Amphicoelias fragillimus, for example).

Color distribution can be viewed using the familiar `value_counts()` method:

```
In []:
grouped.color.value_counts()
Out[]:
label           color
platyhog        light black         195
                purple polka-dot     174
                pink gold           151
rabbosaurus     light black         168
                pink gold           156
                space gray          156
Name: color, dtype: int64
```

We can represent this in a more appealing form, using `unstack()` and `plot()` methods:

```
In []:
plot = grouped.color.value_counts().unstack().plot(kind='barh',
stacked=True, figsize=[16,6], colormap='autumn')
Out[]:
```

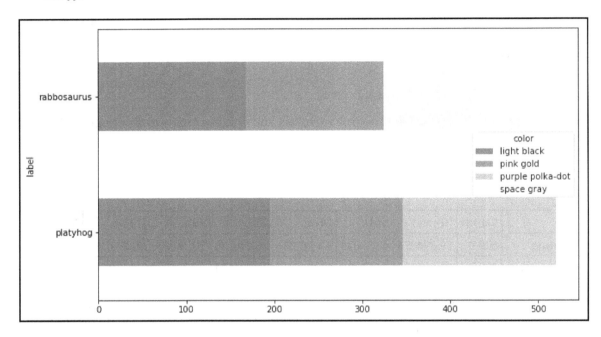

Figure 2.2: Color distribution

Looks like purple polka dot is a strong predictor of a `platyhog` class. But if we see a space-gray individual, we can be sure we should run quickly.

In a similar manner, fluffiness distribution can be visualized using:

```
In []:
plot = grouped.fluffy.value_counts().unstack().plot(kind='barh',
stacked=True, figsize=[16,6], colormap='winter')
Out[]:
```

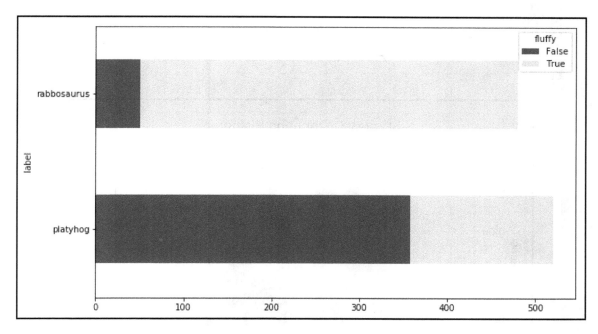

Figure 2.3: Fluffiness distribution

Rabbosauruses go in three colors: light black, pink gold, and space gray. 90% of them are fluffy (the remaining 10% are probably old and bald). Platyhogs, on the other hand, can be light black, pink gold, or purple polka dot. 30% of them are fluffy (mutants, maybe?).

For more complex data visualization, we need the matplotlib plotting library:

```
In []:
import matplotlib.pyplot as plt
```

Drawing the histogram of length distribution:

```
In []:
plt.figure()
plt.hist(df[df.label == 'rabbosaurus'].length, bins=15, normed=True)
plt.hist(df[df.label == 'platyhog'].length, bins=15, normed=True)
plt.title("Length Distribution Histogram")
plt.xlabel("Length")
plt.ylabel("Frequency")
fig = plt.gcf()
plt.show()
Out []:
```

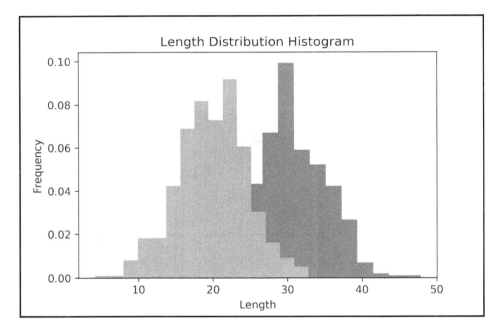

Figure 2.4: Length distribution

In general, one can say that the platyhogs are smaller, but there is significant range of overlap approximately between 20 and 30 meters, where the length alone is not enough to discriminate between two classes.

Data preprocessing

In the following sections we will take a look at the different data processing techniques.

Converting categorical variables

As you already have noticed, a data frame can contain columns with the data of different types. To see which type has each column, we can check the `dtypes` attribute of the data frame. You can think about Python attributes as being similar to Swift properties:

```
In []:
df.dtypes
Out[]:
length      float64
color        object
fluffy         bool
label        object
dtype: object
```

While `length` and `fluffy` columns contain the expected datatypes, the types of `color` and `label` are less transparent. What are those objects? This means those columns can contain any type of the object. At the moment, we have strings in them, but what we really want them to be are categorical variables. In case you don't remember from the previous chapter, categorical variables are like Swift enums. Fortunately for us, data frame has handy methods for converting columns from one type to another:

```
In []:
df.color = df.color.astype('category')
df.label = df.label.astype('category')
```

That's it. Let's check:

```
In []:
df.dtypes
Out []:
length      float64
color       category
fluffy         bool
label       category
dtype: object
```

`color` and `label` are categories now. To see all colors in those categories, execute:

```
In []:
colors = df.color.cat.categories.get_values().astype('string')
colors
Out[]:
array(['light black', 'pink gold', 'purple polka-dot', 'space gray'],
dtype='|S16')
```

As expected, we have four colors. `'|S16'` stands for strings of 16 characters in length.

Separating features from labels

Let's separate our features from the labels, as we will feed them into the model separately:

```
In []:
features = df.loc[:,:'fluffy']
labels = df.label
```

This horrible construction `df.loc[:,:'fluffy']` tells the data frame that we want all the rows (the first column), and the columns starting from the first, finishing with `'fluffy'`.

One-hot encoding

Most of the machine learning algorithms can't work with the categorical variables, so usually we want to convert them to the one-hot vectors (statisticians prefer to call them **dummy variables**). Let's convert first, and then I will explain what this is:

```
In []:
features = pd.get_dummies(features, columns = ['color'])
features.head()
Out[]:
```

	length	fluffy	color_light black	color_pink gold	color_purple polka-dot	color_space gray
0	27.545139	True	0	1	0	0
1	12.147357	False	0	1	0	0
2	23.454173	True	1	0	0	0
3	29.956698	True	0	1	0	0

4	34.884065	True	1	0	0	0

So now, instead of one column, `color`, we have four columns: `color_light black`, `color_pink gold`, `color_purple polka dot`, and `color_space gray`. The color of each sample is encoded as 1 in the corresponding column. Why do we need this if we could simply replace colors with the numbers from 1 to 4? Well, this is the problem: why to prefer 1 to 4 over the 4 to 1, or powers of 2, or prime numbers? These colors on their own don't carry any quantitative information associated to them. They can't be sorted from the largest to the smallest. If we introduce this information artificially, the machine learning algorithm may attempt to utilize that meaningless information, and we will end up with the classifier that sees regularities where there are none.

Splitting the data

Finally, we want to split our data into training and test sets. We will train our classifier only on the training set, so it will never see the test set until we want to evaluate its performance. This is a very important step, because as we will see in the future, the quality of predictions on the test set can differ dramatically from the quality measured on the training set. Data splitting is an operation specific to machine learning tasks, so we will import scikit-learn (a machine learning package) and use some functions from it:

```
In []:
from sklearn.model_selection import train_test_split
X_train, X_test, y_train, y_test = train_test_split(features, labels,
test_size=0.3, random_state=42)
X_train.shape, y_train.shape, X_test.shape, y_test.shape
Out[]:
  ((700, 6), (700,), (300, 6), (300,))
```

Now we have 700 training samples with 6 features each, and 300 test samples with the same number of features.

Decision trees everywhere

The algorithm that we're going to use for our first machine learning exercise is called a **decision tree classifier**. A decision tree is a set of rules that describe the process of decision making (see *figure 2.5* for example).

Decision trees are widely used outside the machine learning in different domains; for example, in business analysis. The popularity of decision trees is understandable: they are easy to interpret, and nice to visualize. For many years, they were built manually using the domain expert knowledge. Fortunately, now we have machine learning algorithms that can easily turn almost any labeled dataset into a decision tree.

Training the decision tree classifier

Let's learn how to train the decision tree classifier as shown in the following code snippet:

```
In []:
from sklearn import tree
tree_model = tree.DecisionTreeClassifier(criterion='entropy',
random_state=42)
tree_model = tree_model.fit(X_train, y_train)
tree_model
Out[]:
DecisionTreeClassifier(class_weight=None,
          criterion='entropy', max_depth=None,
          max_features=None, max_leaf_nodes=None,
          min_impurity_split=1e-07, min_samples_leaf=1,
          min_samples_split=2, min_weight_fraction_leaf=0.0,
          presort=False, random_state=42, splitter='best')
```

The most interesting for us are the class attributes of `DecisionTreeClassifier`:

- `criterion`: The way to estimate the best partition (see the *How decision tree learning works* section).
- `max_depth`: Maximum tree depth.
- `max_features`: The maximum number of attributes to account in one split.
- `min_samples_leaf`: The minimum number of objects in the leaf; for example, if it is equal to 3, then the tree will generate only those classification rules that are true for at least three objects.

These attributes are known as **hyperparameters**. They are different from model parameters: the former is something that users can tweak, and the latter is something that machine learning algorithm learns. In a decision tree, parameters are specific rules in its nodes. The tree hyperparameters must be adjusted depending on the input data, and this is usually done using cross-validation (stay tuned).

Decision tree classifier documentation:
http://scikit-learn.org/stable/modules/tree.html.

The properties of the model, which are not adjusted (learned) by the model itself, but are available for the user's adjustments, are known as hyperparameters. In the case of the decision tree model, these hyperparameters are class_weight, criterion, max_depth, max_features, and so on. They are like knobs you can turn to adjust the model to your specific needs.

Tree visualization

Let us take a look at the code to visualize a tree as follows:

```
In []:
labels = df.label.astype('category').cat.categories
labels = list(labels)
labels
Out[]:
[u'platyhog', u'rabbosaurus']
```

Define a variable to store all the names for the features:

```
In []:
feature_names = map(lambda x: x.encode('utf-8'),
features.columns.get_values())
feature_names
Out[]:
['length',
 'fluffy',
 'color_light black',
 'color_pink gold',
 'color_purple polka-dot',
 'color_space gray']
```

Then, create the graph object using the export_graphviz function:

```
In []:
import pydotplus
dot_data = tree.export_graphviz(tree_model, out_file=None,
                            feature_names=feature_names,
                            class_names=labels,
                            filled=True, rounded=True,
                            special_characters=True)
dot_data
Out[]:
u'digraph Tree {nnode [shape=box, style="filled, rounded", color="black",
fontname=helvetica] ;nedge [fontname=helvetica] ;n0 [label=<length &le;
26.6917<br/>entropy = 0.9971<br/>samples = 700<br/>value = [372, ...
In []:
graph = pydotplus.graph_from_dot_data(dot_data.encode('utf-8'))
graph.write_png('tree1.png')
Out[]:
True
```

Put a markdown to the next cell to see the newly-created file as follows:

```
![](tree1.png)
```

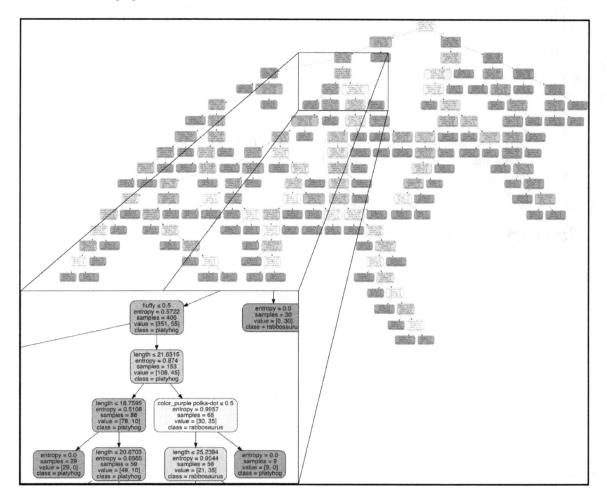

Figure 2.5: Decision tree structure and a close-up of its fragment

The preceding diagram shows what our decision tree looks like. During the training, it grows upside-down. Data (features) travels through it from its root (top) to the leaves (bottom). To predict the label for a sample from our dataset using this classifier, we should start from the root, and move until we reach the leaf. In each node, one feature is compared to some value; for example, in the root node, the tree checks if the length is < 26.0261. If the condition is met, we move along the left branch; if not, along the right.

Let's look closer at a part of the tree. In addition to the condition in each node, we have some useful information:

- Entropy value
- Number of samples in the training set which supports this node
- How many samples support each outcome
- The most likely outcome at this stage

Making predictions

We use the `predict` function to get outcome labels for two samples. The first one is light-black, fluffy creature, 24 meters long. The second one is purple polka dot, non-fluffy, and 34 meters long. If you already don't remember the meaning of each feature, consult the `feature_names` variable:

```
In []:
samples = [[24,1,0,1,0,0], [34,0,0,0,1,0]]
tree_model.predict(samples)
Out[]:
array([u'platyhog', u'rabbosaurus'], dtype=object)
```

Our model predicted `platyhog` for the first sample, and `rabbosaurus` for the second one. A decision tree can also provide probabilistic output (how sure it is about the prediction):

```
In []:
tree_model.predict_proba(samples)
Out[]:
array([[ 1.,   0.],
       [ 0.,   1.]])
```

The array contains two nested arrays, one for every prediction. Elements in the nested arrays are probabilities of the sample belonging to the corresponding class. This means that our model is 100% sure that the first sample belongs to the first class, and 100% sure that the second sample belongs to the second class.

But how sure can we be about these predictions? We have a whole set of different tools to evaluate the model's accuracy, and the simplest one is the built-in scoring functions.

Evaluating accuracy

Score function calculates accuracy of the model using the data. Let's calculate the accuracy of our model on the training set:

```
In []:
tree_model.score(X_train, y_train)
Out[]:
1.0
```

Wow, looks like our model is 100% accurate. Isn't it a great result? Let's not hurry and check our model on held-out data. Evaluation on the test set is the golden standard of success in machine learning:

```
In []:
tree_model.score(X_test, y_test)
Out[]:
0.87666666666666671
```

Worse now. What's just happened? Here, the first time we were faced with the problem of overfitting, when the model is trying to fit itself to every quirk in the data. Our model adjusted itself to the training data so much, that on the previously unseen data, it lacks the ability to generalize. As any real-world data contains noise and signal, we want our models to fit to the signal and to ignore the noise component. Overfitting is the most common problem in machine learning. It's common when datasets are too small, or models are too flexible. The opposite situation is called underfitting—when the model is not able to fit the complex data well enough:

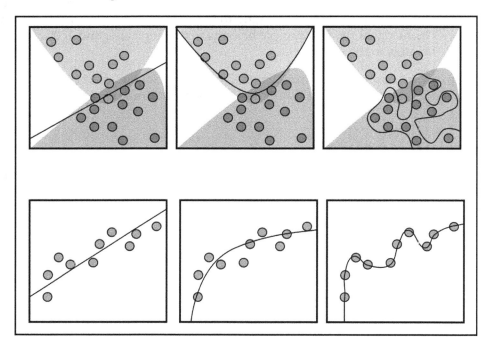

Figure 2.6: Underfitting (right column) versus good fit (central column) versus overfitting (right column). Top row shows classification problem, bottom row shows regression problem.

An overfitting problem is familiar to anyone who looked at some item at the online store, and then was presented with targeted advertisement of the same item everywhere on the internet. This item most likely is not relevant anymore, but the machine learning algorithm already overfitted to the limited dataset, and now you have trinket rabbits (or whatever you've looked at on the e-store) on every page you open.

In any case, we must fight overfitting somehow. So, what can we do? The simplest solution is to make the model simpler and less flexible (or, speaking machine learning, to reduce model capacity).

Tuning hyperparameters

The simplest way to simplify the decision tree is to limit its depth. How deep is it now? You can see 20 splits, or 21 layers, in *Figure 2.5*. At the same time, we have only three features. There are six of them actually, if we are taking into account one-hot encoded categorical color. Let's limit the maximum depth of the tree aggressively to be comparable with the number of features. `tree_model` object has a `max_depth` property, and so we're setting it to be less than the number of features:

```
In []:
tree_model.max_depth = 4
```

After these manipulations, we can retrain our model and reevaluate its accuracy:

```
In []:
tree_model = tree_model.fit(X_train, y_train)
tree_model.score(X_train, y_train)
Out[]:
0.90571428571428569
```

Note that accuracy on training is now set less by about 6%. How about test set?

```
In []:
tree_model.score(X_test, y_test)
Out[]:
0.9200000000000004
```

Accuracy on previously unseen data is now higher, by about 4%. This doesn't look like a great achievement, until you realize that it's an additional 40 correctly classified creatures from our initial set of 1,000. In modern machine learning contests, the final difference between 1st and 100th place can easily be about 1%.

Let's draw a tree structure after pruning. Code for this visualization is the same as before:

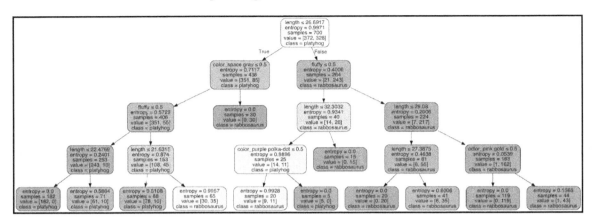

Figure 2.7: Tree structure after limiting its depth

Understanding model capacity trade-offs

Let's train trees with different depths: starting from 1 split, and to maximal 23 splits:

```
In []:
train_losses = []
test_losses = []
for depth in xrange(1, 23):
    tree_model.max_depth = depth
    tree_model = tree_model.fit(X_train, y_train)
    train_losses.append(1 - tree_model.score(X_train, y_train))
    test_losses.append(1 - tree_model.score(X_test, y_test))
figure = plt.figure()
plt.plot(train_losses, label="training loss", linestyle='--')
plt.plot(test_losses, label="test loss")
plt.legend(bbox_tc_anchor=(0., 1.02, 1., .102), loc=3, ncol=2,
mode="expand", borderaxespad=0.)
Out []:
```

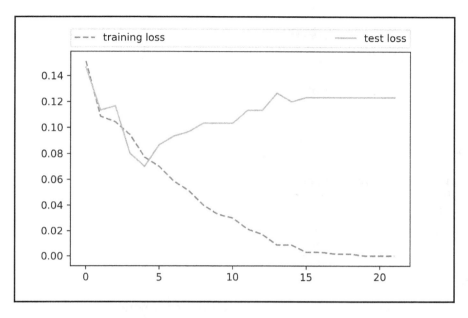

Figure 2.8: Training loss versus test loss, depending on the maximum tree depth

On the x axis, we've plotted the tree depth, and on the y axis, we've plotted the model's error. An interesting phenomenon that we're observing here is well familiar to any machine learning practitioner: as the model gets more complex, it gets more prone to overfitting. At first, as the model's capacity grows, both training and test loss (error) decreases, but then something strange happens: while error on the training set continues to go down, test error starts growing. This means that the model fits itself to the training examples so well, that it is not able to generalize well on unseen data anymore. That's why it's so important to have a held-out dataset, and perform your model validation on it. From the above plot, we can see that our more-or-less random choice of max_depth=4 was lucky: test error at this point became even less than training error.

How decision tree learning works

Decision tree learning is a supervised, non-parametric algorithm used for classification and regression.

Building a tree automatically from data

The *Twenty Questions* game is a traditional game where one of the players is the answerer who chooses an object (or a famous person in some variants), not revealing what it is to the other participants. All the other players are trying to guess what the object is by asking questions like *Can I eat this?* or *Is it a human?* where answers can only be *yes* or *no*.

If you have never heard about this game, refer to Wikipedia:
https://en.wikipedia.org/wiki/Twenty_Questions.

This is essentially a tree learning algorithm. To win in a game, you should pose such questions that discriminate the most; for example, the question, *Is it alive?* in the beginning of the game is clearly better than *Is it a cucumber?*. This ability to dissect the hypothesis space in an optimal way is formalized in the notion of information gain criterion.

Combinatorial entropy

Information gain criterion is based on the Shannon entropy notion. The Shannon entropy is a very important topic in the information theory, physics, and other domains. Mathematically, it is expressed as:

$$H = \sum_{i=1}^{N} p_i log_2 \left(\frac{1}{p_i} \right)$$

Where i is a state of a system, N is a total number of possible states, and p_i is a probability of the system being in the state i. Entropy describes the amount of uncertainty in the system. The more order you have in the system, the less entropy there is.

For the visual introduction to the information theory, check *Visual Information Theory* by Christopher Olah at:
http://colah.github.io/posts/2015-09-Visual-Information/.

If you want to learn more about entropy, check the nice, interactive blog *Entropy Explained, With Sheep* by Aatish Bhatia at:
https://aatishb.com/entropy/.

Let's show a simple example of how entropy can be useful for decision tree construction. For this, we'll simplify a task of alien creature classification, assuming that we can measure only one feature: body length. We have 10 individuals (Ö= platyhog and ⅍= rabbosaurus) with the following body lengths:

True label	Ö	Ö	Ö	Ö	Ö	⅍	Ö	⅍	⅍	⅍
Body length, meters	1	2	3	4	5	6	7	8	9	10

If we take one random individual from the group, it can be a platyhog with the probability of 0.6, or a rabbosaurus with the probability of 0.4. We have two states in this system for two outcomes. Let's calculate the entropy of it:

$$H = \frac{6}{10} \times log_2(\frac{10}{6}) + \frac{4}{10} \times log_2(\frac{10}{4}) = 0.97$$

So, the amount of uncertainty in this dataset is 0.97. Is it a lot, or a little? We don't have anything yet to compare it with, so let's divide the set at the middle (> 5 meters), and calculate the entropy for both subsets:

True label	Ö	Ö	Ö	Ö	Ö	⅍	Ö	⅍	⅍	⅍
Body length	1	2	3	4	5	6	7	8	9	10

$$H = \frac{5}{5} \times log_2(\frac{5}{5}) = 0$$

$$H = \frac{1}{5} \times log_2(\frac{5}{1}) + \frac{4}{5} \times log_2(\frac{5}{4}) \approx 0.72$$

H and *H* are now less than the original *H*. This demonstrates how you can reduce the entropy by splitting the dataset in the right place. This idea lies in the fundamentals of decision tree learning algorithms.

We can calculate how effectively we reduced the entropy by splitting the set using the **Information Gain** (**IG**) criterion:

Information Gain = Entropy(parent) - Weighted Sum of Entropy (Children), or:

$$IG = H_0 - \sum_{i=1}^{q} \frac{N_i}{N} H_i$$

q is a number of groups after splitting, N_i is a count of elements in the i-th group, N—is the total count of elements before split. In our example, $q = 2$, $N = 10$, and $N_1 = N_2 = 5$:

$$IG_{length>5} = 0.97 - (\frac{5}{10} \times 0 + \frac{5}{10} \times 0.72) = 0.61$$

This means that asking the question *Is the body length greater than 5?* gives us an information gain of *0.61*. Is it a lot, or a little? Let's compare it to the information loss of the split around length > 7:

$$IG_{length > 7} = 0.97 - [\frac{7}{10} \times (\frac{1}{7} \times \log_2(7) + \frac{6}{7} \times \log_2(\frac{7}{6}))] \approx 0.56$$

Apparently, the choice of the middle point was lucky, because all other splits don't look promising. But you are free to check them if you want.

There is no sense to split the left part further, but we can continue splitting the right subset until entropy of each of its children will not be equal to zero (see *Figure 2.9*).

So, this is our decision tree, and a recursive algorithm for its building. But now comes an interesting question: how to know which split yields the maximal information gain? The simplest way is a greedy search: just check all possible variants.

Information gain is only one of the heuristics, there are more of them; for instance, in our scikit-learn decision tree learner, we used Gini impurity as a heuristic. According to the Michigan State University (`http://www.cse.msu.edu/~cse802/DecisionTrees.pdf`):

> *"Gini impurity is the expected error rate at node N if the category label is selected randomly from the class distribution present at N."*

Check the documentation on the `criterion` property of `DecisionTreeClassifier` for more information about different heuristics available for tree learning in scikit-learn. In practice, Gini works very similarly to the information gain. A historical fact to dilute the theoretical exposition: Corrado Gini was an Italian statistician and the author of *The Scientific Basis of Fascism* (1927):

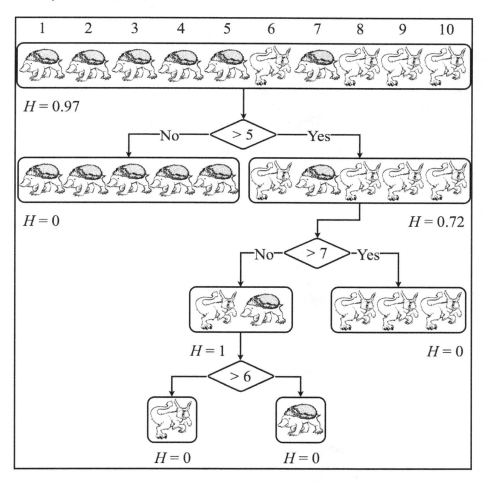

Figure 2.9: Building a decision tree. *H* stands for entropy in each group. Picture by Mykola Sosnovshchenko.

Evaluating performance of the model with data

The ways to assess the quality of a model's predictions quantitatively are known as **metrics**. The simplest metric in classification is accuracy, a proportion of correctly classified cases. Accuracy metric can be misleading. Imagine that you have a training set with 1000 samples. 999 of them are of class A, and 1 of class B. Such a kind of dataset is called **imbalanced**. The baseline (the simplest) solution in this case would be to always predict class A. Accuracy of such a model would then be 0.999, which can be pretty impressive, but only if you don't know about the ratio of classes in the training set. Now imagine that class A corresponds to an outcome of healthy, and class B to cancer, in the medical diagnostic system. It's clear now that 0.999 accuracy is worth nothing, and totally misleading. Another thing to consider is that the cost of different errors can be different. What's worse: to diagnose a healthy person as ill, or an ill person as healthy? This leads to the notion of two types of error (*Figure 2.10*):

- Type I error, also known as **false positive**: algorithm predicts **cancer**, while there is no cancer
- Type II error, also known as, **false negative**: algorithm predicts **no cancer**, while there is.

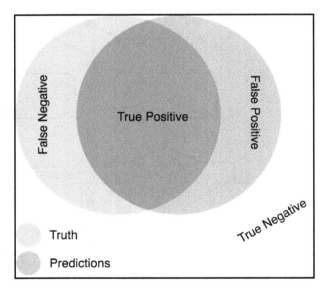

Figure 2.9: Two types of errors represented as a Venn diagram

Precision, recall, and F1-score

To assess the quality of the algorithm considering the two types of error, accuracy metric is useless. That's why different metrics were proposed.

Precision and **recall** are metrics used to evaluate a prediction's quality in information retrieval and binary classification. Precision is a proportion of true positives among all predicted positives. It shows how relevant results are. Recall, also known as **sensitivity**, is a proportion of true positives among all truly positive samples. For example, if the task is to distinguish cat photos from non-cat photos, precision is a fraction of correctly predicted cats to all predicted cats. Recall is a fraction of predicted cats to the total number of true cats.

If we denote the number of true positive cases as T_p, and number of false positive cases as F_p, then precision P is calculated as:

$$P = \frac{T_p}{T_p + F_p}$$

Recall R is calculated as:

$$R = \frac{T_p}{T_p + F_n},$$

Where F_n is a number of false negative cases.

F1 measure is calculated as:

$$F_1 = 2\frac{P \times R}{P + R}$$

Now the same in Python:

```
In []:
import numpy as np
predictions = tree_model.predict(X_test)
predictions = np.array(map(lambda x: x == 'rabbosaurus', predictions),
dtype='int')
true_labels = np.array(map(lambda x: x == 'rabbosaurus', y_test),
dtype='int')
from sklearn.metrics import precision_score, recall_score, f1_score
precision_score(true_labels, predictions)
Out []:
0.87096774193548387
```

```
In []:
recall_score(true_labels, predictions)
Out[]:
0.88815789473684215
In []:
f1_score(true_labels, predictions)
Out[]:
0.87947882736156346
```

K-fold cross-validation

This method was invented and gained popularity in those days when the big date was not yet a problem, everyone had little data, but still needed to build reliable models. First thing we do is shuffle our dataset well, and then divide it randomly into several equal parts, say 10 (this is the k in k-fold). We hold out the first part as a test set, and on the remaining nine parts we train the model. The trained model is then assessed on the test set that did not participate in the training as usual. Next, we hold out the second of 10 parts, and train the model on the remaining nine (including those previously served as a test set). We validate the new model again on the part that did not participate in the training. We continue this process until each of the 10 parts is in the role of the test set. The final quality metrics are determined by the averaging metrics from each of the 10 tests:

```
In []:
from sklearn.model_selection import cross_val_score
scores = cross_val_score(tree_model, features, df.label, cv=10)
np.mean(scores)
Out[]:
0.8830000000000001
In []:
plot = plt.bar(range(1,11), scores)
Out[]:
```

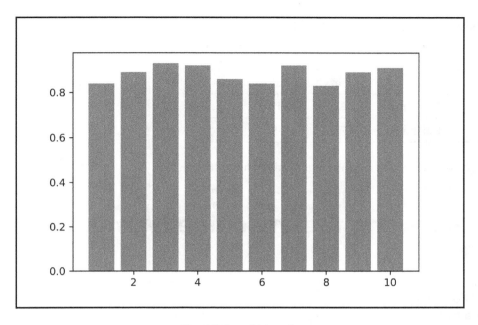

Figure 2.10: Cross-validation results

From the preceding graph, you can see that the model's accuracy depends on how you split the data, but not much. By taking the average and variance of the cross-validation results, you can make a sense of how well your model can generalize on different data, and how stable it is.

Confusion matrix

Confusion matrix helps to see what types of errors occur more often:

```
In []:
from sklearn.metrics import confusion_matrix
confusion_matrix(y_test, tree_model.predict(X_test))
Out[]:
array([[128,  20],
       [ 17, 135]])
```

This is how to read and interpret such matrices:

	Predicted labels		
		Platyhog	Rabbosaurus
True labels	Platyhog	128	20
	Rabbosaurus	17	135

The bigger the numbers on the matrix diagonally, the better.

Implementing first machine learning app in Swift

You can transfer your model from Python to Swift in two ways: transfer a trained model, or train a model from the ground up in Swift. The first option is easy in the case of decision trees, as a trained model can be expressed as a set of if-else conditions, which is trivial to code manually. Training the model from the ground up is required only in the situation where you want your app to learn in runtime. We will stick to the first approach in this example, but instead of coding rules manually, we will export the scikit-learn model for iOS using Core ML tools.

Introducing Core ML

Core ML was first presented at Apple WWDC 2017. Defining Core ML as machine learning framework is not fair, because it lacks learning capabilities; it's rather a set of conversion scripts to plug the pre-trained model into your Apple applications. Still, it is an easy way for newcomers to start running their first models on iOS.

Core ML features

Here is a list of Core ML features:

- `coremltools` Python package includes several converters for popular machine learning frameworks: scikit-learn, Keras, Caffe, LIBSVM, and XGBoost.
- Core ML framework allows running inference (making predictions) on a device. Scikit-learn converter also supports some data transformation and model pipelining.
- Hardware acceleration (Accelerate framework and Metal under the hood).
- Supports iOS, macOS, tvOS, and watchOS.
- Automatic code generation for OOP-style interoperability with Swift.

The biggest Core ML limitation is that it doesn't support models training.

Exporting the model for iOS

In our Jupyter notebook, execute the following code to export the model:

```
In []:
import coremltools as coreml
coreml_model = coreml.converters.sklearn.convert(tree_model, feature_names,
'label')
coreml_model.author = "Author name goes here..."
coreml_model.license = "License type goes here ..."
coreml_model.short_description = "Decision tree classifier for
extraterrestrials."
coreml_model.input_description['data'] = "Extraterrestrials features"
coreml_model.output_description['prob'] =  "Probability of belonging to
class."
coreml_model.save('DecisionTree.mlmodel')
```

Scikit-learn converter documentation:
`http://pythonhosted.org/coremltools/generated/coremltools.conver`
`ters.sklearn.convert.html#coremltools.converters.sklearn.convert`

The code creates the `tree.mlmodel` file next to the Jupyter notebook file. This file can contain a single model, a model pipeline (several models chained one after another), or a list of scikit-learn models. According to the documentation, the scikit-learn converter supports the following types of machine learning models:

- Decision tree learning
- Tree ensembles
- Random forests
- Gradient boosting
- Linear and logistic regression (see `Chapter 5`, *Association Rule Learning*)
- Support vector machines (several types)

It also supports the following data transformations:

- Normalizer
- Imputer
- Standard scaler
- DictVectorizer
- One-hot encoder

Note that you can embed one-hot encoding as a part of pipeline, so you don't need to do it yourself in your Swift code. This is handy, because you don't need to keep track of the proper order of categorical variable levels.

The `.mlmodel` file can be one of three types: classifier, regressor, or a transformer, depending on the last model in the list, or a pipeline. It is important to understand that there is no direct correspondence between scikit-learn models (or other source framework) and Core ML models that run on a device. Because Core ML sources are closed, we don't know how it operates under the hood, and can't be sure that the model before and after the conversion will produce identical results. This means you need to validate the model after device deployment, to measure its performance and accuracy.

Ensemble learning random forest

One-sentence explanation for LOTR fans: if decision trees were Ents, the random forest would be an Entmoot. For everyone else, random forest algorithm works like this:

- Split data into random subsets of equal size, maybe with replacement
- On each of those subsets, build a decision tree, choosing for every split a random feature subset of fixed size
- To perform inference, perform a voting among the trees (classification), or average their predictions (regression)

Such tree ensembles are very popular in certain domains, because their prediction quality beats most other models.

Most likely, this is not the model you want to train on a mobile device, due to the memory and time limitations, but you can still use it for inference thanks to Core ML. The workflow looks like this:

- Pre-train random forest in scikit-learn
- Export the model in the scikit-learn format
- Convert it to the Apple `mlmodel` format with the help of the `coremltool` Python package
- Import it in your iOS project using Core ML framework

By the way, if you look at the inner structure of the GameplayKit's tree learner in a debugger or playground, you'll see that it also uses random forest under the hood.

Training the random forest

Training the random forest model is not very different from training the decision tree:

```
In []:
from sklearn.ensemble import RandomForestClassifier
rf_model = RandomForestClassifier(criterion = 'entropy', random_state=42)
rf_model = rf_model.fit(X_train, y_train)
print(rf_model)
Out[]:
RandomForestClassifier(bootstrap=True, class_weight=None,
criterion='entropy',
            max_depth=None, max_features='auto', max_leaf_nodes=None,
            min_impurity_split=1e-07, min_samples_leaf=1,
            min_samples_split=2, min_weight_fraction_leaf=0.0,
```

```
        n_estimators=10, n_jobs=1, oob_score=False, random_state=42,
        verbose=0, warm_start=False)
```

 Documentation at: `http://scikit-learn.org/stable/modules/generated/sklearn.ensemble.RandomForestClassifier.html`.

Random forest accuracy evaluation

Loss on training data:

```
In []:
rf_model.score(X_train, y_train)
Out[]:
0.98999999999999999
```

Loss on test data:

```
In []:
rf_model.score(X_test, y_test)
Out[]:
0.90333333333333332
```

Cross-validation:

```
In []:
scores = cross_val_score(rf_model, features, df.label, cv=10)
np.mean(scores)
Out[]:
0.89700000000000002
In []:
print("Accuracy: %0.2f (+/- %0.2f)" % (scores.mean(), scores.std() * 2))
Accuracy: 0.90 (+/- 0.06)
```

Precision and recall:

```
In []:
predictions = rf_model.predict(X_test)
predictions = np.array(map(lambda x: x == 'rabbosaurus', predictions),
dtype='int')
true_labels = np.array(map(lambda x: x == 'rabbosaurus', y_test),
dtype='int')
precision_score(true_labels, predictions)
Out[]:
0.9072847682119205
In []:
recall_score(true_labels, predictions)
Out[]:
0.90131578947368418
```

F1-score:

```
In []:
f1_score(true_labels, predictions)
Out[]:
0.90429042904290435
```

Confusion matrix:

```
In []:
confusion_matrix(y_test, rf_model.predict(X_test))
Out[]:
array([[134,  14],
       [ 15, 137]])
```

You export a random forest for the iOS in the same way you do for a decision tree.

Importing the Core ML model into an iOS project

Create a new iOS project and drag and drop the DecisionTree.mlmodel into a project tree in Xcode. Click on it to see a machine learning model navigator screen:

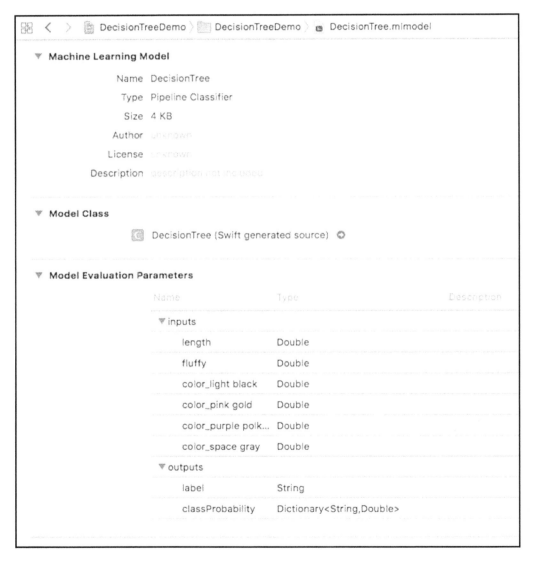

Figure 2.11: Machine learning navigator screen

On this screen, you can find a familiar model description, model type (pipeline by some reason, in this case), the name of the Swift class that represents the model in the app, and lists of inputs and outputs. If you click on the small arrow next to the class name in the **Model Class** section, the autogenerated file `DecisionTree.swift` is opened. This reminds a Core Data framework, where you have autogenerated files for `NSMangedObject` subclasses. `DecisionTree.swift` contains three classes:

- `DecisionTreeInput: MLFeatureProvider`, contains the input features (six of them, all Double).
- `DecisionTreeOutput: MLFeatureProvider`, contains class label and class probability.
- `DecisionTree: NSObject`, the class of the model itself. It contains methods for initialization and making predictions.

The method `init(contentsOf: url)` allows to replace the model in runtime, but only if you preserve the input and output structure. For example, this is how the model is loaded from the file in the bundle:

```
let bundle = Bundle.main
let assetPath = bundle.url(forResource: "DecisionTree",
withExtension:"mlmodelc")
let sklDecisionTree = DecisionTree(contentsOf: assetPath!)
```

In a same way, you can create a model with the content of a remote URL.

Drag and drop the `RandomForest.ml` model to the project to also compare accuracy of the models on the iOS.

Evaluating performance of the model on iOS

I'm not describing here a `.csv` parsing in Swift; if you are interested in the details, please see the supplementary materials. Assuming that you've successfully loaded the test data in the form of two arrays, `[Double]` for features and `[String]` for labels, have a go at the following code:

```
let (xMat, yVec) = loadCSVData()
```

To create a decision tree and evaluate it, try this:

```
let sklDecisionTree = DecisionTree()

let xSKLDecisionTree = xMat.map { (x: [Double]) -> DecisionTreeInput in
    return DecisionTreeInput(length: x[0],
                             fluffy: x[1],
                             color_light_black: x[2],
                             color_pink_gold: x[3],
                             color_purple_polka_dot: x[4],
                             color_space_gray: x[5])
}

let predictionsSKLTree = try! xSKLDecisionTree
    .map(sklDecisionTree.prediction)
    .map{ prediction in
        return prediction.label == "rabbosaurus" ? 0 : 1
}

let groundTruth = yVec.map{ $0 == "rabbosaurus" ? 0 : 1 }

let metricsSKLDecisionTree = evaluateAccuracy(yVecTest: groundTruth,
predictions: predictionsSKLTree)
print(metricsSKLDecisionTree)
```

To create a random forest and evaluate it, trying using the following code:

```
let sklRandomForest = RandomForest()

let xSKLRandomForest = xMat.map { (x: [Double]) -> RandomForestInput in
    return RandomForestInput(length: x[0],
                             fluffy: x[1],
                             color_light_black: x[2],
                             color_pink_gold: x[3],
                             color_purple_polka_dot: x[4],
                             color_space_gray: x[5])
}

let predictionsSKLRandomForest = try!
xSKLRandomForest.map(sklRandomForest.prediction).map{$0.label ==
"rabbosaurus" ? 0 : 1}

let metricsSKLRandomForest = evaluateAccuracy(yVecTest: groundTruth,
predictions: predictionsSKLRandomForest)
print(metricsSKLRandomForest)
```

This is an example of how you can evaluate your model's prediction quality in the Swift application. The structure, that contains the results of evaluation is as follows:

```
struct Metrics: CustomStringConvertible {
let confusionMatrix: [[Int]]
let normalizedConfusionMatrix: [[Double]]
let accuracy: Double
let precision: Double
let recall: Double
let f1Score: Double

var description: String {
    return """
    Confusion Matrix:
    (confusionMatrix)
    Normalized Confusion Matrix:
    (normalizedConfusionMatrix)
    Accuracy: (accuracy)
    Precision: (precision)
    Recall: (recall)
    F1-score: (f1Score)
    """
}
}
```

For the function for quality assessment, here's the code:

```
func evaluateAccuracy(yVecTest: [Int], predictions: [Int]) -> Metrics {
```

Calculating the confusion matrix

We'll use a straightforward approach here to calculate the confusion matrix; however, this would not work for multiclass classification. Here, p stands for predicted value, and t is for ground truth:

```
let pairs: [(Int, Int)] = zip(predictions, yVecTest).map{ ($0.0, $0.1) }
var confusionMatrix = [[0,0], [0,0]]
for (p, t) in pairs {
    switch (p, t) {
    case (0, 0):
        confusionMatrix[0][0] += 1
    case (0, _):
        confusionMatrix[1][0] += 1
    case (_, 0):
        confusionMatrix[0][1] += 1
    case (_, _):
```

```
        confusionMatrix[1][1] += 1
    }
  }
  let totalCount = Double(yVecTest.count)
```

Normalize the matrix by total count:

```
let normalizedConfusionMatrix =
confusionMatrix.map{$0.map{Double($0)/totalCount}}
```

As we already know, accuracy is a number of true predictions divided by the total number of cases.

To calculate accuracy, try using the following code:

```
let truePredictionsCount = pairs.filter{ $0.0 == $0.1 }.count
let accuracy = Double(truePredictionsCount) / totalCoun
```

To calculate true positive, false positive, and false negative counts, you can use the numbers from the confusion matrix, but let's do it the proper way:

```
let truePositive = Double(pairs.filter{ $0.0 == $0.1 && $0.0 == 0 }.count)
let falsePositive = Double(pairs.filter{ $0.0 != $0.1 && $0.0 == 0 }.count)
let falseNegative = Double(pairs.filter{ $0.0 != $0.1 && $0.0 == 1 }.count)
```

To calculate precision:

```
let precision = truePositive / (truePositive + falsePositive)
```

To calculate recall:

```
let recall = truePositive / (truePositive + falseNegative)
```

To calculate *F1*-score:

```
let f1Score = 2 * precision * recall / (precision + recall)
return Metrics(confusionMatrix: confusionMatrix, normalizedConfusionMatrix:
normalizedConfusionMatrix, accuracy: accuracy, precision: precision,
recall: recall, f1Score: f1Score)
}
```

Here is my result for the decision tree on iOS:

```
Confusion Matrix:
[[135, 17],
[20, 128]]

Normalized Confusion Matrix:
[[0.45000000000000001, 0.056666666666666664],
[0.066666666666666666, 0.42666666666666669]]

Accuracy: 0.876666666666667
Precision: 0.870967741935484
Recall: 0.888157894736842
F1-score: 0.879478827361563
```

And for the random forest:

```
Confusion Matrix:
[[138, 14],
[18, 130]]

Normalized Confusion Matrix:
[[0.46000000000000002, 0.046666666666666669],
[0.059999999999999998, 0.43333333333333335]]

Accuracy: 0.893333333333333
Precision: 0.884615384615385
Recall: 0.907894736842105
F1-score: 0.896103896103896
```

Congratulations! We've trained two machine learning algorithms, deployed them to the iOS, and evaluated their accuracy. Interesting that while decision tree metrics match perfectly, the random forest performance is slightly worse on Core ML. Don't forget to always validate your model after any type of conversion.

Decision tree learning pros and cons

Advantages:

- Easy to understand and interpret, perfect for visual representation. This is an example of a white box model, which closely mimics the human decision-making process.
- Can work with numerical and categorical features.
- Requires little data preprocessing: no need for one-hot encoding, dummy variables, and so on.
- Non-parametric model: no assumptions about the shape of data.
- Fast for inference.
- Feature selection happens automatically: unimportant features will not influence the result. The presence of features that depend on each other (multicollinearity) also doesn't affect the quality.

Disadvantages:

- It tends to overfit. This usually can be mitigated in one of three ways:
  - Limiting tree depth
  - Setting the minimal number of objects in leaves
  - Tree pruning by deleting unimportant splits moving from the leaves to the root
- It is unstable—small changes in data can dramatically affect the structure of the tree and the final prediction.
- The problem with finding the globally optimal decision tree is NP-complete. That's why we use different heuristics and greedy search. Unfortunately, this approach doesn't guarantee learning the globally best tree, only locally optimal ones.
- Inflexible, in the sense that you can't incorporate a new data into them easily. If you obtained new labeled data, you should retrain the tree from scratch on the whole dataset. This makes decision trees a poor choice for any applications that require dynamic model adjustment.

Summary

In this chapter, we had our first experience of building a machine learning application, starting from the data and all the way over to the working iOS application. We went through several phases in this chapter:

- Exploratory data analysis using Jupyter, pandas, and Matplotlib
- Data preparation—splitting, and handling categorical variables
- Model prototyping using scikit-learn
- Model tuning and evaluation
- Porting prototype for the mobile platform using Core ML
- Model validation on a mobile device

There are several machine learning topics that we've learned about in this chapter: model parameters vs. hyperparameters, overfitting vs. underfitting, evaluation metrics: cross-validation, accuracy, precision, recall, and *F1*-score. These are the basic things that will be recurring topics throughout this book.

We've become acquainted with two machine learning algorithms, namely decision trees and random forest, a type of model ensemble.

In the next chapter, we're going to continue exploring classification algorithms, and will learn about instance-based learning algorithms. We will also build an iOS app that can learn right on the device, this time not for alien classification, but for some real-world problem, I promise.

K-Nearest Neighbors Classifier

3

This chapter is devoted to an important class of machine learning algorithms, known as instance-based models. The name comes from the fact that they are built around the notion of similarity between instances (distance) and the geometrical intuition behind it. As a practical application of our newly learned skills, we will build an app that recognizes types of user movements based on the data from motion sensors and learns completely on device (no Python this time).

The algorithms that we are discussing and implementing in this chapter are **k-nearest neighbors** (**KNN**) and **dynamic time warping** (**DTW**).

In this chapter, we will cover the following topics:

- Choosing a distance metric—Euclidean, edit distance, taxicab, and DTW
- Building a KNN multiclass classifier
- Geometrical intuition behind machine learning models
- Reasoning in high-dimensional spaces
- Choosing hyperparameters

Calculating the distance

How do we calculate a distance? Well, that depends on the kind of problem. In two-dimensional space, we used to calculate the distance between two points, (x_1, y_1) and (x_2, y_2), as $\sqrt{(x_1 - x_2)^2 + (y_1 - y_2)^2}$—the **Euclidean distance**. But this is not how taxi drivers calculate distance because in the city you can't cut corners and go straight to your goal. So, they use (knowing it or not) another distance metric: **Manhattan distance** or **taxicab distance**, also known as l_1 norm: $|x_1 - x_2| + |y_1 - y_2|$. This is the distance if we're only allowed to move along coordinate axes:

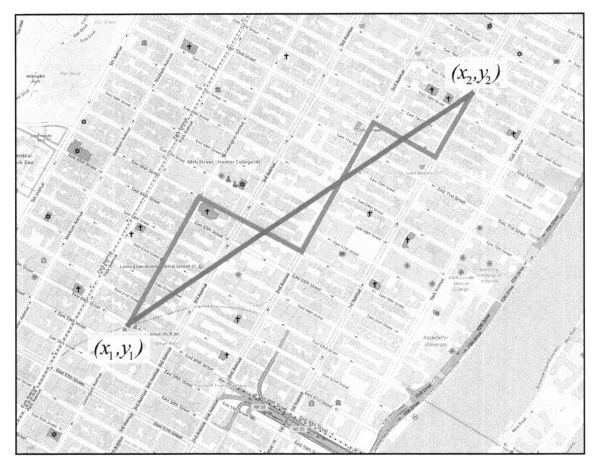

Figure 3.1: The blue line represents the Euclidean distance, the red line represents the Manhattan distance. Map of Manhattan by OpenStreetMap

Jewish German mathematician Hermann Minkowski proposed a generalization of both Euclidean and Manhattan distances. Here is the formula for the Minkowski distance:

$$d(p, q) = (\sum_{i=1}^{n} |p_i - q_i|^c)^{\frac{1}{c}}$$

where p and q are n-dimensional vectors (or coordinates of points in n-dimensional space if you wish). But what does c stand for? It is an order of the Minkowsi distance: under the $c = 1$, it gives an equation of Manhattan distance, and under $c = 2$ it gives Euclidean distance.

Vector operations, including the calculation of Manhattan and Euclidean distances, can be parallelized for efficiency. Apple's Accelerate framework provides APIs for fast vector and matrix computations.

In machine learning, we generalize the notion of distance to any kind of objects for which we can calculate how similar they are, using a function: distance metric. In this way, we can define the distance between two pieces of text, two pictures, or two audio signals. Let's take a look at two examples.

When you deal with two pieces of text of equal length, you use **edit distance**; for example, **Hamming distance**—the minimum number of substitutions needed to transform one string into another. To calculate the edit distance, we use dynamic programming, an iterative approach where the problem is broken into small subproblems, and the result of each step is remembered for future computations. Edit distance is an important measure in applications that deal with text revisions; for example, in bioinformatics (see the following diagram):

	cT c C C + + T t G A A g c c c C C a T t C G t A T a a T A A
	430 432 434 436 438 440 442 444 446 448 450 452 454 456 458 460
Homo sapiens	C T C C C G A T T G A A G C C C C A T T C G T A T A A T A A
Homo sapiens neanderthalensis	C T C C C G G T T G A A G C C C C A T T C G T A T A A T A A
Gorilla gorilla	C T T C C A G T T G A A G C C C C G T C C G T A T A A T A A
Felis catus	T T A C C A A T A G A A A T G A C C A T T C G C A T G T T A A

Figure 3.2: Four pieces of DNA from different species aligned together: modern human, neanderthal, gorilla, and cat. The Hamming edit distance from modern human to others is 1, 5, and 11 respectively.

Often, we store different signals (audio, motion data, and so on) as arrays of numbers. How do we measure the similarity of such two arrays? We use the combination of Euclidean distance and edit distance, called DTW.

DTW

Despite its Sci-Fi name, DTW has little to do with time travel, except for the fact that this technique was popular for speech recognition back in the 1980s. Imagine two signals as two springs oriented along the time axis. We place them next to each other on the table, and want to measure how similar (or how different... what's the same?) they are. One of them will serve as a template. And we start stretching and compressing another one, piece by piece, until it looks exactly as the first one (or the most similar). Then we account for how much effort we put into align two springs—we sum up all tensions and stretches together, and get the DTW distance.

DTW distance between two sound signals tells us how similar to each other they are. For example, having the record of an unknown voice command, we can compare it to voice commands in the database, and find the most similar one. DTW can be used not only with audio, but with many other types of signals. We will use it to calculate distance between signals from motion sensors:

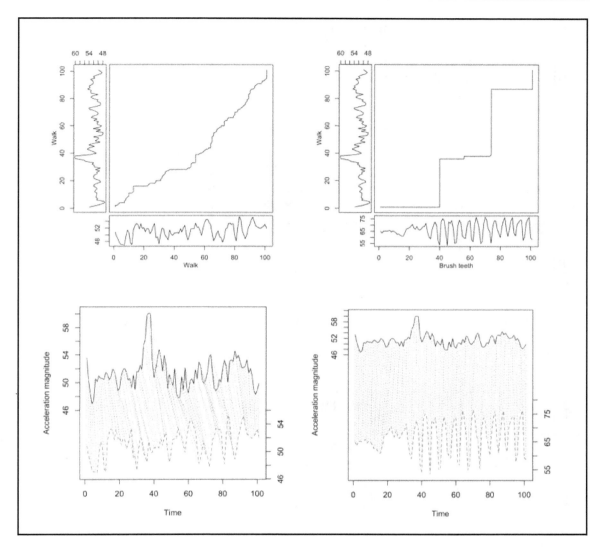

Figure 3.3: DTW alignment of two accelerometer signals. On the left: walking sample against another walking sample. On the right: brushing teeth against walking. The shorter the alignment is, the closer the two signals are to one another. Plots created using [1] and [2].

Let's demonstrate this with a simple example. Say we have two arrays: *[5, 2, 1, 3]* and *[10, 2, 4, 3]*. How do we calculate the distance between two arrays of length one: *[5]* and *[10]*? You can use squared difference as a measure; for example, $(5 - 10)^2 = 25$. Okay, now let's extend one of them: *[5, 2]* and *[10]*, and calculate the cumulative difference:

	[5]	[2]
[10]	25	$25 + (2-10)^2 = 89$

Let's extend another array to have *[5, 2]* and *[10, 2]*. Now, how to calculate the cumulative difference is not as clear as it was before, but let's assume that we are interested in the simplest way to transform one array into another (minimal distance, in other words):

	[5]	[2]
[10]	25	89
[2]	$25 + (5-2)^2 = 34$	$min (25, 89, 34) + (2-2)^2 = 25$

By extending arrays in such a way further, eventually we will get the following table:

	[5]	[2]	[1]	[3]
[10]	25	89	$89 + (1-10)^2 = 170$	$170 + (3-10)^2 = 219$
[2]	34	25	$min (89, 170, 25) + (1-2)^2 = 26$	$min (170, 219, 26) + (3-2)^2 = 27$
[4]	$34+(5-4)^2=35$	$min (34, 25, 35) + (2-4)^2 = 29$	$min (25, 26, 29) + (1-4)^2 = 34$	$min (26, 27, 34) + (3-4)^2 = 27$
[3]	$35+(5-3)^2=39$	$min (35, 29, 39) + (2-3)^2 = 30$	$min (29, 34, 30) + (1-3)^2 = 33$	$min (34, 27, 33) + (3-3)^2 = 27$

The bottom-right cell of the table contains the quantity we're interested in: DTW distance between two arrays, the measure of how hard it is to transform one array into another. We've just checked all the possible ways to transform arrays, and found the easiest of them (marked with a gray shading in the table). Movement along the diagonal of the table indicates the perfect match between arrays, while horizontal direction stands for deletion of the elements from the first array, and vertical movement indicates insertion into it (compare with *Figure 3.3*). The final array alignment looks like this:

[5, 2, 1, 3, -]

[10, 2, -, 4, 3]

 By the way, DTW can be applied not only to arrays of single numbers. Replace squared difference with Euclidean or Manhattan distance, and you can compare trajectories in a three-dimensional space or taxi routes.

Implementing DTW in Swift

There are two versions of the algorithm (with locality constraint, and without it). We'll implement both.

 The full source code for the application we are developing in this chapter can be found in the `MotionClassification` folder of supplementary materials.

Let's define a DTW structure, and create a static function `distance` in it:

```
func distance(sVec: [Double], tVec: [Double]) -> Double {
```

First, we're creating a distance matrix of size *(n+1 x m+1)*, and populating it with some values: the first cell of the matrix should be equal to zero, and the first row and the first column should be equal to a maximum double value. This is needed to handle border conditions in a proper way later. The first cell plays a role of initial value: initially, the distance is zero. All other cells are unimportant for now, as we'll overwrite their values later:

```
let n = sVec.count
let m = tVec.count
var dtwMat = [[Double]](repeating: [Double](repeating:
Double.greatestFiniteMagnitude, count: m+1), count: n+1)
dtwMat[0][0] = 0
```

After this, we iterate through both arrays from *1* to *n* and *1* to *m*, filling the distance matrix. At each position *[i, j]*, we calculate the cost for the previous position *(i-1, j-1)* as the squared difference between corresponding positions in the arrays: $(s_{i-1} - t_{j-1})^2$:

```
for i in 1...n {
    for j in 1...m {
        let cost = pow(sVec[i-1] - tVec[j-1], 2)
        let insertion = dtwMat[i-1][j]
        let deletion = dtwMat[i][j-1]
        let match = dtwMat[i-1][j-1]
        let prevMin = min(insertion, deletion, match)
        dtwMat[i][j] = cost + prevMin
    }
}
```

The value we are now looking for is in the last cell of the matrix: *dtw[n, m]*. To make the result comparable between series with different lengths, we normalize it by the length of the longest series:

```
    return dtwMat[n][m]/Double(max(n, m))
}
```

This gives us an average distance between two series.

To avoid warping the whole sequence to the small segment of its counterpart, locality constraint was introduced. It sets the upper limit to how many deletions/insertions can be found in a row.

And a version of the algorithm with locality constraint w:

```
func distance(sVec: [Double], tVec: [Double], w: Int) -> Double {
    let n = sVec.count
    let m = tVec.count
    var dtwMat = [[Double]](repeating: [Double](repeating:
Double.greatestFiniteMagnitude, count: m+1), count: n+1)
    dtwMat[0][0] = 0
    let constraint = max(w, abs(n-m))
    for i in 1...n {
        for j in max(1, i-constraint)...min(m, i+constraint) {
            let cost = pow(sVec[i-1] - tVec[j-1], 2)
            let insertion = dtwMat[i-1][j]
            let deletion = dtwMat[i][j-1]
            let match = dtwMat[i-1][j-1]
            dtwMat[i][j] = cost + min(insertion, deletion, match)
        }
    }
    return dtwMat[n][m]/Double(max(n, m))
```

```
}
```

Let's test our algorithm. The first two vectors are similar :

```
let aVec: [Double] = [1,2,3,4,5,6,7,6,5,4,3,2,1]
let bVec: [Double] = [2,3,4,5,7,7,6,5,4,3,2,1,0,-2]

let distance1 = DTW.distance(sVec: aVec, tVec: bVec)
let distance2 = DTW.distance(sVec: aVec, tVec: bVec, w: 3)
```

The result is about 0.857 in both cases.

Now we have two very different vectors:

```
let cVec: [Double] = [1,2,3,4,5,6,7,6,5,4,3,2,1,0]
let dVec: [Double] = [30,2,2,0,1,1,1,14,44]

let distance3 = DTW.distance(sVec: cVec, tVec: dVec)
let distance4 = DTW.distance(sVec: cVec, tVec: dVec, w: 3)
```

The results are 216.571 and 218.286 correspondingly. Note that the distance with locality constraint is even bigger than without it.

 Our implementation of DTW is naïve, and can be accelerated using parallel computing. To calculate the new row/column in a distance matrix, you don't need to wait until the previous one is finished; you only need it to be filled one cell ahead of your row/column. DTW can be effectively parallelized using GPU. See *Accelerating Dynamic Time Warping Subsequence Search with GPUs and FPGAs* for more details [3].

Using instance-based models for classification and clustering

Instance-based machine learning algorithms are usually easy to understand as they have some geometrical intuition behind them. They can be used to perform different kinds of tasks, including classification, regression, clustering, and anomaly detection.

It's easy to confuse classification and clustering at first. Just to remind you, classification is one of the many types of supervised learning. The task is to predict some discrete label from the set of features (*Figure 3.4*, left pane). Technically, classification goes in two types: binary (check *yes* or *no*), and multiclass (*yes/no/maybe/I don't know/can you repeat the question?*). But in practice, you can always build a multiclass classifier from several binary classifiers.

On the other hand, clustering is the task of unsupervised learning. This means that, unlike classification, it knows nothing about data labels, and works out clusters of similar samples in your data on its own. In the next chapter, we are going to discuss an instance-based clustering algorithm called *k*-means (KNN), and in this chapter, we focus on applications of instance-based algorithm KNN to multiclass classification:

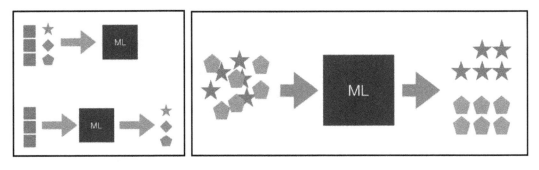

Figure 3.4: Classification process (on the left) and clustering (on the right). Classification consists of two steps: training with the labelled data and inference with unlabeled data. Clustering groups samples according to their similarity.

People motion recognition using inertial sensors

Wouldn't it be awesome at the end of every day to see the statistics of it: how much time have you spent doing things you like, and how much time you've wasted? With this kind of report, you could make your time management decisions based on real data, not just a gut feeling. Wait, but there are a lot of time trackers out there on the App Store, right? Sure, but there is one problem with most of them: you have to fill them in manually, because they can't detect what are you doing at every moment. You can't teach them to recognize types of your activities. Fortunately, we can fix this using machine learning; specifically, **time series classification**.

Time series is a special kind of dataset in which samples are arranged according to the time. Usually, time series are generated when samples are taken repeatedly after equal time intervals (sampling interval). In other words, the time series is a sequence of values measured at successive moments in time, after regular intervals, and describing a process unrolling in a time dimension.

Time series data type is common in iOS applications: among examples are signals from inertial sensors, measurements from HealthKit, and any other data that has a clear time correspondence and sampled regularly. Some other types of data, such as application logs or records of user activity, can be reduced to a special type of time series: categorical time series, where categories are in place of numbers.

The motion recognition task is important in health monitoring and fitness applications, but can also have some unusual use cases. For example, the *Walk Me Up! Alarm Clock* app makes you get out of your bed, because it doesn't allow you to snooze your alarm until you take a number of steps. It distinguishes real steps from attempts to cheat by shaking the device.

The Core Motion framework provides APIs to get a history of a user's movements or a real-time stream of data from motion sensors. It can also distinguish a limited set of movement types, but we're going to teach our app to recognize more types than the Core Motion can. With the growth in popularity of wearable accessories, the motion sensor became a very common source of data; however, the method described in this chapter is not specific to sensor data, so you can apply these algorithms to many other practical problems. That's the good thing about general-purpose machine learning algorithms: you can apply them to any kind of data, you only need to find an appropriate representation for the data.

Understanding the KNN algorithm

To recognize different types of motion activities, we will train the KNN classifier. The idea of the method is to find k training samples closest to the sample with an unknown label, and predict the label as a most frequent class among those k. That's it:

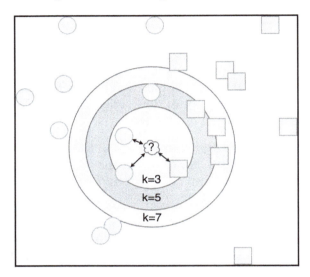

Figure 3.5: KNN classification algorithm. The new data point marked with ? gets classified based on the classes of its neighbors.

 Note how the choice of neighbor number affects the result of classification.

In fact, the algorithm is so simple, that it's tempting to formulate it in more complicated terms. Let's do it. The secret sauce of a KNN is a distance metric: function, which defines how close to each other two samples are. We have discussed several of them already: Euclidean, Manhattan, Minkowski, edit distance, and DTW. Following the terminology, samples are points in some n-dimensional space, where n equals to the number of features in each sample. This space is called **feature space**, and samples are distributed in it as clouds of points. Classification of an unknown data point happens in three steps:

1. Calculate distances from the point to all points in a training set
2. Choose the k-closest neighbors to the unknown point
3. Perform a majority vote among them

The surface that separates one class of points from another class is known as a **decision boundary**. The KNN algorithm creates piecewise linear decision boundaries that can approximate a decision boundary of any complexity by adding more and more training samples:

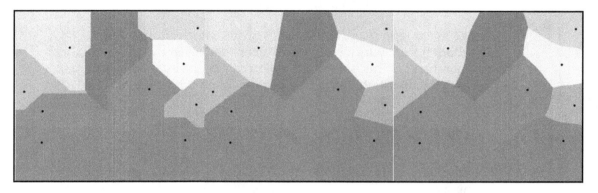

Figure 3.6: Voronoi cells graph shows the closest neighbor at each point with a color. Depending on the distance metric you choose, the graph looks quite different. From the left to the right: Manhattan ($c = 1$), Euclidean ($c = 2$), and Minkowski ($c = 3$) distance metrics.

Algorithms similar to KNN are also known as **non-generalizing machine learning**. In Chapter 6, *Linear Regression and Gradient Descent*, we will discuss a linear regression, an algorithm that constructs general representation of all data points—a straight line, because it assumes that all data points lie along the line. Unlike linear regression, KNN makes no assumption about the underlying structure of the data, it just stores all the training samples. Both approaches have their advantages and downsides.

You may think that this algorithm is too simple to be used for anything but some toy tasks. But over the years, KNN has demonstrated to be successfully employed for a wide range of problems, such as handwriting recognition, and satellite photo classification. It's also worth noting that it's easy to turn this classification algorithm into regression—you just need to replace categorical labels with the real numbers, and add an interpolation function.

Parametric versus non-parametric models

Many restrictions of the linear regressions come from the fact that it assumes that data is normally distributed. The class of statistical models which makes explicit assumptions about the statistical distribution underlying data is called **parametric models**.

Unlike linear regression, KNN makes no assumptions about the distribution from which samples are generated. That's why we call them **non-parametric**. This is the right tool to choose in situations where data has unusual distribution, and the decision boundary is irregular.

Implementing KNN in Swift

Fast implementations of KNN and DTW can be found in many machine learning and DSP libraries, for example `lbimproved` and `matchbox` C++ libraries:

- `github.com/lemire/lbimproved`
- `github.com/hfink/matchbox`

The KNN classifier works with virtually any type of data since you define distance metric for your data points. That's why we define it as a generic structure parameterized with types for features and labels. Labels should conform to a `Hashable` protocol, as we're going to use them for dictionary keys:

```
struct kNN<X, Y> where Y: Hashable { ... }
```

KNN has two hyperparameters: k—the number of neighbors `var k: Int`, and distance metric. We'll define it elsewhere, and pass during the initialization. Metric is a function, returning double distance for any two samples x1 and x2:

```
var distanceMetric: (_ x1: X, _ x2: X) -> Double
```

During the initialization, we just record the hyperparameters inside our structure. The definition of `init` looks like this:

```
init (k: Int, distanceMetric: @escaping (_ x1: X, _ x2: X) -> Double) {
    self.k = k
    self.distanceMetric = distanceMetric
}
```

KNN stores all its training data points. We are using the array of pairs *(features, label)* for this purposes:

```
private var data: [(X, Y)] = []
```

As usual with supervised learning models, we'll stick to the interface with two methods, `train` and `predict`, which reflect the two phases of a supervised algorithm's life. The `train` method in the case of KNN just saves the data points to use them later in the `predict` method:

```
mutating func train(X: [X], y: [Y]) {
    data.append(contentsOf: zip(X, y))
}
```

The `predict` method takes the data point and predicts the label for it:

```
func predict(x: X) -> Y? {
    assert(data.count > 0, "Please, use method train() at first to provide
training data.")
    assert(k > 0, "Error, k must be greater then 0.")
```

For this, we iterate through all samples in the training dataset, and compare them with the input sample x. We use *(distance, label)* tuples to keep track of distances to each of the training samples. After this, we sort all the samples descending by distances, and take the (`prefix`) first k elements:

```
    let tuples = data
        .map { (distanceMetric(x, $0.0), $0.1) }
        .sorted { $0.0 < $1.0 }
        .prefix(upTo: k)
```

This implementation is not optimal, and can be improved by keeping track of only the best k samples at each step, but the goal of it is to demonstrate the simplest machine learning algorithm without diving into the complex data structures, and show that even such naïve versions of it can perform well on complex tasks.

Now we arrange majority voting among top k samples. We count the frequency of each label, and sort them from descending:

```
    let countedSet = NSCountedSet(array: tuples.map{$0.1})
    let result = countedSet.allObjects.sorted {
        countedSet.count(for: $0) > countedSet.count(for: $1)
        }.first
    return result as? Y
}
```

The `result` variable holds a predicted class label.

Recognizing human motion using KNN

Core Motion is an iOS framework that provides an API for inertial sensors of mobile devices. It also recognizes some user motion types, and stores them to the HealthKit database.

If you are not familiar with Core Motion API, please check the framework reference: `https://developer.apple.com/reference/coremotion`.

The code for this example can be found in the `Code/02DistanceBased/ MotionClassification` folder of supplementary materials.

As per iOS 11 beta 2, the `CMMotionActivity` class includes the following types of motion:

- Stationary
- Walking
- Running
- Automotive
- Cycling

Everything else falls into an unknown category or is recognized as one of the preceding. Core Motion doesn't provide a way to recognize custom motion types so we'll train our own classifier for this purpose. Unlike decision trees from the previous chapter, KNN will be trained on device end-to-end. It will also not be frozen inside Core ML because as we keep all the control on it, we'll be able to update it in the application runtime.

iOS devices have three types of motion sensors:

- **Gyroscope**: This measures device orientation in space
- **Accelerometer**: This measures device acceleration
- **Magnetometer or compass**: This measures magnetism

They also have a barometer to detect elevation and some other sensors, but they are less relevant for our purposes. We will use an accelerometer data stream to train our KNN classifier and predict different motion types, like shaking a phone or squatting.

The following listing shows how to get updates from the accelerometer:

```
let manager = CMMotionManager()
manager.accelerometerUpdateInterval = 0.1
manager.startAccelerometerUpdates(to: OperationQueue.main) { (data:
CMAccelerometerData?, error: Error?) in
    if let acceleration = data?.acceleration {
        print(acceleration.x, acceleration.y, acceleration.z)
    }
}
```

The accelerometer APIs in Core Motion provide a time series of three-dimensional vectors, as shown in the following diagram:

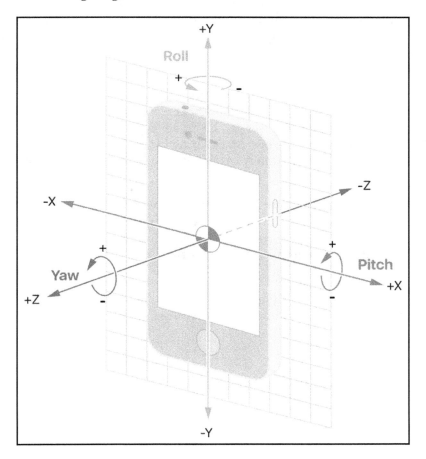

Figure 3.7: Core Motion coordinate system for accelerometer and gyroscope

To train our classifier, we need some labeled data. As we don't have a ready dataset and motion signals can be very different from person to person, we are going to allow the user to add new samples and improve the model. In the interface, the user selects the type of motion he wants to record, and presses the **Record** button, as shown in the next screenshot. The application samples 25 acceleration vectors, takes the magnitude of each vector, and feeds them with the label of the selected motion type into the KNN classifier. The user records as many samples as he wants.

Cold start problem

A very common situation is when a machine learning system starts functioning in a new environment, where no information to pre-train is available. The situation is known as a **cold start**. Such a system requires a certain amount of time to collect enough training data, and start producing meaningful predictions. The problem often arises in the context of personalization and recommender systems.

One solution for this it is so-called **active learning**, where the system can actively seek new data that could improve its performance. Usually, this means that the system queries a user to label some data. For instance, the user can be asked to provide some labeled examples before the start of the system, or the system can ping him when it stumbles upon especially hard cases asking to label them manually. Active learning is a special case of semi-supervised learning.

The second component of active learning is estimating which samples are the most useful by associating weights to them. In the case of KNN, these can be the samples that the model is less confident about, for example, the samples for whom their neighbors' classes are divided almost equally or the samples that are far from all others (outliers).

However, some researchers point out that active learning is built on flawed assumptions: the user is always available and willing to answer questions and he is always right in his/her answers. This is also something worth keeping in mind when building an active learning solution.

I guess when the Twitter app pings you at 4 AM with push notifications like *Take a look at this and 13 other Highlights*, it just wants to update its small personalized binary classifier of *interesting/not interesting* content using active learning.

Figure 3.8: App interface

In the classification phase, we feed unlabeled chunks of the same size into the classifier and get predictions which display to the user. We use DTW as a distance measure with locality constraint 3. In my experiments, k as 1 gave the best results but you can experiment with other number of neighbors. I will show here only the machine learning part, without the data collection part and user interface.

Creating the classifier:

```
classifier = kNN(k: 1, distanceMetric: DTW.distance(w: 3))
```

Training the classifier:

```
self.classifier.train(X: [magnitude(series3D: series)], y: [motionType])
```

The `magnitude()` function converts three-dimensional series into one-dimensional by calculating vector magnitude $\sqrt{x^2 + y^2 + z^2}$ to simplify the computations.

Making the predictions:

```
let motionType = self.classifier.predict(x: magnitude(series3D: series))
```

Balanced dataset

The application allows you to record samples of different motion types. As you train the model, you may notice one interesting effect: to get accurate predictions, you need not only enough samples, but you also need the proportion of different classes in your dataset to be roughly equal. Think about it: if you have 100 samples of two classes (`walk` and `run`), and 99 of them belong to one class (`walk`), the classifier that delivers 99% accuracy may look like this:

```
func predict(x: [Double]) -> MotionType {
    return .walk
}
```

But this is not what we want, obviously.

This observation lead us to the notion of the balanced data set; for most machine learning algorithms, you want the data set in which samples of different classes are represented equally frequently.

Choosing a good k

It is important to pick a proper value of hyperparameter k, since it can improve a model's performance as well as degrade it when chosen incorrectly. One popular rule of thumb is to take a square root of the number of training samples. Many popular software packages use this heuristic as a default k value. Unfortunately, this doesn't always work well, because of the differences in the data and distance metrics.

There is no mathematically-grounded way to come up with the optimal number of neighbors from the very beginning. The only option is to scan through a range of *k*s, and choose the best one according to some performance metric. You can use any performance metric that we've already described in the previous chapter: accuracy, *F1*, and so on. The cross-validation is especially useful when the data is scarce.

In fact, there is a variation of KNN, which doesn't require *k* at all. The idea is to make the algorithm take the radius of a ball to search the neighbors within. The *k* will be different for each point then, depending on the local density of points. This variation of the algorithm is known as **radius-based neighbor learning**. It suffers from the *n*-ball volume problem (see next section), because the more features you have, the bigger the radius should be to catch at least one neighbor.

Reasoning in high-dimensional spaces

Working with feature spaces of high dimensions requires special mental precautions, since our intuition used to deal with three-dimensional space starts to fail. For example, let's look at one peculiar property of *n*-dimensional spaces, known as an *n*-ball volume problem. *N*-ball is just a ball in *n*-dimensional Euclidean space. If we plot the volume of such *n*-ball (*y* axis) as a function of a number of dimensions (*x* axis), we'll see the following graph:

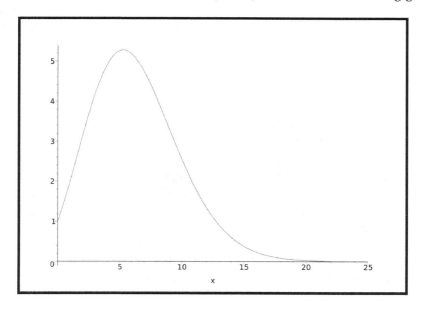

Figure 3.9: Volume of *n*-ball in *n*-dimensional space

Note that at the beginning the volume rises, until it reaches its peak in five-dimensional space, and then starts decreasing. What does it mean for our models? Specifically, for KNN, it means that starting from five features, the more features you have the greater should be the radius of the sphere centered on the point you're trying to classify to cover KNN.

The counter-intuitive phenomena that arise in a high-dimensional space are colloquially known as the **curse of dimensionality**. This includes a wide range of phenomena that can't be observed in the three-dimensional space we used to deal with. Pedro Domingos, in his *A Few Useful Things to Know about Machine Learning*, provides some examples:

> *"In high dimensions, most of the mass of a multivariate Gaussian distribution is not near the mean, but in an increasingly distant shell around it; and most of the volume of a high-dimensional orange is in the skin, not the pulp. If a constant number of examples is distributed uniformly in a high-dimensional hypercube, beyond some dimensionality most examples are closer to a face of the hypercube than to their nearest neighbor. And if we approximate a hypersphere by inscribing it in a hypercube, in high dimensions almost all the volume of the hypercube is outside the hypersphere. This is bad news for machine learning, where shapes of one type are often approximated by shapes of another."*

Speaking specifically of KNN, it treats all dimensions as equally important. This creates problems when some of the features are irrelevant, especially in high dimensions, because the noise introduced by these irrelevant features suppresses the signal comprised in the good features. In our example, we bypassed multidimensional problems by taking into account only the magnitude of each three-dimensional vector in our motion signals.

KNN pros

- It's simple to implement if you are not going for optimized versions which use advanced data structures.
- It's easy to understand and interpret. The algorithm is well studied theoretically, and much known about its mathematical properties in different settings.
- You can plug in any distance metric. This allows working with complex objects, like time series, graphs, geographical coordinates, and basically anything you can define distance metric for.
- Algorithms can be used for classification, ranking, regression (using neighbors average or weighted average), recommendations, and can even provide (a kind of) probabilistic output—what proportion of neighbors voted for this class.

- It's easy to incorporate new data in the model or remove outdated data from it. This makes KNN a good choice for online learning (see `Chapter 1`, *Getting Started with Machine Learning*) systems.

KNN cons

- The algorithm is fast for training but slow for inference.
- You need to choose the best k somehow (see *Choosing a good k* section).
- With the small values of k, the model can be badly affected by outliers; in other words, it's prone to overfitting.
- You need to choose a distance metric. For usual real value features, one can choose among many available options (see *Calculating the distance* section) resulting in different closest neighbors. The metric used by default in many machine learning packages is the Euclidean distance; however, this choice is nothing more than a tradition and for many applications is not the optimal.
- Model size grows with the new data incorporated.
- What should we do if there are several identical samples with different labels? In this case, the result can be different depending on the order in which samples are stored.
- The model suffers from the curse of dimensionality.

Improving our solution

There are several directions in which we can proceed to improve our algorithm for motion recognition.

Probabilistic interpretation

The `CMMotionActivity` class provides a confidence level for each predicted motion type. We can also add this feature to our algorithm. Instead of returning one label, we can return the proportion of labels among neighbors.

More data sources

We've used only accelerometer, but we could use gyroscope and magnetometer also. This can be done in several ways: you can just merge three time series into one three-dimensional time series or you can train an ensemble of three independent classifiers.

We've also merged x, y, and z of accelerometer into one magnitude value, but you can try to use them as separate time series. In this case, for three motion sensors, you'd have nine time series.

Smarter time series chunking

We split our time series into chunks of 25 elements length. This introduces delay when the motion type changes from one to another. This can also be fixed relatively easily by introducing sliding windows instead of chunks. With this approach, we don't need to wait for the new chunk to be delivered; we just record a frame or predict a new label every time when we get a new value from the motion sensor.

Hardware acceleration

The KNN algorithm is inherently parallel because to calculate the distance between two data points you don't need to know anything about other data points. This makes it a perfect candidate for GPU acceleration. DTW, as we've mentioned, can also be optimized for parallel execution.

Trees to speed up the inference

An array is not the only possible candidate for KNN's memory implementation. To make neighbors search faster, many implementations use special data structures such as a KD tree or a ball tree.

Check scikit-learn documentation if you're interested in more details: `http://scikit-learn.org/stable/modules/neighbors.html#nearest-neighbor-algorithms`.

Utilizing state transitions

Transitions between some motion types are more likely than between others: it's easy to imagine how a user can start walking after being still, but it's much harder to imagine how he could start running immediately after squatting. The popular way of modelling such probabilistic state changes is **hidden Markov model** (**HMM**), but that's a long story for some other time.

Summary

In this chapter, we implemented a working machine learning solution for motion data classification and trained it end-to-end on a device. The simplest of the instance-based models is the nearest neighbors classifier. You can use it to classify any type of data, the only tricky thing is to choose a suitable distance metric. For feature vectors (points in n-dimensional space), many metrics have been invented, such as the Euclidean and Manhattan distances. For strings, editing distances are popular. For time series, we applied DTW.

The nearest neighbors method is a non-parametric model, which means that we can apply it without regard to statistical data distributions. Another advantage is that it is well suited for online learning and is easy to parallelize. Among the shortcomings is the curse of dimensionality and the algorithmic complexity of predictions (lazy learning).

In the next chapter, we're going to proceed with instance-based algorithms, this time focusing on the unsupervised clustering task.

Bibliography

1. Lichman, M. (2013), UCI Machine Learning Repository (http://archive.ics.uci.edu/ml), Irvine, CA: University of California, School of Information and Computer Science, *Dataset for ADL Recognition with Wrist-worn Accelerometer Data Set*
2. Toni Giorgino (2009), *Computing and Visualizing Dynamic Time Warping Alignments in R: The dtw Package,* Journal of Statistical Software, 31(7), 1-24, doi:10.18637/jss.v031.i07

3. *Accelerating Dynamic Time Warping Subsequence Search with GPUs and FPGAs*, Doruk Sart, Abdullah Mueen, Walid Najjar, Vit Niennattrakul, Eamonn Keogh, in the Proceedings of IEEE ICDM 2010. pp. 1001-1006 at: `http://alumni.cs.ucr.edu/~mueen/pdf/icdm2010.pdf`

4. Domingos P. 2012, *A Few Useful Things to Know about Machine Learning*, Communications of the ACM, October, 55(10), pp. 78-87

4
K-Means Clustering

In this chapter, we're going to switch our attention from supervised learning to unsupervised learning. The algorithms that we'll discuss and implement in this chapter are k-means and k-means++ clustering.

In this chapter, we will cover the following topics:

- Instance-based algorithm of k-means clustering
- The shortcomings of the k-means and how to fix them with the k-means++
- Where you can use k-means and where you shouldn't use it
- Application of clustering for signal quantization
- How to choose the number of clusters

Unsupervised learning

Unsupervised learning is a way of making hidden patterns in data visible:

- Clustering finds groups or hierarchy of similar objects
- Unsupervised anomaly detection finds outliers (weird samples)
- Dimensionality reduction finds which details of data are the most important
- Factor analysis reveals the latent variables that influence the behavior of the observed variables
- Rule mining finds associations between different entities in the data

As usually, these tasks overlap pretty often, and many practical problems inhabit the neutral territory between supervised and unsupervised learning.

We will focus on clustering in this chapter and on rule mining in the next chapter. Others will remain mostly beyond the scope of this book, but in `Chapter 10`, *Natural Language Processing*, we will nevertheless briefly discuss autoencoders; they can be used for both dimensionality reduction and anomaly detection.

Here are some examples of real-world tasks where clustering would be your tool of choice:

- Cluster face photos by identity of a person depicted
- Find groups of customers for a targeted advertisement using the database of their transactions (market segmentation)
- Having a set of text documents, sort them into a folder according to the personal style (stylometry) of their author (authorship attribution) or according to their topics (topic modelling)
- Having DNA markers of relatives, build a phylogenetic or family tree (hierarchical clustering; clusters are nested in this case)

Note, that these are clustering tasks only as long as groups/categories/clusters are not predefined in advance. As soon as you have predefined classes of objects, you would be better off with the classification algorithms.

Where might clustering be needed in the context of mobile development? Clustering pins on a map may look like the most natural idea. Having clusters of a user's locations, you can guess the location of his important locations, like house and workplace, for example. We will start from this and later discuss more complex applications of clustering. For now, we will concentrate on the classical clustering algorithm: *k*-means.

K-means clustering

The name of this algorithm comes from the *k* clusters into which the samples are divided, and the fact that each cluster is grouped around some mean value, a **centroid** of a cluster. This centroid serves as a prototype of a class. Each data point belongs to the cluster which centroid is the closest.

The algorithm was invented in 1957 at Bell Labs.

In this algorithm, each data point belongs to only one cluster. As a result of this algorithm, we get the feature space partitioned into Voronoi cells.

Because of the *k* in its name, this algorithm is often confused with the KNN algorithm, but as we already have seen with *k*-fold cross-validation, not all *k*s are the same. You may wonder why machine learning people are so obsessed with this letter that they put it in every algorithm's name. I don't *k*-now.

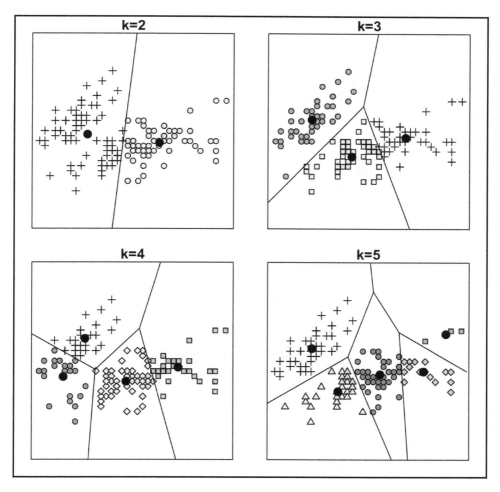

Figure 4.1: Four different ways to cluster the same data using *k*-means algorithm. Bald black dots are centroids of clusters. The samples are from the classical Iris dataset, plotted petals length against petal width.

Let's define the algorithm's aim more formally. If n is the number of your data points (samples, represented as real vectors of length d), then k-means algorithm splits them into k sets (clusters, $k < n$), such that within each cluster sum of distances from the points to the center (mean) is minimal. In other words, the objective of the algorithm is to find a set of clusters with the minimal WCSS:

$$WCSS = \sum_{i=1}^{k} \sum_{x_j \in S_i} (x_j - \mu_i)^2$$

Where:

- k is a number of clusters
- S_i clusters, $i = 1, 2, ..., k$,
- x_j is a sample (vector),
- μ_i is a mean of samples in the cluster , in other words—centroid of the cluster.

For the beginning we usually initialize centroids at random or with the values of some random samples from the dataset. Algorithm is iterative and each iteration consists of two steps:

1. Calculate the centroids for each cluster
2. Rreassign samples to clusters, according to the closest centroids

Algorithm ends, when after some iteration the coordinates of centroids haven't changed (convergence achieved) or after some predefined number of steps.

Implementing k-means in Swift

Similar to the KNN from the previous chapter, we'll have a structure to represent an algorithm and keep all its hyperparameters:

```
struct KMeans {
    public let k: Int
```

The standard k-means algorithm was designed to be used only with Euclidean distance:

```
internal let distanceMetric = Euclidean.distance
```

We need several arrays to store different kinds of data during the clustering.

Storage for samples:

```
internal var data: [[Double]] = []
```

Coordinates of centroids:

```
public var centroids: [[Double]] = []
```

An array that matches each sample to its cluster. It should be of the same length as the data, and for every sample, it stores an index of centroid in the `centroids` array:

```
private(set) var clusters: [Int] = []
```

Within-cluster sum of squares is a measure that we'll use later to assess the quality of the result:

```
internal var WCSS: Double = 0.0
```

For now, the only parameter that we pass on the initialization is the number of clusters:

```
public init (k: Int) {
  self.k = k
}
}
```

Unlike KNN, k-means has only one method in its interface: `train(data:)`, which returns the results of clustering, the index of cluster each sample belongs to:

```
public mutating func train(data: [[Double]]) -> [Int] {
```

Before starting actual calculations, there are several inevitable ceremonies to perform.

The count of data points should be greater or equal to `k`, and the number of samples (n) should be greater than zero:

```
let n = data.count
precondition(k <= n)
precondition(n > 0)
```

Calculate the dimensionality of samples (number of features in each sample) and check that it is greater than zero:

```
let d = data.first!.count
precondition(d > 0)
```

If everything is fine, store the data:

```
self.data = data
```

If the number of clusters is equal to the number of data points, then we can just create a cluster for each data point and return the result:

```
if k == n {
  centroids = data
  clusters = Array<Int>(0..<k)
  return clusters
}
```

Populating the clusters array with zeros:

```
clusters = [Int](repeating: 0, count: n)
```

The important detail of the k-means is an initial choice of centroids. The result of the algorithm may be significantly different, depending on the initialization step. Let's not overthink it for now, and go on with the random initialization:

```
chooseCentroidsAtRandom() // The function body will be described later.
```

The main part of the algorithm is a while loop, which breaks when the convergence conditions are met:

```
while true {
```

Inside those loops, the algorithm consists of two steps: update step, and assignment step.

Within-cluster sum of squares (WCSS) is an important performance measure for k-means. We set it to be zero on every iteration start and as it changes every time, we update the cluster centroids:

```
WCSS = 0.0
```

Update step

After the initial choice of centroids, we need to iterate over data points and update information about cluster assignment according to the distance to the closest centroid:

```
for (pointIndex, point) in data.enumerated() {
  var minDistance = Double.infinity
  for (clusterID, centroid) in centroids.enumerated() {
    let distance = pow(distanceMetric(point, centroid), 2)
```

Remember the newly calculated distance if it is less than the previously saved minimum distance for the corresponding data point:

```
if minDistance > distance {
   clusters[pointIndex] = clusterID
   minDistance = distance
}
}
```

Save information about WCSS for the future:

```
WCSS += minDistance
}
```

Assignment step

Calculate new centroids of clusters:

```
var centroidsCount = [Double](repeating: 0.0, count: k)
let rowStub = [Double](repeating: 0.0, count: d)
var centroidsCumulative = [[Double]](repeating: rowStub, count: k)

for (point, clusterID) in zip(data, clusters) {
  centroidsCount[clusterID] += 1
  centroidsCumulative[clusterID] = vecAdd(centroidsCumulative[clusterID],
point)
}

var newCentroids = centroidsCumulative
for (j, row) in centroidsCumulative.enumerated() {
  for (i, element) in row.enumerated() {
    let new = element/centroidsCount[j]
    assert(!new.isNaN)
    newCentroids[j][i] = new
  }
}
```

After this, we have to check whether the new centroids are different from those previously calculated. If they are different, we perform another iteration of optimization, if not, we've reached the convergence and can break the loop:

```
var convergence = false
convergence = zip(centroids, newCentroids).map{$0.0 == $0.1}.reduce(true,
and)
// and(_: Bool, _:Bool) was added for convenience
if convergence { break }
centroids = newCentroids
}

return clusters
}
```

Do you remember, we've skipped the cluster centroid's initialization implementation? So, here it goes:

```
internal mutating func chooseCentroidsAtRandom() {
  let uniformWeights = [Double](repeating: 1.0, count: data.count)
  let randomIndexesNoReplacement =
Random.Weighted.indicesNoReplace(weights:uniformWeights, count: k)

  var centroidID = 0
  for index in randomIndexesNoReplacement {
    centroids.append(data[index])
    clusters[index] = centroidID
    centroidID += 1
  }
}
```

This `Random.Weighted.indicesNoReplace(weights:uniformWeights, count: k)` looks mysterious, but it's just a utility function for random sampling with predefined weights from an array. It samples without replacement and returns an array of indices. In this case, all weights are equal so the probability of each element to be sampled is equal. Later, we'll change this to improve the quality of clustering and speed of convergence. I ported this function from the R standard library.

Clustering objects on a map

Where can we apply k-means in the context of mobile development? Clustering pins on a map may look like the most natural idea. Having the clusters of user locations, you can guess the location of the user's important locations like home and workplace, for example. We will implement pin clustering to visualize k-means, some of its unfortunate properties, and show why such an application of it may be not the best idea.

You can find a demo application under the 4_kmeans/MapKMeans folder of supplementary code. Everything interesting happens in the ViewController.swift. Clustering happens in the clusterize() method:

```
func clusterize() {
  let k = Settings.k
  colors = (0..<k).map{_ in Random.Uniform.randomColor()}
  let data = savedAnnotations.map{ [Double]($0.coordinate) }
  var kMeans = KMeans(k: k)
  clusters = kMeans.train(data: data)
  centroidAnnotations = kMeans.centroids
    .map { CLLocationCoordinate2D(latitude: $0[0], longitude: $0[1]) }
    .map { coordinate in
      let annotation = MKPointAnnotation()
      annotation.coordinate = coordinate
      annotation.title = "(coordinate)"
      return annotation
    }
}
```

CLLocationCoordinate2D gets converted to the Double in the following way:

```
extension Array where Element == Double {
  init(_ coordinates: CLLocationCoordinate2D) {
    self.init(arrayLiteral: Double(coordinates.latitude),
Double(coordinates.longitude))
  }
}
```

The app shows the map and you can put in as many pins as you wish by tapping on it. Try to form several clusters and run the algorithm by pressing the circular arrow button several times. Note that the results of the algorithm are usually unstable: it can give different results every time. Check how the result differs when you chose another number of clusters.

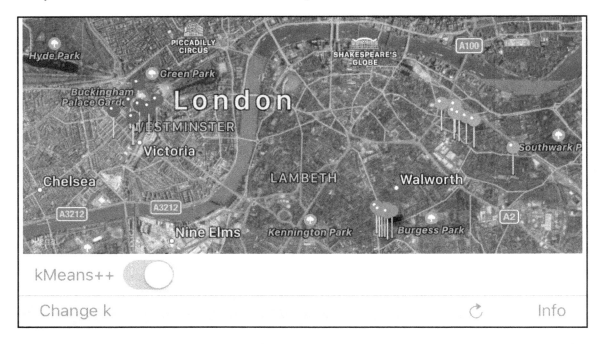

Figure 4.2: The results of the demo app work. Combine this with locations from the photo library metadata and you can guess where the user lives, works and spends his/her free time.

Now to the problems with using k-means with geospatial data. You may notice that it looks like algorithm treats horizontal and vertical space unequally important. That's because one degree of longitude is always about 111 km, but one degree of latitude has a different length depending on how far from the equator you are. Basically, you should not use geographical coordinates as features for Euclidean distance. More to the point, if you put some points on the border between Alaska and Russia, you would observe that KNN treats points in Russia as very different from points close to Alaska. This is due to the 180° Meridian. Basically, we can say that using k-means for pin clustering was a mistake. It could work on some relatively small scale. for example, it could work fine on a city scale. Just don't use it on the world map scale. Maps are just ideal for vanilla k-means problem demonstrations.

But wait. Cut can't we replace the Euclidean distance with some other distance metric, like we did with KNN in the previous chapter? No, unfortunately not this time. Strictly speaking, k-means is not a distance-based algorithm. The objective of the algorithm is to minimize the within-cluster variance (or squared error). The formula of a variance happened to be identical to the formula of Euclidean distance. This makes it impossible to plug in to your custom distance metrics because the algorithm can stop converge. For pin clustering, it's better to choose some other algorithm, and for k-means it's better to choose some other application, and indeed we will. But first, let's discuss some problems that became apparent after our first experiment:

- https://datascience.stackexchange.com/questions/761/clustering-geo-location-coordinates-lat-long-pairs
- https://stats.stackexchange.com/questions/81481/why-does-k-means-clustering-algorithm-use-only-euclidean-distance-metric

Choosing the number of clusters

If you don't know in advance how many clusters you have, then how do you choose the optimal *k*? This is essentially an egg-and-chicken problem. Several approaches are popular and we'll discuss one of them: the elbow method.

Do you remember those mysterious WCSS that we calculated on every iteration of k-means? This measure tells us how much points in every cluster are different from their centroid. We can calculate it for several different k values and plot the result. It usually looks somewhat similar to the plot on the following graph:

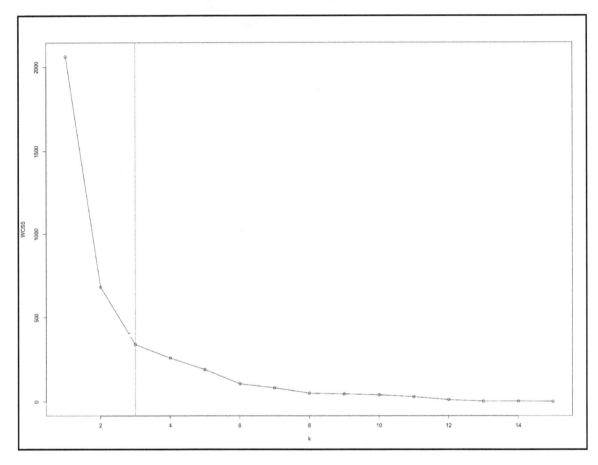

Figure 4.3: WCSS plotted against the number of clusters

This plot should remind you about the similar plots of loss functions from Chapter 3, *K-Nearest Neighbors Classifier*. It shows how well our model fits the data. The idea of the elbow method is to choose the k value after which the result is not going to improve sharply anymore. The name comes from the similarity of the plot to an arm. We choose the point at the elbow, marked with the red line on the graph.

For more information refer to the following links:

- https://en.wikipedia.org/wiki/Determining_the_number_of_clusters_in_a_data_set
- http://stackoverflow.com/questions/18042290/implementing-the-elbow-method-for-finding-the-optimum-number-of-clusters-for-k-m

K-means clustering – problems

Refer to the following for more information about k-means and k-means++:

- https://en.wikipedia.org/wiki/K-means_clustering
- https://en.wikipedia.org/wiki/K-means%2B%2B

K-means algorithm suffers from at least two shortcomings:

- The worst-case time complexity of the algorithm is super polynomial in the input size, meaning that it is not bounded above by any polynomial
- Standard algorithm can perform arbitrarily poor in comparison to the optimal clustering because it finds only an approximation of the real optimum

Try it out yourself: put four pins on a map, as shown in the following image. After running clustering several times, you may notice that the algorithm often converges to the suboptimal solution:

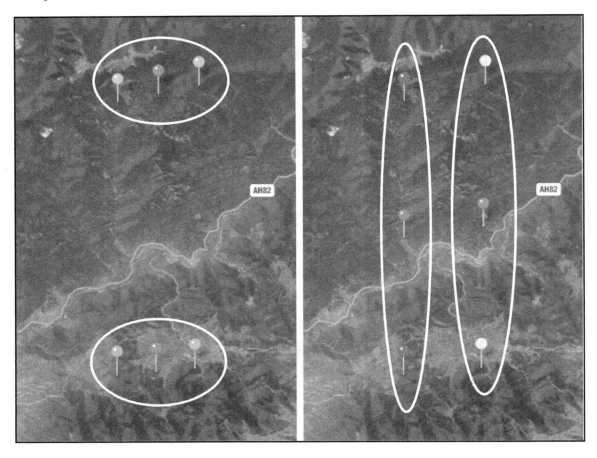

Figure 4.4: Optimal and non-optimal clustering results on the same dataset

K-means++

An improved algorithm was proposed in 2007. K-means++ addresses the problem of suboptimal clustering by introducing an additional step for a good centroids initialization.

An improved algorithm of initial centers selection looks like this:

1. Select randomly any data point to be the first center
2. For all other data points, calculate the distance to the first center $d(x)$
3. Sample the next center from the weighted probability distribution, where the probability of each data point to become a next center is proportional to the square of distance $d(x)^2$
4. Until k centers are chosen, repeat step 2 and step 3
5. Proceed with the standard k-means algorithm

In Swift, it looks like this:

```
internal mutating func chooseCentroids() {
    let n = data.count

    var minDistances = [Double](repeating: Double.infinity, count: n)
    var centerIndices = [Int]()
```

`clusterID` is an integer identifier of a cluster: the first cluster has identifier zero, the second has one, and so on:

```
for clusterID in 0 ..< k {
    var pointIndex: Int
    if clusterID == 0 {
```

Choose the first centroid randomly from data points:

```
pointIndex = Random.Uniform.int(n)
} else {
```

In all other cases, choose center from the weighted distribution, proportionally to the squared distance to the closest centroid:

```
if let nextCenter = Random.Weighted.indicesNoReplace(weights: minDistances,
count: 1).first {
  pointIndex = nextCenter
} else {
  fatalError()
}
}
centerIndices.append(pointIndex)
let center = data[pointIndex]
centroids.append(center)
```

The distance to the closest center is zero. Hence, the probability of sampling once again is also zero:

```
minDistances[pointIndex] = 0.0
clusters[pointIndex] = clusterID
```

After this, we have to perform one iteration of the assign step so that all points are assigned to the corresponding clusters when we proceed with the usual k-means algorithm.

Calculate the distance from each of the data points to the centroid:

```
var nextI = (0, centerIndices.first ?? Int.max)
for (pointIndex, point) in data.enumerated() {
```

Skip the data point if it was selected as a center already:

```
if pointIndex == nextI.1 {
```

Check if all centroids were attended:

```
if nextI.0 < clusterID {
  let nextIndex = nextI.0+1
  nextI = (nextIndex, centerIndices[nextIndex])
}
continue
}
```

If the data point is not selected as a center yet, calculate the distance from it to the last selected center:

```
let distance = pow(distanceMetric(point, center), 2)
```

Remember the newly calculated distance if it is less than the minimum distance saved for the corresponding data point previously:

```
let currentMin = minDistances[pointIndex]
if currentMin > distance {
  minDistances[pointIndex] = distance
  clusters[pointIndex] = clusterID
}
}
}
}
```

That's it. Now don't forget to update the rest of the code to work with the ++ part:

```
public struct KMeans {
  public enum InitializationMethod {
    case random
    case plusplus
  }
  ...
  public var initialization: InitializationMethod = .plusplus
  ...
}

public mutating func train(data: [[Double]]) -> [Int] {
  ...
  switch initialization {
    case .random:
    chooseCentroidsAtRandom()
    case .plusplus:
    chooseCentroids()
  }
  ...
}
```

Image segmentation using k-means

The k-means algorithm was invented in the field of digital signal processing and is still in common use in that field for signal quantization. For this task, it performs much better than for pin clustering. Let's look at an example on the following diagram. The picture can be segmented into meaningful parts using color space quantization. We choose the number of clusters, then run k-means on every pixel's RGB values, and find the cluster's centroids. Then we replace each pixel with the color of its corresponding centroid. This can be used in image editing for separating objects from the background or for lossy image compression. In Chapter 12, *Optimizing Neural Networks for Mobile Devices*, we're going to use this approach for deep learning neural network compression:

Figure 4.5: Image segmentation using k-means

Here is a code sample in Objective-C++ using fast OpenCV implementation of k-means. You can find the whole iOS application in the folder 4_kmeans/ImageSegmentation:

```
- (cv::Mat)kMeansClustering:(cv::Mat)input withK:(int)k {
  cv::cvtColor(input, input, CV_RGBA2RGB);
  cv::Mat samples(input.rows * input.cols, 3, CV_32F);

  for (int y = 0; y < input.rows; y++){
    for (int x = 0; x < input.cols; x++){
      for (int z = 0; z < 3; z++){
        samples.at<float>(y + x*input.rows, z) =
input.at<cv::Vec3b>(y,x)[z];
      }
    }
  }

  int clusterCount = k;
  cv::Mat labels;
  int attempts = 5;
  cv::Mat centers;
  kmeans(samples, clusterCount, labels,
cv::TermCriteria(CV_TERMCRIT_ITER|CV_TERMCRIT_EPS, 100, 0.01), attempts,
cv::KMEANS_PP_CENTERS, centers);

  cv::Mat outputMatrix( input.rows, input.cols, input.type());

  for (int y = 0; y < input.rows; y++) {
    for (int x = 0; x < input.cols; x++) {
      int cluster_idx = labels.at<int>(y + x*input.rows,0);
      outputMatrix.at<cv::Vec3b>(y,x)[0] = centers.at<float>(cluster_idx,
0);
      outputMatrix.at<cv::Vec3b>(y,x)[1] = centers.at<float>(cluster_idx,
1);
      outputMatrix.at<cv::Vec3b>(y,x)[2] = centers.at<float>(cluster_idx,
2);
    }
  }

  return outputMatrix;
}
```

Summary

In this chapter, we've discussed an important unsupervised learning task: clustering. The simplest clustering algorithm is k-means. It doesn't provide stable results and is computationally complex, but this can be improved using k-means++. The algorithm can be applied to any data for which Euclidean distance is a meaningful measure, but the best area to apply it is a signal quantization. For instance, we've used it for image segmentation. Many more clustering algorithms exist for different types of tasks.

In the next chapter, we're going to explore unsupervised learning more deeply. Specifically, we're going to talk about algorithms for finding association rules in data: association learning.

5
Association Rule Learning

In many practical applications data comes in the form of lists (ordered or unordered): grocery lists, playlists, visited locations or URLs, app logs, and so on. Sometimes those lists are generated as a byproduct of business processes, but they still contain potentially useful information and insights for process improvement. To extract some of that hidden knowledge, one can use a special kind of unsupervised learning algorithm—association rule mining. In this chapter, we are going to build an app that can analyze your shopping lists to find out your preferences in the form of rules such as *"If you've bought oatmeal and cornflakes, you also want to buy milk."* This can be used to create an adaptable user experience, for instance, contextual suggestions or reminders.

In this chapter, we will cover the following topics:

- Association rules
- Association measures
- Association rule mining algorithms
- Building an adaptable user experience

Seeing association rules

There are many situations where we're interested in patterns demonstrating the co-occurrence of some items. For example, marketers want to know which goods are often bought together, clinical personnel need to know symptoms associated with certain medical conditions, and in information security we want to know which activity patterns are associated with intrusion or fraud. All of these problems have a common structure: there are items (goods, symptoms, records in logs) organized in transactions (shopping list, medical case, user activity transaction). With this type of data, we can then analyze it to find association rules, such as *If the client bought a lemon and some cookies, he is also likely to buy tea*, or in more formal notation: (cookies, lemon → tea).

 We will use pictograms throughout this chapter to facilitate the visual notation of item sets and rules: {● ● → ●}.

These rules allow us to make informed decisions, such as putting associated items on the same shelf, providing patients with the appropriate care, and alerting security staff if suspicious activity is suspected in a system. The unsupervised learning algorithms that find these rules are known as **association rule mining** or **association rule learning** algorithms. These are considered a type of unsupervised learning, as you do not need labeled data to generate a rule.

 Association rule learning is not the type of algorithm that one typically sees in an introductory-level book about machine learning. This is perhaps due to their relatively narrow use case. However, in the following sections, we will see how rule learning can become the engine of an adaptable user interface, and used in other important applications. After this, we hope you will agree that the power of these methods has been underestimated.

Defining data structures

What we want to have by the end of this chapter is a rule learning algorithm called Apriori. We will learn about the algorithm details later; for now, we only want to define the data structures that we will work with throughout the chapter, along with some utility functions.

The generic structure for the algorithm is as follows:

```
public struct Apriori<Item: Hashable & Equatable> {
```

In the simplest case, the ordering of the items in the transaction doesn't matter, and neither does their number nor the associated timestamps. This means that we consider our item sets and transactions as mathematical or Swift sets:

```
public typealias ItemSet = Set<Item>
```

The parameter I is a type of item in your transactions. Next, we have to implement some structures for subsets and rules:

```
class Subsets: Sequence {
  var subsets: [ItemSet]
  init(_ set: ItemSet) {
    self.subsets = Array(set).combinations().map(Set.init)
  }
  func makeIterator() -> AnyIterator<ItemSet> {
    return AnyIterator { [weak self] in
    guard let `self` = self else {
      return nil
    }
    return self.subsets.popLast()
  }
}
public struct Rule {
  let ifPart: Set<I>
  let thenPart: Set<I>
}
```

Apriori's structure variables are as follows:

```
public var elements: Set<Int>
public let transactions: ContiguousArray<ItemSet>
public let map: [I: Int]
public let invertedMap: [Int: I]
```

Supports are stored here to prevent multiple computations:

```
public convenience init(transactions: [[I]]) {
    self.init(transactions: transactions.map(Set<I>.init))
}

public init(transactions: [Set<I>]) {
    // delete

    var indexedTransactions = [ItemSet]()
    var counter = 0
    var map = [I: Int]()
    var invertedMap = [Int: I]()
```

```
    for transaction in transactions {
        var indexedTransaction = ItemSet()
        for item in transaction {
            if let stored = map[item] {
                indexedTransaction.insert(stored)
            } else {
                map[item] = counter
                invertedMap[counter] = item
                indexedTransaction.insert(counter)
                counter += 1
            }
        }
        indexedTransactions.append(indexedTransaction)
    }
    self.transactions = ContiguousArray(indexedTransactions)
    self.elements = self.transactions.reduce(Set<Int>()) {$0.union($1)}
    self.map = map
    self.invertedMap = invertedMap

    self.total = Double(self.transactions.count)
}
```

Using association measures to assess rules

Look at these two rules:

- {Oatmeal, corn flakes → Milk}
- {Dog food, paperclips → Washing powder}

Intuitively, the second rule looks more unlikely than the first one, doesn't it? How can we tell that for sure, though? In this case, we need some quantitative measures that will show us how likely each rule is. What we are looking for here are association measures, as we call them in machine learning and data mining. Rule mining algorithms revolve around this notion in a similar manner to how distance-based algorithms revolve around distance metrics. In this chapter, we're going to use four association measures: support, confidence, lift, and conviction (see *Table 5.1*).

Note that these measures tell us nothing about how useful or interesting the rules are, but only quantify their probabilistic characteristics. A rule's usefulness and practicality can be hard to grasp mathematically and often requires human judgment in each case. As usual in statistics, interpreting analysis results is something left to the discretion of a domain expert or developer.

Supporting association measures

Let's say that we have the following six shopping lists (six transactions) composed of only four items: a hot dog, tomatoes, tea, and cookies. This is our database:

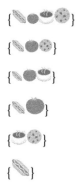

We say that the item set {} covers the transactions 1, 3, and 5, because the item set is a subset of each of those transactions. There are $2^n = 2^4 = 16$ possible item sets in our example, including the empty item set.

The support of the item set shows how often this set occurs as part of a transaction; in other words, what proportion of transactions is covered in this item set. For example:

$$supp(\{\bullet\ \bullet\}) = \frac{2}{6} \approx 0.333$$

Support for an empty item set is assumed to be equal to the number of transactions in the dataset ($supp(\{\}) = 6$, in our case). If you represent all the item sets as a graph (see *Figure 5.1*), you may notice that support always decreases as the length of item sets grows. When mining for association rules, we are usually interested in the larger item sets that have support greater than a given threshold; for instance, for the support threshold 0.5, such item sets are {\ \ }, {\ }, and {\ }. In other words, this means that each of the item sets cover at least half of all transactions.

Here, we are extracting association measures to the separate structure extension for convenience:

```
public extension Apriori {
    public mutating func support(_ set: ItemSet) -> Double {
```

We store support values that we've already calculated because they don't change during algorithm running, and we will be able to prevent the repetition of a costly operation. On the other hand, however, this solution increases the memory footprint:

```
if let stored = supports[set] {
  return stored
}
let support = transactions.filter{set.isSubset(of: $0)}.count
let total = transactions.count
let result = Double(support)/Double(total)
supports[set] = result
return result
}
```

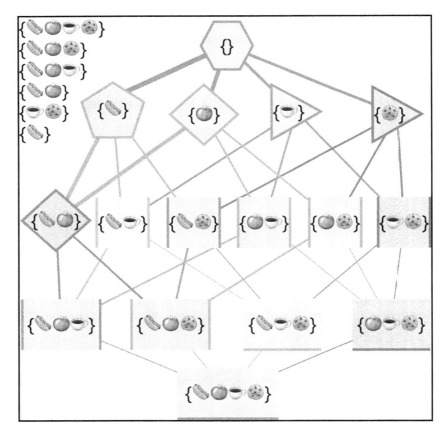

Figure 5.1: The graph of item sets for the transactions depicted in the top-left corner. The number of bold sides for each item set depicts the support value (for instance, a triangle means that support = 3). The width of the incoming edges for each node is proportional to its support. Note how the support monotonically decreases from the top (6) to the bottom (1) as the item set size grows

Confidence association measures

The confidence association measures shows how likely it is for an item to occur in a transaction including other items:

$$conf\left(\{\text{🔪}\text{⚫}\rightarrow\text{🍵}\}\right) = \frac{supp\left(\{\text{🔪}\text{⚫}\text{🍵}\}\right)}{supp\left(\{\text{🔪}\text{⚫}\}\right)} = \frac{2}{4} = 0.5$$

Note that confidence can't be greater than *1*. The problem with this measure is that it doesn't take into account the general support of the item; if {🍵} is common in the dataset, then it's likely that it will occur in the transaction independently of any associations.

Note that:

$$conf\left(\{\text{🔪}\rightarrow\text{⚫}\}\right) \neq conf\left(\{\text{⚫}\rightarrow\text{🔪}\}\right)$$

In Swift:

```
public mutating func confidence(_ rule: Rule) -> Double {
    return support(rule.ifPart.union(rule.thenPart))/support(rule.ifPart)
}
```

Lift association measures

Lift is confidence normalized by the support of the item of interest, shown as follows:

$$lift\left(\{\text{🔪}\text{⚫}\rightarrow\text{🍵}\}\right) = \frac{supp\left(\{\text{🔪}\text{⚫}\text{🍵}\}\right)}{supp\left(\{\text{🔪}\text{⚫}\}\right)\times supp\left(\{\text{🍵}\}\right)} = \frac{2}{4\times3} \approx 0.167$$

Lift takes into consideration the support of both sets {🔪⚫} and {🍵}. The *lift > 1* shows that items are associated positively, meaning that items after the arrow are likely to be bought if items before the arrow are present. The *lift < 1* implies a negative association; in our case, this means that if the customer has taken already bought a hot dog and tomatoes it's unlikely he will add tea to the basket. *Lift = 1* means no association at all.

Unlike confidence:

$$lift\left(\{\text{🔪}\rightarrow\text{⚫}\}\right) = lift\left(\{\text{⚫}\rightarrow\text{🔪}\}\right)$$

In Swift:

```
public mutating func lift(_ rule: Rule) -> Double {
    return
support(rule.ifPart.union(rule.thenPart))/support(rule.ifPart)/support(rule
.thenPart)
}
```

Conviction association measures

Conviction is a measure that helps to judge if the rule happened to be there by chance or not. It was introduced by Sergey Brin and coauthors in 1997 [1] as a replacement for confidence, which can't capture the direction of an association. Conviction is a comparison of the probability of *if* appearing without *then*, if they were dependent on the actual frequency of *if* without *then*:

$$conv(\{ \searrow \to \bullet \}) = \frac{1 - supp(\{ \bullet \})}{1 - conf(\{ \searrow \to \bullet \})} = \frac{1 - 4/6}{1 - 4/5} \approx 1.667$$

In the nominator, we have the expected frequency of item sets without {●}. (In other words, how often the rule doesn't hold true.) In the denominator, we have an observed frequency of false predictions. In our example, it shows that the rule { ＼ → ● } holds true approximately 67% more often (*1.667* as often) if the association between { ＼ } and { ● } was by chance.

Association measure	Formula	Range	Notes
Support	$supp(X) = P(X^+)$ $supp(X \cup Y) = P(X^+ \cap Y^+)$	[0, 1]	How often does X occur in the dataset? How often do X and Y occur in the dataset together?
Confidence	$conf(X \to Y) = \frac{supp(X \cup Y)}{supp(X)}$ $= \frac{P(X^+ \cap Y^+)}{P(X^+)} = P(Y^+ \| X^+)$	[0, 1]	Given the presence of X, what is the probability that Y is also present?

Lift	$lift(X \to Y) = \dfrac{conf(X \to Y)}{supp(Y)} = \dfrac{P(X^+ \cap Y^+)}{P(X^+)P(Y^+)}$	$[0, \infty]$	*1 means independence between X and Y, because for independent events P(A ∩ B) = P(A)P(B).*
Conviction	$conv(X \to Y) = \dfrac{1 - supp(Y)}{1 - conf(X \to Y)} = \dfrac{P(X^+)P(Y^-)}{P(X^+ \cap Y^-)}$	$[0, \infty]$	*1 means independence, ∞ means always true.*

Table 5.1: Common association measures

X and Y stand for the item sets themselves, and they stand for the events of their presence in a transaction, so $P(X^+ \cap Y^+)$ denotes the probability that both X and Y are present in a transaction.

For the comprehensive list of association measures used in rule learning with explanations, formulas, and references, see *A Probabilistic Comparison of Commonly Used Interest Measures for Association Rules* by Michael Hahsler at `http://michael.hahsler.net/research/association_rules/measures.html`.

Decomposing the problem

The task of extracting all association rules with the given confidence and support from the dataset is non-trivial. Let's approach it by decomposing it into smaller subtasks:

- Find all item sets with the support above the given threshold
- Generate all possible rules from the item sets that have confidence above the given threshold

Generating all possible rules

We need a method to generate all possible combinations of elements of this array. Combinations are found via the binary representation of subsets, as shown in the following snippet:

```
public extension Array {
public func combinations() -> [[Element]] {
      if isEmpty { return [] }
      let numberOfSubsets = Int(pow(2, Double(count)))
      var result = [[Element]]()
      for i in 0..<numberOfSubsets {
          var remainder = i
          var index = 0
          var combination = [Element]()
          while remainder > 0 {
              if remainder % 2 == 1 {
                  combination.append(self[index])
              }
              index += 1
              remainder /= 2
          }
          result.append(combination)
      }
      return result
   }
}
```

The following usage example:

```
let array = [1,2,3]
print(array.combinations())
```

Produces:

```
[[], [1], [2], [1, 2], [3], [1, 3], [2, 3], [1, 2, 3]]
```

Finding frequent item sets

The first step of the algorithm that we implement is based on the support measure. This function returns a set of all item sets with support larger than `minSupport`:

```
func frequentItemSets(minSupport: Double) -> Set<ItemSet> {
    var itemSets = Set<ItemSet>()
    let emptyItemSet: ItemSet = ItemSet()
    supporters[emptyItemSet] = Array(0 ..< transactions.count)
```

Here we use the priority queue data structure to keep track of possible extensions.

There is no priority queue implementation in the Foundation or Swift standard libraries, and standard data structures are out of the scope of this book. We are using the open source implementation by David Kopec (MIT license): https://github.com/davecom/SwiftPriorityQueue.

To make it work with item sets we had to change the code a bit—instead of being parameterized with the comparable types, it is now parameterized with types conforming to the equatable protocol:

```
    var queue = PriorityQueue<ItemSet>(order: { (lh, rh) -> Bool in
        lh.count > rh.count
    }, startingValues: [emptyItemSet])
    while let itemset = queue.pop() {
        var isMax = true

        for anExtension in allExtensions(itemset) {
            if isAboveSupportThreshold(anExtension, extending: itemset,
threshold: minSupport) {
                isMax = false
                queue.push(anExtension)
            }
        }
        if isMax == true {
            itemSets.insert(itemset)
        }
    }
    return itemSets
}
```

Note that this algorithm has one bad characteristic: it generates the same item sets multiple times. We'll return to this later.

The Apriori algorithm

The most famous algorithm for association rule learning is Apriori. It was proposed by Agrawal and Srikant in 1994. The input of the algorithm is a dataset of transactions where each transaction is a set of items. The output is a collection of association rules for which support and confidence are greater than some specified threshold. The name comes from the Latin phrase *a priori* (literally, "from what is before") because of one smart observation behind the algorithm: *if the item set is infrequent, then we can be sure in advance that all its subsets are also infrequent.*

You can implement Apriori with the following steps:

1. Count the support of all item sets of length 1, or calculate the frequency of every item in the dataset.
2. Drop the item sets that have support lower than the threshold.
3. Store all the remaining item sets.
4. Extend each stored item set by one element with all possible extensions. This step is known as candidate generation.
5. Calculate the support value of each candidate.
6. Drop all candidates below the threshold.
7. Drop all stored items from step 3 that have the same support as their extensions.
8. Add all the remaining candidates to storage.
9. Repeat steps 4 to step 8 until there are no more extensions with support greater than the threshold.

This is not a very efficient algorithm if you have a lot of data, but mobile applications are not recommended for use with big data anyway. This algorithm was influential in its time, and is also elegant and easy to understand today.

If you want to extract rules from your data as part of your server-side data processing pipeline, you may want to check Apriori's implementation in the mlxtend Python library: http://rasbt.github.io/mlxtend/user_guide/frequent_patterns/apriori/.

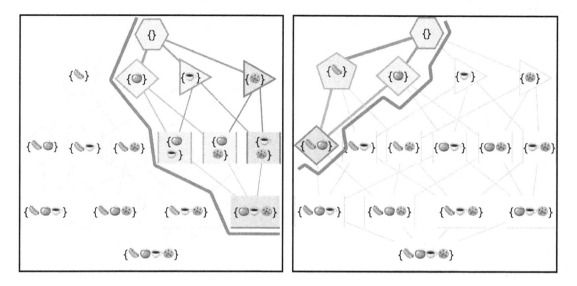

Figure 5.2: By excluding only one node we can reduce the number of possible rules twice. By excluding two nodes, we reduce the hypothesis space four times

Implementing Apriori in Swift

What will follow is a simplified version of a code that can be found in supplementary materials. We will skip some of the less important parts here.

The main method, which returns association rules with the given support and confidence, is as follows:

```
public func associationRules(minSupport: Double, minConfidence: Double) ->
[Rule] {
    var rules = [Rule]()
    let frequent = frequentItemSets(minSupport: minSupport)
    for itemSet in frequent {
        for (ifPart, thenPart) in nonOverlappingSubsetPairs(itemSet) {
            if confidence(ifPart, thenPart) >= minConfidence {
                let rule = Rule(ifPart: convertIndexesToItems(ifPart),
thenPart: convertIndexesToItems(thenPart))
                rules.append(rule)
            }
        }
    }
    return rules
}
```

```
func nonOverlappingSubsetPairs(_ itemSet: ItemSet) -> [(ItemSet, ItemSet)]
{
    var result = [(ItemSet, ItemSet)]()
    let ifParts = Subsets(itemSet)
    for ifPart in ifParts {
        let nonOverlapping = itemSet.subtracting(ifPart)
        let thenParts = Subsets(nonOverlapping)
        for thenPart in thenParts {
            result.append((ifPart, thenPart))
        }
    }
    return result
}
```

Running Apriori

And finally, this is how we use the algorithm with our toy example:

```
let transactions = [[" ", " ", " ", " "],
                    [" ", " ", " "],
                    [" ", " ", " "],
                    [" ", " "],
                    [" ", " "],
                    [" ", " "],
                    [" "]
]

let apriori = Apriori<String>(transactions: transactions)
let rules = apriori.associationRules(minSupport: 0.3, minConfidence: 0.5)
for rule in rules {
    print(rule)
    print("Confidence: ", apriori.confidence(rule), "Lift: ",
apriori.lift(rule), "Conviction: ", apriori.conviction(rule))
}
```

It produces the following:

```
{   →  }
Confidence:  0.8 Lift:  1.4 Conviction:  2.14285714285714
{   →  }
Confidence:  1.0 Lift:  1.4 Conviction:  inf
```

```
{ 🍪 → 🍪 }
Confidence:   0.75 Lift:   1.3125 Conviction:   1.71428571428571
{ 🍪 → 🍪 }
Confidence:   0.75 Lift:   1.3125 Conviction:   1.71428571428571
```

Let's analyze what's going on here. The second rule has the maximum confidence as well as conviction.

Running Apriori on real-world data

In this example, we collected real-world shopping lists from an apartment and composed a small, but nevertheless realistic, dataset. Let's see if we'll be able to extract any meaningful rules from it using our algorithm. Please note that this dataset is extremely small. For any production application of Apriori, you will need much larger datasets:

```
let transactions =
[["Grapes", "Cheese"],
["Cheese", "Milk"],
["Apples", "Oranges", "Cheese", "Gingerbread", "Marshmallows", "Eggs",
"Canned vegetables"],
["Tea", "Apples", "Bagels", "Marshmallows", "Icecream", "Canned
vegetables"],
["Cheese", "Buckwheat", "Cookies", "Oatmeal", "Banana", "Butter", "Bread",
"Apples", "Baby puree"],
["Baby puree", "Cookies"],
["Cookies"],
["Chicken", "Grapes", "Pizza", "Cheese", "Marshmallows", "Cream"],
["Potatoes"],
["Chicken"],
["Cornflakes", "Cookies", "Oatmeal"],
["Tea"],
["Chicken"],
["Chicken", "Eggs", "Cheese", "Oatmeal", "Bell pepper", "Bread", "Chocolate
butter", "Buckwheat", "Tea", "Rice", "Corn", "Cornflakes", "Juice",
"Sugar"],
["Bread", "Canned vegetables"],
["Carrot", "Beetroot", "Apples", "Sugar", "Buckwheat", "Rice", "Pasta",
"Salt", "Rice flour", "Dates", "Tea", "Butter", "Beef", "Cheese", "Eggs",
"Bread", "Cookies"]
]
```

After some experimentation with the threshold values, you can see that we ended up with 0.15 for support and 0.75 for confidence. This gives the 15 rules you can see in the following table:

```
let apriori = Apriori<String>(transactions: transactions)
let rules = apriori.associationRules(minSupport: 0.15, minConfidence: 0.75)
```

The resulting rules are sorted according to their lift:

Rules	Confidence	Lift	Conviction
{Cheese, bread → Buckwheat}	1	5.333333333	∞
{Buckwheat → Cheese, bread}	1	5.333333333	∞
{Cheese, buckwheat → Bread}	1	4	∞
{Buckwheat → Bread}	1	4	∞
{Bread → Cheese, buckwheat}	0.75	4	3.25
{Bread → Buckwheat}	0.75	4	3.25
{Eggs → Cheese}	1	2.285714286	∞
{Buckwheat, bread → Cheese}	1	2.285714286	∞
{Buckwheat → Cheese}	1	2.285714286	∞
{Bread → Cheese}	0.75	1.714285714	2.25
{Apples → Cheese}	0.75	1.714285714	2.25

Table 5.2: 15 rules

Buckwheat is a type of cereal popular in Eastern Europe, Western Asia, and elsewhere. People usually eat buckwheat porridge with butter and bread (but not in Poland). In our case, however, it looks as though we prefer it with cheese rather than butter, which is not completely true. Seven out of the 11 rules recommend that we buy cheese, which is not surprising as it's the most common item across all transactions. The remaining four rules point at an association between bread and buckwheat, which is not a fluke because here in Ukraine many people consume these products together, and so the rules are valid. What is important here is that the algorithm is able to extract patterns that correspond to real-world phenomena: user preferences, cultural traditions, and so on.

The pros and cons of Apriori

The pros of Apriori are as follows:

- This is the most simple and easy-to-understand algorithm among association rule learning algorithms
- The resulting rules are intuitive and easy to communicate to an end user
- It doesn't require labeled data as it is fully unsupervised; as a result, you can use it in many different situations because unlabeled data is often more accessible
- Many extensions were proposed for different use cases based on this implementation—for example, there are association learning algorithms that take into account the ordering of items, their number, and associated timestamps
- The algorithm is exhaustive, so it finds all the rules with the specified support and confidence

The cons of Apriori are as follows:

- If the dataset is small, the algorithm can find many false associations that happened simply by chance. You can address this issue by evaluating obtained rules on the held-out test data for the support, confidence, lift, and conviction values.
- As Agrawal and Srikant note at the end of their original paper, the algorithm doesn't take into account hierarchies of products or quantities of the items bought in a transaction. This additional information, while useful for market basket analysis, may be irrelevant in other rule mining domains and is out of the scope of this particular machine learning approach.
- The algorithm is computationally expensive, but there are many variants of Apriori that improve its algorithmic complexity.

Building an adaptable user experience

Human-computer interaction is never easy. Computers don't understand speech, sentiments, or body language. However, we are all used to communicating with our smart devices using not-so-smart buttons, drop downs, pickers, switches, checkboxes, sliders, and hundreds of other controls. They comply with a new kind of language that is commonly referred to as UI. Slowly but unavoidably, machine learning has made its way into all areas where computers interact directly with humans: voice input, handwriting input, lip reading, gesture recognition, body pose estimation, face emotion recognition, sentiment analysis, and so on. This may not be immediately obvious, but machine learning is the future of both UI and UX. Today, machine learning is already changing the way users interact with their devices. Machine learning-based solutions are likely to become widely-adopted in UIs because of their convenience. Furthermore, ranking, contextual suggestions, automatic translation, and personalization are also elements that most internet users have got used to. A nice example of how machine learning may fuel the UI is with the Facebook app, which runs on-device machine learning (even offline) to automatically sort posts in your timeline.

In the design community, such patterns of user interactions are commonly referred to as **anticipatory** or **algorithmic design** and are often described as **new trends** or **black magic**. Essentially, all the examples of anticipatory design that you may see in blogs or in presentations are cases of machine learning (just don't tell the design folks that). Machine learning can not only fuel big data analytics, but also small UI tweaks such as moving buttons on a screen or guessing what a user wants to do next and helping them with that. Such things when properly designed and tested can make your apps more enjoyable and easy to use. The main goal of such design patterns is to free the user from cognitive load when he or she uses the app. When you start using a new app, it's often like being in a new environment: you learn where different objects are placed, where to go to find whatever you want, and where short paths and pitfalls are located. By allowing the computer to also learn from the user, we can adjust the UX to make the user's learning curve steeper.

Laura Busche explains this concept in her blog *What You Need To Know About Anticipatory Design* at Smashing magazine particularly well:

> *"In psychology, we use the term cognitive load to describe the amount of mental effort being used in the working memory at any given moment in time. For everyone involved in user experience design, cognitive load is a crucial consideration. Are we doing everything in our power to relieve the strain caused by learning something new to use our product? How can we reduce the number of elements that our users need to worry about at any given time? Reducing cognitive load is one of the cornerstones of anticipatory design, as it helps create a more pleasurable experience by foreseeing our users' needs."*

The main idea behind anticipatory design is the principle of having fewer choices — in other words, we reduce the number of options for the user in an intelligent way.

In practice, you can do this in plenty of different ways depending on your app; you can filter out irrelevant results, push the most likely options to the top of the list or increase their size, and so on.

Going back to the topic of this chapter, you can use association rule learning to analyze user activity in your app and narrow the space of possibilities for them. For example, in a photo editing app, a user applies a set of filters to their photo. When a user has chosen the first filter, rules can be used to predict which filter (or even which set of filters) are most likely to be applied next. Here, you can sort the candidates according to one of the association measures. In `Chapter 7`, *Linear Classifier and Logistic Regression*, you will see another example of anticipatory design that will be based on supervised learning.

Summary

In this chapter, we explored association rule learning, which is a branch of unsupervised learning. We implemented the Apriori algorithm, which can be used to find patterns in the form of rules in different transactional datasets. Apriori's classical use case is market basket analysis. However, it is also important conceptually, because rule learning algorithms bridge the gap between classical artificial intelligence approaches (logical programming, concept learning, searching graphs, and so on) and logic-based machine learning (decision trees).

In the following chapter, we're going to return to supervised learning, but this time we will switch our attention from non-parametric models, such as KNN and k-means, to parametric linear models. We will also discuss linear regression and the gradient descent optimization method.

Bibliography

1. Sergey Brin, Rajeev Motwani, Jeffrey D. Ullman, and Shalom Tsur, *Dynamic itemset counting and implication rules for market basket data*, in SIGMOD 1997, Proceedings ACM SIGMOD international conference on Management of data, pages 255-264, Tucson, Arizona, USA, May 1997
2. Rakesh Agrawal and Ramakrishnan Srikant, *Fast Algorithms for Mining Association Rules*, Proceedings of the 20th international conference on very large databases, VLDB, pages 487-499, Santiago, Chile, September 1994 at: http://www.vldb.org/conf/1994/P487.PDF

6
Linear Regression and Gradient Descent

In the previous chapters, we've implemented non-parametric models including kNN and *k*-means and their applications to supervised classification and unsupervised clustering. In this chapter, we will proceed with the supervised learning by discussing algorithms for regression, this time focusing on the parametric models. **Linear regression** is the simple yet powerful tool for this kind of task. Linear regression was historically the first machine learning algorithm, so the math behind it is well developed, and you can find many books dedicated to this one topic exclusively. We will see when to use linear regression and when not to, how to analyze its errors, and how to interpret its results. As for the Swift part, we will get our feet wet with Apple's numerical libraries—the **Accelerate framework**.

Linear regression will serve as an example to explain an important mathematical optimization technique, **gradient descent**. This iterative algorithm will haunt us until the book's very end, because it is heavily used for training artificial neural networks.

The algorithms to be discussed and implemented in this chapter are:

- Simple linear regression for datasets with one feature
- Multiple linear regression for datasets with more than one feature
- Gradient descent algorithm
- Data normalization

Understanding the regression task

Recall that the regression task is of a particular case of supervised learning, where real numbers take the place of labels. It is the primary difference from the classification, where all labels are categories. You can use regression analysis to study the interactions between two or more variables; for example, the way personal computer price depends on the computer's characteristics, such as a number of CPU cores and the type, memory size, video card characteristics, and storage type and size. In the context of regression, we usually call features *independent variables* and labels *dependent variables*. In our example, independent variables are the computer's characteristics and the dependent variable is its price. Having a regression model, we can predict which machine is better to buy. Moreover, regression allows you to make educated guesses about the contribution of each feature to the final price. Could be an idea for the next viral app.

Regression analysis is a subfield of statistics that investigates how dependent variable changes depend on changes of an independent variable. It also can be used for determining which independent variables are essential and which are not. In some cases, regression analysis can even be used to infer a causal relationship between variables.

Different regression algorithms are implemented in several Swift libraries: AIToolbox, MLKit, multilinear-math, and YCML.

Introducing simple linear regression

Linear regression is a kind of steampunk machine learning. It was invented in the time of Sherlock Holmes, long before the first electronic computer was invented and the term *machine learning* was coined. The term *regression* and its calculation algorithm was introduced by the English polymath Sir Francis Galton in 1886, in the publication named *Regression towards Mediocrity in Hereditary Stature*. Galton proposed the concept while performing research on how to create the perfect breed of people. The task of regression emerged from the need to predict the child's body parameters given the parent's body measurements. So nowadays, Sir Galton is mostly remembered as the father of eugenics rather than as an inventor of the first machine learning algorithm. Later in this chapter, we will follow the footsteps of Galton (but not too far), and employ the linear regression to predict some biological data. Linear regression often is the best choice of machine learning algorithm for fitness apps. You can model all kinds of simple dependencies using it: muscle growth depending on drills; weight loss depending on calorie intake; and so on:

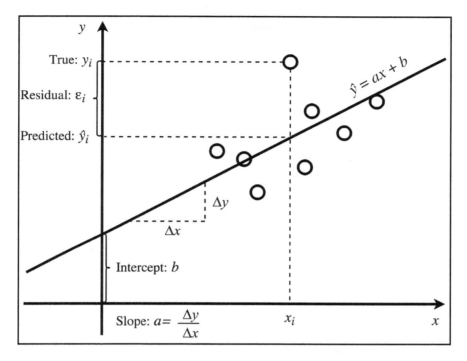

Figure 6.1: Linear regression terminology

From the preceding diagram, you can find the following:

- **x**: Independent variable or feature
- **y**: Dependent variable or targets
- $\hat{y}$: Predicted values of dependent variable
- **yi**: True value of dependent variable for a given data point
- $\hat{y}$**i**: Predicted value of dependent variable for a given data point
- **a**: Slope—rate of predicted changes for **y** scores for each unit increase in **x**
- **b**: y-intercept—predicted value of **y**, when **x** is zero
- ε_i: Residual (error) for a given data point

The idea of linear regression is quite simple. As we remember from the previous chapter, the model in the supervised learning is a mathematical function $f(x)$, which predicts output label y (height of sons, in Galton's research) for the input feature x (height of parents). Perhaps, every reader keeps fond school memories about a simple formula for a straight line: $y = ax + b$, where coefficient a regulates the slope of a line, and the b term is a y-intercept. Given that dependency between x and y is linear, we can suppose that the function underlying our dataset is $y_i = ax_i + b + \varepsilon_i$, where ε stands for errors (in measurements or of any other kind). The straight line plays the role of a model (or hypothesis function, $h(x)$) in task. For now, let's focus on the situation when y is determined by only one feature x. This kind of regression is called **simple linear regression**. To start predicting something, we need the parameters a and b. In fact, the goal of the learning process is to choose the best parameters for our model, such that the line fits the dataset in the best possible way. In other words, the best parameters allow making the most accurate predictions. To tell accurate predictions apart from inaccurate, we use another function: loss (or what's the same, cost) function. Sir Francis Galton used the least squares method to estimate the model parameters.

The linear regression algorithm greatly relies on linear algebra. To implement it in Swift, we are using Accelerate framework. Don't forget to import it:

```
import Accelerate
```

Accelerate framework

Accelerate contains low-level functions optimized for maximum performance on Apple hardware. vDSP sublibrary contains functions for vector operations and digital signal processing. We will go into the details of the Accelerate and other low-level numerical libraries in Chapter 11, *Machine Learning Libraries*, For now, all you need to know is that it's fast and it's low-level.

First, let's create a class `SimpleLinearRegression`. It contains two double variables: model parameters `slope` (a) and `intercept` (b):

```
class SimpleLinearRegression {
var slope = 1.0
var intercept = 0.0
}
```

The main functionality of this class is to train the model and then make predictions using it. For this, we need to add the following methods:

- `predict()`, which goes in two forms: for one sample (takes feature value *x* and returns prediction *h(x)*) and for an array of samples (takes `Double` array of samples and returns `Double` array of predictions)
- `train()`, which takes the sample vector `xVec` and label vector `yVec` of equal length, and updates the parameters `slope` and `intercept`

Both `predict()` functions just call corresponding hypothesis functions, as shown in the following code. Later, we will add more functionality to them:

```
func predict(x: Double) -> Double {
    return hypothesis(x: x)
}
```

And for several samples:

```
func predict(xVec: [Double]) -> [Double] {
    return hypothesis(xVec: xVec)
}
```

Now let's add the hypothesis function $h(x) = ax + b$ as follows:

```
func hypothesis(x: Double) -> Double {
    return slope*x + intercept
}
```

In vectorized form, for several samples at once:

```
func hypothesis(xVec: [Double]) -> [Double] {
    let count = UInt(xVec.count)
    var scaledVec = [Double](repeating: 0.0, count: Int(count))
    vDSP_vsmulD(UnsafePointer(xVec), 1, &slope, &scaledVec, 1, count)
    var resultVec = [Double](repeating: 0.0, count: Int(count))
    vDSP_vsaddD(UnsafePointer(scaledVec), 1, &intercept, &resultVec, 1,
count)
    return resultVec
}
```

The model can be trained as follows:

```
func train(xVec: [Double], yVec: [Double], learningRate: Double, maxSteps:
Int) {
        precondition(xVec.count == yVec.count)
        precondition(maxSteps > 0)
// The goal of training is to minimize cost function.
}
```

Loss function

We've already given the loss function definition in, Chapter 1, *Getting Started with Machine Learning* (see the *Mathematical optimization* section), but here is the first time we actually implement real-value loss function in our code, so let's refresh what we know already.

In machine learning, loss function (or cost function) maps model parameters onto a real-valued cost.

Fitting a regression line using the least squares method

As you remember from Chapter 1, *Getting Started with Machine Learning*, for supervised learning we need two functions: the model and the loss function. We will use the least squares loss function to assess the quality of the model. The method was proposed by Carl Friedrich Gauss at the end of the 17th century. The essence of it is to minimize the distance between data points to the regression line. The difference (deviation) between the true value y_i and the predicted value $h(x_i)$ is called **residual** and denoted as ε_i. Our loss function J will be a **residual sum of squares** (RSS), modified just a bit. If there are n samples of feature x_i and label y_i, then the RSS can be calculated as:

$$RSS = \sum_{i=1}^{n} \epsilon_i^2 = \sum_{i=1}^{n} (h(x_i) - y_i)^2 = ||h(x) - y||^2$$

Note that all residuals are squared before summation to prevent residuals with the opposite sign from cancelling out each other. To make it independent of the size of dataset, we will divide the *RSS* by n. Also, to make some future calculations simpler, we divide those by two.

The final loss function written in Swift is as follows:

```
func cost(trueVec: [Double], predictedVec: [Double]) -> Double {
    let count = UInt(trueVec.count)
```

Let's now calculate the squared Euclidean distance as follows:

```
    var result = 0.0
    vDSP_distancesqD(UnsafePointer(trueVec), 1,
UnsafePointer(predictedVec), 1, &result, 1)
```

You can normalize by vector length, as shown in the following code:

```
    result /= (2*Double(count))
    return result
}
```

It shows how well our hypothesis fits our data. Our goal is to minimize this function: changing the parameters *a* and b finds the minimum of loss function: $\min_{a,b} J(a,b)$. Using a bit of calculus (or looking at Wikipedia), one can show that *a* and *b*, which yield minimum value of loss function, can be calculated using the following formulas:

$$b = \rho_{xy} \frac{\sigma_y}{\sigma_x}$$

$$a = \mu_x - b\mu_y$$

In these formulas, ρ is a correlation coefficient, σ—a standard deviation, and μ—the mean.

Where to use GD and normal equation

If the goal is just to add linear regression to your app, at this point you are done; however, there is another more interesting way to obtain the same coefficients—an optimization technique known as **gradient descent**. The gradient descent algorithm and its multiple descendants are used to find loss function minimums in many machine learning algorithms, including deep neural networks, where a direct analytical solution, like with linear regression is not possible. So, we'd better try it on a simple example like linear regression, so we're already familiar with it when we discuss more complex algorithms.

Using gradient descent for function minimization

If the machine learning algorithm is a car, then the optimization algorithm is its engine. For more information, refer to http://www.pyimagesearch.com/2016/10/10/gradient-descent-with-python/.

From your math classes, you should remember that geometrical interpretation is a derivative $\frac{df(x)}{dx}$ of a function $f(x)$ is a slope at any given point (x) of the function. Now, if we have a function of two parameters $f(x, y)$, we can't calculate just derivative as we did previously. Nevertheless, we can calculate partial derivatives: $\left[\frac{\partial f(y)}{\partial x}, \frac{\partial f(x)}{\partial y}\right]$. The vector composed of these partial derivatives is known as a gradient, and the corresponding operator is denoted by the Nabla symbol ∇.

The gradient of a regression loss function $J(a, b)$ is a vector $\nabla J(a,b) = \left[\frac{\partial J(b)}{\partial a}, \frac{\partial J(a)}{\partial b}\right]$. In a similar manner as a derivative is a slope of the curve at each point, the gradient is a map of heights with the vectors showing the steepest direction at each point of the map.

The loss function of the linear regression has the shape of a bowl (see *Figure 6.2*). Imagine a snail sitting on the edge of the bowl. It doesn't have good sight, it only can sense the direction of the surface slope. How can it reach the bottom of the bowl? The snail just needs to take small steps in the steepest direction, which is exactly against the direction that the gradient shows at each given point of the path.

The gradient descent algorithm for linear regression works in the following way:

1. Initialize a and b at random (or with some predefined values)
2. Take an α (alpha) step in the direction opposite to where the gradient points
3. The coordinates of the point where you ended up are your new a and b
4. Repeat from step 2 until convergence

In mathematical notation, it can be expressed as follows:

$$a' = a - \alpha\frac{\partial}{\partial\alpha}J(a,b)$$

$$b' = b - \alpha\frac{\partial}{\partial b}J(a,b)$$

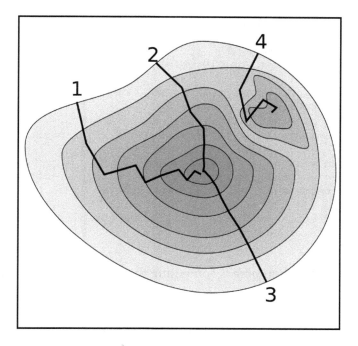

Figure 6.2: Gradient descent trajectories for some hypothetical functions of two variables. This is a heights map depicted on the left and 3D-surface on the right

Now let's implement the same algorithm in Swift. The gradient descent is an iterative algorithm, so we will utilize a loop and some stopping conditions: `maxSteps` (the maximum number of algorithm iterations), which will be checked for the convergence condition. The function explicitly takes input vectors x and y, a learning rate α, and modifies the weights a and b implicitly:

```
func gradientDescent(xVec: [Double], yVec: [Double], α: Double, maxSteps:
Int) {
    for _ in 0 ..< maxSteps {
        let (newSlope, newIntercept) = gradientDescentStep(xVec: xVec,
yVec: yVec, α: α)
        if (newSlope==slope && newIntercept==intercept) { break } //
convergence
        slope = newSlope
        intercept = newIntercept
    }
}
```

Note that a and b (`slope` and `intercept`) should be updated simultaneously.

Following is one step of the gradient descent:

```
// alpha is a learning rate
func gradientDescentStep(xVec: [Double], yVec: [Double], α: Double) ->
(Double, Double) {
    // Calculate hypothesis predictions.
    let hVec = hypothesis(xVec: xVec)
    // Calculate gradient with respect to parameters.
    let slopeGradient = costGradient(trueVec: yVec, predictedVec: hVec,
xVec: xVec)
    let newSlope = slope + α*slopeGradient
    let dummyVec = [Double](repeating: 1.0, count: xVec.count)
    let interceptGradient = costGradient(trueVec: yVec, predictedVec: hVec,
xVec: dummyVec)
    let newIntercept = intercept + α*interceptGradient
    return (newSlope, newIntercept)
}
```

The derivative of a cost function here is something that we simply derive using a pencil and paper:

```
// derivative of a cost function
func costGradient(trueVec: [Double], predictedVec: [Double], xVec:
[Double]) -> Double {
    let count = UInt(trueVec.count)
    var diffVec = [Double](repeating: 0.0, count: Int(count))
    vDSP_vsubD(UnsafePointer(predictedVec), 1, UnsafePointer(trueVec), 1,
&diffVec, 1, count)
    var result = 0.0
    vDSP_dotprD(UnsafePointer(diffVec), 1, UnsafePointer(xVec), 1, &result,
count)
    // Normalize by vector length.
    return result/Double(count)
}
func gradientDescentStep(x: Vector<Double>,
y: Vector<Double>, α: Double) -> (Double, Double) {
    let new = Vector([b, a]) - α*cost_d(x: x, y: y)
    return (new[1], new[0])
}
```

Don't forget to update the `train` function:

```
func train(xVec: [Double], yVec: [Double], learningRate: Double, maxSteps:
Int) {
    gradientDescent(xVec: xVec, yVec: yVec, α: learningRate, maxSteps:
maxSteps)
}
```

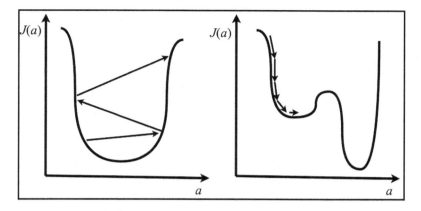

Figure 6.3: The plot shows the graph of some loss function versus parameter w. The learning rate α: on the left it is too large and causes overshooting; on the right it is too small and leads to slow convergence and trapping in local minimum

Forecasting the future with simple linear regression

While writing this book, I was using simple linear regression to estimate the approximate finish date. From time to time, I recorded the total number of pages I had written up to that moment, and then incorporated the data into linear regression. The number of pages here is a feature and the date is a label.

Linear trend is a useful feature for any application that deals with some gradually progressing processes or tasks, especially in the combination with charts. Later in this chapter, we will learn how to build non-linear trend lines, namely polynomial.

Let's make some forecasts:

```
let xVec: [Double] = [2,3,4,5]
let yVec: [Double] = [10,20,30,40]

let regression = SimpleLinearRegression()
regression.train(xVec: xVec, yVec: yVec, learningRate: 0.1, maxSteps: 31)

regression.slope
regression.intercept

regression.predict(x: 7)
regression.cost(trueVec: yVec, predictedVec: regression.predict(xVec:
xVec))
```

Feature scaling

If you have several features and their ranges differ significantly, many machine learning algorithms may have taught times with your data: the large feature may overwhelm the features with small absolute values. A standard way to deal with this obstacle is **feature scaling** (also known as **feature/data normalization**). There are several methods to perform it, but the two most common are rescaling and standardization. This is something you want to do as a preprocessing step before feeding your data into the learner.

The least squares method is almost the same as the Euclidean distance between two points. If we want to calculate how close two points are, we want each dimension to make an equal contribution to the result. In the case of the linear regression features, contributions depend on absolute values of each feature. That's why feature scaling is a must before linear regression. Later, we will meet similar technique batch normalization when we talk about deep learning neural networks.

Features in the input data can have different ranges. For example: user age 0 to 120 years, user height 0 to 5 meters. Many loss functions would have a problem dealing with such data. Under the Euclidean distance feature with the large absolute values will suppress feature with the small absolute values. That's why usually, before passing the data into a machine learning algorithm, we want to normalize them. This is how we do it:

$$x' = \frac{x - max(x)}{max(x) - min(x)}$$

 For scikit-learn, follow this link: http://scikit-learn.org/stable/
modules/preprocessing.html.

Feature standardization

An alternative approach is feature standardization:

$$x' - \frac{x - \mu}{\sigma}$$

Which of the two to use in your app is up to you, but be sure to use at least one of them.

As usual, we have an accelerate function for that:

```
func normalize(vec: [Double]) -> (normalizedVec: [Double], mean: Double,
std: Double) {
    let count = vec.count
    var mean = 0.0
    var std = 0.0
    var normalizedVec = [Double](repeating: 0.0, count: count)
    vDSP_normalizeD(UnsafePointer(vec), 1, &normalizedVec, 1, &mean, &std,
UInt(count))
    return (normalizedVec, mean, std)
}
```

Now we need to update the `train` method:

```
func train(xVec: [Double], yVec: [Double], learningRate: Double, maxSteps:
Int) {
    precondition(xVec.count == yVec.count)
    precondition(maxSteps > 0)
    if normalization {
        let (normalizedXVec, xMean, xStd) = normalize(vec: xVec)
        let (normalizedYVec, yMean, yStd) = normalize(vec: yVec)
        // Save means and std-s for prediction phase.
        self.xMean = xMean
        self.xStd = xStd
        self.yMean = yMean
        self.yStd = yStd
        gradientDescent(xVec: normalizedXVec, yVec: normalizedYVec, α:
learningRate, maxSteps: maxSteps)
    } else {
        gradientDescent(xVec: xVec, yVec: yVec, α: learningRate, maxSteps:
maxSteps)
    }
}
```

You also have to update `predict` methods:

```
func predictOne(x: Double) -> Double {
    if normalization {
        return hypothesis(x: (x-xMean)/xStd) * yStd + yMean
    } else {
        return hypothesis(x: x)
    }
}
```

For a vectorized case it looks a bit more complicated, but essentially it does the same thing: shift-scale, unscale-unshift:

```swift
func predict(xVec: [Double]) -> [Double] {
    if normalization {
        let count = xVec.count
        // Normalize
        var centeredVec = [Double](repeating: 0.0, count: count)
        var negMean = -xMean
        vDSP_vsaddD(UnsafePointer(xVec), 1, &(negMean), &centeredVec, 1,
UInt(count))
        var scaledVec = [Double](repeating: 0.0, count: count)
        vDSP_vsdivD(UnsafePointer(centeredVec), 1, &xStd, &scaledVec, 1,
UInt(count))
        // Predict
        let hVec = hypothesis(xVec: scaledVec)
        // Denormalize
        var unScaledVec = [Double](repeating: 0.0, count: count)
        vDSP_vsmulD(UnsafePointer(hVec), 1, &yStd, &unScaledVec, 1,
UInt(count))
        var resultVec = [Double](repeating: 0.0, count: count)
        vDSP_vsaddD(UnsafePointer(unScaledVec), 1, &yMean, &resultVec, 1,
UInt(count))
        return resultVec
    } else {
        return hypothesis(xVec: xVec)
    }
}
```

Let's make some forecasts:

```swift
let xVec: [Double] = [2,3,4,5]
let yVec: [Double] = [10,20,30,40]

let regression = SimpleLinearRegression()
regression.normalization = true
regression.train(xVec: xVec, yVec: yVec, learningRate: 0.1, maxSteps: 31)

regression.slope
1.0
regression.intercept
-1.970....
regression.xMean
3.5
regression.xStd
1.1180...
regression.yMean
25.0
```

```
regression.yStd
11.18033987...
regression.predict(x: 7)
60.0
regression.cost(trueVec: yVec, predictedVec: regression.predict(xVec:
xVec))
1.5777218...
```

Multiple linear regression

If we have a regression task on the dataset with multiple features, we can't use simple linear regression but we can apply its generalization: **multiple linear regression**. The formula to make a prediction now looks like this:

$$y_i = x_i^T w$$

In this formula, x_i^T is a sample (feature vector) with m features, and w is a weights row vector of length m. The dependent variable y_i is a scalar.

The task of loss minimization changes to be:

$$w_{min} = \underset{w}{\operatorname{argmin}} \left\| wX - y \right\|^2 = \underset{w}{\operatorname{argmin}} \sum_{i=0}^{n} \left(h(x_i) - y_i \right)^2$$

In this formula, $\|\|$ is the Euclidean norm (length of a vector): $\|v\| = \sqrt{v_1^2 + \cdots + v_n^2}$. Note that this is the same as the Euclidean distance between vectors wx and y.

One can also see multiple linear regression fitting as a solution of a system of linear equations, where each coefficient is a feature value, and each variable is a corresponding weight value:

$$\begin{cases} 10w_1 + 0.5w_2 - 3w_3 = 15 \\ 2w_1 + 0.3w_2 + 1.5w_3 = 8 \\ 7w_1 - 0.1w_2 - 2w_3 = 4 \\ \cdots \\ X_{i1}w_1 + X_{i2}w_2 + \ldots + X_{ij}w_j = y_i \end{cases}$$

Or:

$$Xw = y$$

The problem here is that such a system may not have the exact solution, so we want to get a solution that, if not exact, nevertheless is optimal in some way.

Implementing multiple linear regression in Swift

The `MultipleLinearRegression` class contains a vector of weights, and staff for data normalization:

```
class MultipleLinearRegression {
public var weights: [Double]!
public init() {}
public var normalization = false
public var xMeanVec = [Double]()
public var xStdVec = [Double]()
public var yMean = 0.0
public var yStd = 0.0
...
}
```

Hypothesis and prediction:

```
public func predict(xVec: [Double]) -> Double {
if normalization {
    let input = xVec
    let differenceVec = vecSubtract([1.0]+input, xMeanVec)
    let normalizedInputVec = vecDivide(differenceVec, xStdVec)
    let h = hypothesis(xVec: normalizedInputVec)
    return h * yStd + yMean
} else {
    return hypothesis(xVec: [1.0]+xVec)
}
}

private func hypothesis(xVec: [Double]) -> Double {
var result = 0.0
vDSP_dotprD(xVec, 1, weights, 1, &result, vDSP_Length(xVec.count))
return result
}
```

```
public func predict(xMat: [[Double]]) -> [Double] {
let rows = xMat.count
precondition(rows > 0)
let columns = xMat.first!.count
precondition(columns > 0)

if normalization {
    let flattenedNormalizedX = xMat.map{
        return vecDivide(vecSubtract($0, xMeanVec), xStdVec)
        }.reduce([], +)
    // Add a column of ones in front of the matrix.
    let basisExpanded = prepentColumnOfOnes(matrix: flattenedNormalizedX,
rows: rows, columns: columns)
    let hVec = hypothesis(xMatFlattened: basisExpanded)
    let outputSize = hVec.count
    let productVec = vecMultiply(hVec, [Double](repeating: yStd, count:
outputSize))
    let outputVec = vecAdd(productVec, [Double](repeating: yMean, count:
outputSize))
    return outputVec
} else {
    // Flatten and prepend a column of ones.
    let flattened = xMat.map{[1.0]+$0}.reduce([], +)
    return hypothesis(xMatFlattened: flattened)
}
}

private func hypothesis(xMatFlattened: [Double]) -> [Double] {
let matCount = xMatFlattened.count
let featureCount = weights.count
precondition(matCount > 0)
let sampleCount = matCount/featureCount
precondition(sampleCount*featureCount == matCount)
let labelSize = 1
let result = gemm(aMat: xMatFlattened, bMat: weights, rowsAC: sampleCount,
colsBC: labelSize, colsA_rowsB: featureCount)
return result
}
```

Least squares cost function, almost the same as for simple regression:

```
public func cost(trueVec: [Double], predictedVec: [Double]) -> Double {
let count = trueVec.count
// Calculate squared Euclidean distance.
var result = 0.0
vDSP_distancesqD(trueVec, 1, predictedVec, 1, &result, 1)
// Normalize by vector length.
result/=(2*Double(count))
```

```
return result
}
```

Gradient descent for multiple linear regression

The gradient descent for multiple linear regression can be calculated as follows:

```
// derivative of a cost function
    private func costGradient(trueVec: [Double], predictedVec: [Double],
xMatFlattened: [Double]) -> [Double] {
        let matCount = xMatFlattened.count
        let featureCount = weights.count
        precondition(matCount > 0)
        precondition(Double(matCount).truncatingRemainder(dividingBy:
Double(featureCount)) == 0)
        let sampleCount = trueVec.count
        precondition(sampleCount > 0)
        precondition(sampleCount*featureCount == matCount)
        let labelSize = 1
        let diffVec = vecSubtract(predictedVec, trueVec)
        // Normalize by vector length.
        let scaleBy = 1/Double(sampleCount)
        let result = gemm(aMat: xMatFlattened, bMat: diffVec, rowsAC:
featureCount, colsBC: labelSize, colsA_rowsB: sampleCount, transposeA:
true, α: scaleBy)
        return result
    }
    // alpha is a learning rate
    private func gradientDescentStep(xMatFlattened: [Double], yVec:
[Double], α: Double) -> [Double] {
        // Calculate hypothesis predictions.
        let hVec = hypothesis(xMatFlattened: xMatFlattened)
        // Calculate gradient with respect to parameters.
        let gradient = costGradient(trueVec: yVec, predictedVec: hVec,
xMatFlattened: xMatFlattened)
        let featureCount = gradient.count
        // newWeights = weights - α*gradient
        var alpha = α
        var scaledGradient = [Double](repeating: 0.0, count: featureCount)
        vDSP_vsmulD(gradient, 1, &alpha, &scaledGradient, 1,
vDSP_Length(featureCount))
        let newWeights = vecSubtract(weights, scaledGradient)
        return newWeights
    }
    private func gradientDescent(xMatFlattened: [Double], yVec: [Double],
α: Double, maxSteps: Int) {
```

```
    for _ in 0 ..< maxSteps {
        let newWeights = gradientDescentStep(xMatFlattened:
xMatFlattened, yVec: yVec, α: α)
        if newWeights==weights {
            print("convergence")
            break
        } // convergence
        weights = newWeights
    }
}
```

Training multiple regression

Let's now see how to train the multiple regression:

```
 private func prepentColumnOfOnes(matrix: [Double], rows: Int, columns:
Int) -> [Double] {
let weightsCount = columns+1

var withFirstDummyColumn = [Double](repeating: 1.0, count: rows *
(columns+1))
for row in 0..<rows {
    for column in 1..<weightsCount {
        withFirstDummyColumn[row*weightsCount + column] =
matrix[row*columns + column-1]
    }
}
return withFirstDummyColumn
}

public func train(xMat: [[Double]], yVec: [Double], learningRate: Double,
maxSteps: Int) {
precondition(maxSteps > 0, "The number of learning iterations should be
grater then 0.")
let sampleCount = xMat.count
precondition(sampleCount == yVec.count, "The number of samples in xMat
should be equal to the number of labels in yVec.")
precondition(sampleCount > 0, "xMat should contain at least one sample.")
precondition(xMat.first!.count > 0, "Samples should have at least one
feature.")
let featureCount = xMat.first!.count
let weightsCount = featureCount+1

weights = [Double](repeating: 1.0, count: weightsCount)
// Flatten and prepend a column of ones.
let flattenedXMat = xMat.reduce([], +)
```

```
if normalization {
    let (normalizedXMat, xMeanVec, xStdVec) = matNormalize(matrix:
flattenedXMat, rows: sampleCount, columns: featureCount)
    let (normalizedYVec, yMean, yStd) = vecNormalize(vec: yVec)
    // Save means and std-s for prediction phase.
    self.xMeanVec = xMeanVec
    self.xStdVec = xStdVec
    self.yMean = yMean
    self.yStd = yStd
    // Add first column of ones to matrix
    let designMatrix = prepentColumnOfOnes(matrix: normalizedXMat, rows:
sampleCount, columns: featureCount)
    gradientDescent(xMatFlattened: designMatrix, yVec: normalizedYVec, α:
learningRate, maxSteps: maxSteps)
} else {
    gradientDescent(xMatFlattened: flattenedXMat, yVec: yVec, α:
learningRate, maxSteps: maxSteps)
}
}
```

Linear algebra operations

Now we will take a look at how linear algebraic operations can be performed:

```
// Add two vectors. Equivalent to zip(a, b).map(+)
func vecAdd(_ a: [Double], _ b: [Double]) -> [Double] {
    let count = a.count
    assert(count == b.count, "Vectors must be of equal length.")
    var c = [Double](repeating: 0.0, count: count)
    vDSP_vaddD(a, 1, b, 1, &c, 1, vDSP_Length(count))
    return c
}

// Subtract vector b from vector a. Equivalent to zip(a, b).map(-)
func vecSubtract(_ a: [Double], _ b: [Double]) -> [Double] {
    let count = a.count
    assert(count == b.count, "Vectors must be of equal length.")
    var c = [Double](repeating: 0.0, count: count)
    vDSP_vsubD(b, 1, a, 1, &c, 1, vDSP_Length(count))
    return c
}

// Multiply two vectors elementwise. Equivalent to zip(a, b).map(*)
func vecMultiply(_ a: [Double], _ b: [Double]) -> [Double] {
    let count = a.count
    assert(count == b.count, "Vectors must be of equal length.")
```

```
        var c = [Double](repeating: 0.0, count: count)
        vDSP_vmulD(a, 1, b, 1, &c, 1, vDSP_Length(count))
        return c
}

// Divide vector a by vector b elementwise. Equivalent to zip(a, b).map(/)
func vecDivide(_ a: [Double], _ b: [Double]) -> [Double] {
        let count = a.count
        assert(count == b.count, "Vectors must be of equal length.")
        var c = [Double](repeating: 0.0, count: count)
        // Note that parameters a and b are swapped.
        vDSP_vdivD(b, 1, a, 1, &c, 1, vDSP_Length(count))
        return c
}

func vecNormalize(vec: [Double]) -> (normalizedVec: [Double], mean: Double,
std: Double) {
        let count = vec.count
        var mean = 0.0
        var std = 0.0
        var normalizedVec = [Double](repeating: 0.0, count: count)
        vDSP_normalizeD(vec, 1, &normalizedVec, 1, &mean, &std,
vDSP_Length(count))
        return (normalizedVec, mean, std)
}
// C←αAB + βC
// Pass flattened matrices in row-major order.
// rowsAC, colsBC, colsA_rowsB - Count of rows/columns AFTER transpose.
func gemm(aMat: [Double], bMat: [Double], cMat: [Double]? = nil,
          rowsAC: Int, colsBC: Int, colsA_rowsB: Int,
          transposeA: Bool = false, transposeB: Bool = false,
          α: Double = 1, β: Double = 0) -> [Double] {
        var result = cMat ?? [Double](repeating: 0.0, count: rowsAC*colsBC)
        // C←αAB + βC
        cblas_dgemm(CblasRowMajor, // Specifies row-major (C) or column-major
(Fortran) data ordering.
        transposeA ? CblasTrans : CblasNoTrans, // Specifies whether to
transpose matrix A.
        transposeB ? CblasTrans : CblasNoTrans, // Specifies whether to
transpose matrix B.
        Int32(rowsAC), // Number of rows in matrices A and C.
        Int32(colsBC), // Number of columns in matrices B and C.
        Int32(colsA_rowsB), // Number of columns in matrix A; number of
rows in matrix B.
        α, // α.
        aMat, // Matrix A.
        transposeA ? Int32(rowsAC) : Int32(colsA_rowsB), // The size of the
first dimention of matrix A; if you are passing a matrix A[m][n], the value
```

```
should be m.
        bMat, // Matrix B.
        transposeB ? Int32(colsA_rowsB) : Int32(colsBC), // The size of the
first dimention of matrix B; if you are passing a matrix B[m][n], the value
should be m.
        β, // β.
        &result, // Matrix C.
        Int32(colsBC) // The size of the first dimention of matrix C; if
you are passing a matrix C[m][n], the value should be m.
    )
    return result
}
```

Feature-wise standardization

Feature-wise standardization can be calculated as follows:

```
// Calculates mean for every matrix column.
func meanColumns(matrix: [Double], rows: Int, columns: Int) -> [Double] {
    assert(matrix.count == rows*columns)
    var resultVec = [Double](repeating: 0.0, count: columns)
    matrix.withUnsafeBufferPointer{ inputBuffer in
        resultVec.withUnsafeMutableBufferPointer{ outputBuffer in
            let inputPointer = inputBuffer.baseAddress!
            let outputPointer = outputBuffer.baseAddress!
            for i in 0 ..< columns {
                vDSP_meanvD(inputPointer.advanced(by: i), columns,
outputPointer.advanced(by: i), vDSP_Length(rows))
            }
        }
    }
    return resultVec
}

// Calculates standard deviation for every matrix column.
func stdColumns(matrix: [Double], rows: Int, columns: Int) -> [Double] {
    assert(matrix.count == rows*columns)
    let meanVec = meanColumns(matrix: matrix, rows: rows, columns: columns)
    var varianceVec = [Double](repeating: 0.0, count: columns)
    var deviationsMat = [Double](repeating: 0.0, count: rows*columns)
    // Calculating the variance for each column.
    matrix.withUnsafeBufferPointer{ inputBuffer in
        deviationsMat.withUnsafeMutableBufferPointer{ deviationsBuffer in
            varianceVec.withUnsafeMutableBufferPointer{ outputBuffer in
                for i in 0 ..< columns {
                    let inputPointer =
```

```
inputBuffer.baseAddress!.advanced(by: i)
                    let devPointer =
deviationsBuffer.baseAddress!.advanced(by: i)
                    let outputPointer =
outputBuffer.baseAddress!.advanced(by: i)
                    var mean = -meanVec[i]
                    // Deviations of each column from its mean.
                    vDSP_vsaddD(inputPointer, columns, &mean, devPointer,
columns, vDSP_Length(rows))
                    // Squared deviations.
                    vDSP_vsqD(devPointer, columns, devPointer, columns,
vDSP_Length(rows))
                    // Sum for every column. Note, that parameters should
be passed in a reverse order.
                    vDSP_sveD(devPointer, columns, outputPointer,
vDSP_Length(rows))
                }
            }
        }
    }
    // -1 for Bessel's correction.
    var devideBy = Double(rows) - 1
    vDSP_vsdivD(varianceVec, 1, &devideBy, &varianceVec, 1,
vDSP_Length(columns))
    // Calculating the standard deviation.
    var length = Int32(columns)
    var stdVec = varianceVec
    vvsqrt(&stdVec, &varianceVec, &length)
    return stdVec
}
// (x-μ)/σ
func matNormalize(matrix: [Double], rows: Int, columns: Int) ->
(normalizedMat: [Double], meanVec: [Double], stdVec: [Double]) {
    var meanVec = meanColumns(matrix: matrix, rows: rows, columns: columns)
    var stdVec = stdColumns(matrix: matrix, rows: rows, columns: columns)
    var result = [Double](repeating: 0.0, count: rows*columns)
    matrix.withUnsafeBufferPointer{ inputBuffer in
        result.withUnsafeMutableBufferPointer{ resultBuffer in
            for i in 0 ..< columns {
                let inputPointer = inputBuffer.baseAddress!.advanced(by: i)
                let resultPointer = resultBuffer.baseAddress!.advanced(by:
i)
                var mean = -meanVec[i]
                var std = stdVec[i]
                // Substract standard deviation.
                vDSP_vsaddD(inputPointer, columns, &mean, resultPointer,
columns, vDSP_Length(rows))
                // Devide by mean.
```

```
                  vDSP_vsdivD(resultPointer, columns, &std, resultPointer,
    columns, vDSP_Length(rows))
               }
          }
     }
     return (result, meanVec, stdVec)
}
```

Normal equation for multiple linear regression

If you want to implement regression in a production code, don't use matrix inversion operation explicitly. The problem with it is that it is very numerically inefficient. Instead, you can use one of the functions for solving a system of linear equations, which is essentially the same as finding regression coefficients. The good fit from the LAPACK package (part of the Accelerate framework) is the QR-decomposition function.

Understanding and overcoming the limitations of linear regression

Before building the predictive model, you should always perform an exploratory analysis. It will help you to select the right model by identifying the relationship and impact of features and samples. Linear regression has a whole bunch of preconditions and hidden assumptions. To get accurate results, you need to be sure that all those conditions are met and all assumptions are true:

- Linear regression assumes all features to be numerical variables. If you have categorical features, you cannot use linear regression. You need to be careful here, because often categorical variables are represented by numbers; for example, country code or E numbers of food additives (found on all food labels in the EU, for example E260 stands for acetic acid). In other words, linear regression can only be applied to quantities (the amount of something) and not to categories, ordered lists, scales, or numerical codes.
- Linear regression models linear relationships; that means that features should be linearly related to labels. Build a scatterplot to be sure that the data you have can be modeled using the line. My favorite quote in this context is Randall Munroe's famous quote from https://xkcd.com/1725/:

"I don't trust linear regressions when it's harder to guess the direction of the correlation from the scatter plot than to find new constellations on it."

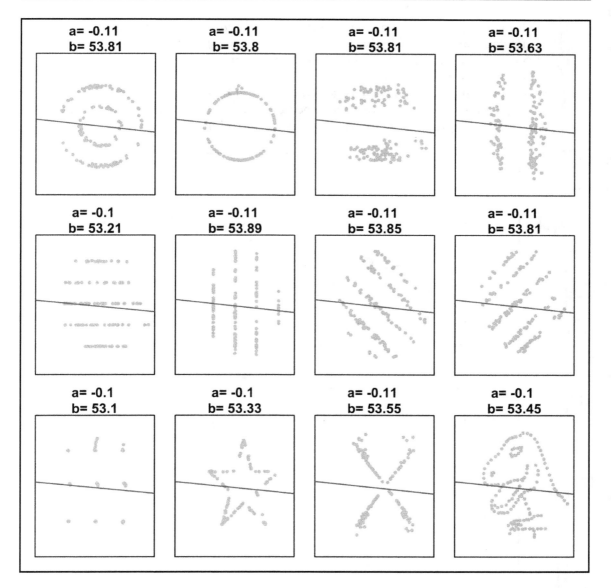

Figure 6.4: Datasaurus Dozen [1] shows how very different datasets can have very similar descriptive statistics. Note how linear regression parameters (*a* and *b*) vary insignificantly among these datasets. Linear regression is a bad model for non-linear data

- Linear regression is sensitive to outliers (see *Figure 6.5*); in other words, it is an unstable algorithm—it gives a bad result on a noisy data. How many outliers do you need to completely spoil the model? One outlier is enough. If you have outliers, be sure to check how they affect your model by building two regressions: one with outliers, and one without them. There are regression algorithms that were developed specifically for the use with the noisy data, such as robust regression, RANSAC, and its modifications:

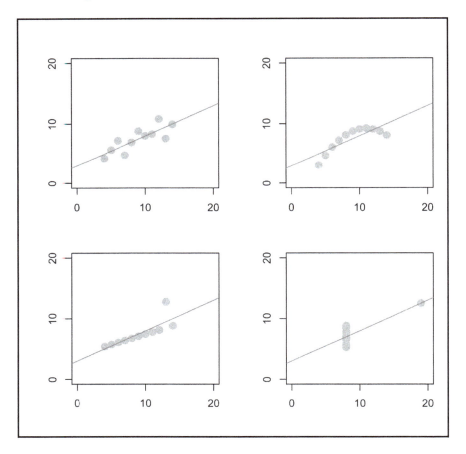

Figure 6.5: Anscombe's quartet [2] is commonly used to demonstrate linear regression limitations. The first graph shows the dataset, which can be modeled by linear regression. The second one shows nonlinearity in the data. The third and fourth show the instability of the algorithm: one outlier is enough to break the model completely

- Linear regression also has some requirements for the errors. Errors should be independent, homoscedastic, and normally distributed around the regression line (see *Figure 6.6*). The homoscedasticity requirement means that variance of errors remains the same over the entire dataset:

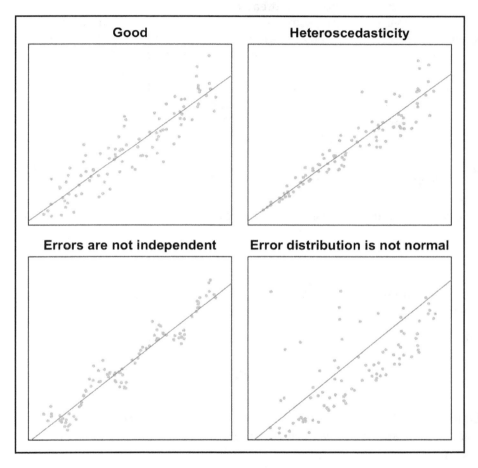

Figure 6.6: Error distribution

There are three spells that break linear regression: multicollinearity (correlation between features), autocorrelation (correlation between samples), heteroscedasticity (error variance changes). Countermeasures are regularization, selecting the most important features by stepwise regression, forward selection, and backward elimination.

Fixing linear regression problems with regularization

As we've seen, one outlier is enough to break the least-squares regression. Such instability is a manifestation of overfitting problems. Methods that help prevent models from overfitting are generally referred to as **regularization** techniques. Usually, regularization is achieved by imposing additional constraints on the model. This can be an additional term in a loss function, noise injection, or something else. We've already implemented one such technique previously, in `Chapter 3`, *K-Nearest Neighbors Classifier*. Locality constraint w in the DTW algorithm is essentially a way to regularize the result. In the case of linear regression, regularization imposes constraints on the weights vector values.

Ridge regression and Tikhonov regularization

Under the standard least squares method, the obtained regression coefficients can vary wildly. We can formulate the least squares regression as an optimization problem:

$$w* = \underset{w}{\operatorname{argmin}} \left(y - \mathbf{X}w \right)^T \left(y - \mathbf{X}w \right)$$

What we have on the right here is just an RSS in a form of a scalar product. Tikhonov regularized least squares regression adds an additional penalty term—squared L_2 norm of weights vector:

$$w* = \underset{w}{\operatorname{argmin}} \left(y - \mathbf{X}w \right)^T \left(y - \mathbf{X}w \right) + \lambda w^T w$$

$$= \underset{w}{\operatorname{argmin}} \left\| y - \mathbf{X}w \right\|_2^2 + \lambda \left\| w \right\|_2^2$$

where L_2 norm $\|w\|_2 = \sqrt{\sum_i w_i^2} \Rightarrow \|w\|_2^2 = \sum_i w_i^2 = w^T w$ and λ is a scalar shrinkage parameter. It allows to control weights variance and keep it low. Similar to other hyperparameters, λ needs to be defined separately, usually using held-out data or cross-validation. The larger it is, the smaller the regression coefficients (weights) will be.

Such an optimization problem has a closed-form solution, similar to the normal equation:

$$\hat{w} = (X^T X + \lambda I)^{-1} X^T y$$

I is an identity matrix, where main diagonal elements are equal to *1*, and all others equal to *0*.

Linear regression regularized in such a way is known as **ridge regression**. One of its advantages is that it can be used even if features in a training data are highly correlated (multicollinearity). Unlike usual linear regression, ridge regression doesn't assume the normal distribution of errors. It reduces the absolute values of features but they don't reach zero, which means that this regression also performs badly if there are irrelevant features.

LASSO regression

To fix the problem with irrelevant features, one can replace the L_2 norm with the L_1 norm in a penalty term, and instead of penalizing squares of regression coefficients, penalize their absolute values:

$$w* = \underset{w}{\operatorname{argmin}} \|y - Xw\|_2^2 + \lambda \|w\|_1$$

where L_1 norm $\|w\|_1 = \sum_i |w_i|$. This is so-called **Least Absolute Shrinkage and Selection Operator (LASSO)** regression. Some of the weight coefficients under such a penalty can become exactly zero, which you can think of as a feature selection. If there are several highly correlated features in your dataset, LASSO picks one of them and sets all others to zero. This also means that LASSO often results in sparse weight vectors.

This type of regression also doesn't assume the normality of error distribution.

ElasticNet regression

ElasticNet regression is a combination of ridge and LASSO methods: add both penalty terms to the usual least squares loss function and you will get the ElasticNet regression. It also has two shrinkage parameters:

$$w* = \underset{w}{\operatorname{argmin}} \|y - Xw\|_2^2 + \lambda_2 \|w\|_2^2 + \lambda_1 \|w\|_1$$

It is especially helpful when you have multiple correlated features. When two features are correlated, LASSO tends to choose one of them randomly, while ElasticNet keeps both. Similar to the ridge regression, ElasticNet is also more stable in many cases:

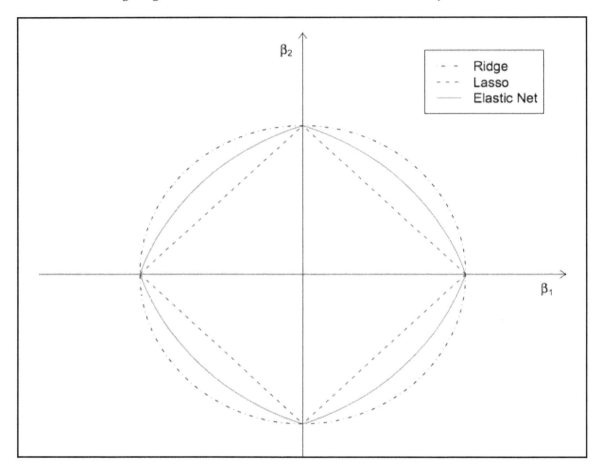

Figure 6.7: Penalty terms in the space of the model parameters.

Regularized linear regression is available in multiple machine learning packages, including Scikit-learn for integration with Core ML and AIToolbox for on-device training.

Summary

In this chapter, we've explored linear regression and gradient descent. Linear regression is a simple parametric model. It makes a certain assumption about data shape and error distribution. We were also acquainted with the Accelerate framework, a powerful hardware-accelerated framework from Apple for numerical computations.

In the next chapter, we'll continue by building different, more complex models on top of linear regression: polynomial regression, regularized regression, and logistic regression.

Bibliography

1. Justin Matejka, George Fitzmaurice (2017), *Same Stats, Different Graphs: Generating Datasets with Varied Appearance and Identical Statistics through Simulated Annealing*, CHI 2017 Conference Proceedings: ACM SIGCHI Conference on Human Factors in Computing Systems
2. F. J. Anscombe, *Graphs in Statistical Analysis*, The American Statistician, V-27 (1): 17-21 (1973), JSTOR 2682899

7
Linear Classifier and Logistic Regression

In the previous chapter, we added several useful supervised learning algorithms for regression tasks to our toolbox. Continuing with building on top of linear regression, in this chapter, we are going to build two classification algorithms: **linear classifier** and **logistic regression**. Both of them take familiar feature vectors as input, similar to multiple linear regression. The difference is in their output. The linear classifier will output true or false (binary classification) and logistic regression will provide the probability of some event happening.

The topics to discuss in this chapter are:

- Bias and variance
- Linear classifier
- Logistic regression

Revisiting the classification task

We already used and implemented some classification algorithms in the previous chapters: decision tree learning, random forest, and KNN are all well suited for solving this task. However, as Boromir used to say, *"One cannot simply walk into neural networks without knowing about logistic regression"*. So, to remind you, classification is almost the same as regression, except that response variable y is not a continuous (float) but takes values from some set of discrete values (enum). In this chapter, we're primarily concerned with the binary classification, where y can be either true or false, one or zero, and belong to a positive or negative class.

Although, if you think about this for a moment, it's not too hard to build a multiclass classifier from several binary classifiers by chaining them one after the other. In the classification domain, response variable y is usually called a **label**.

Linear classifier

Linear regression can be trivially adapted for binary classification: just predict a positive class for all regression outputs above some threshold and a negative class for everything below it. For example, in the following diagram, the threshold is 0.5. Everything with $x < 0.5$ gets classified as a negative class and everything with $x > 0.5$ as positive. The line that separates feature values of one class from another is called a **decision boundary**. With more than one feature, the decision boundary will not be a line but a hyperplane:

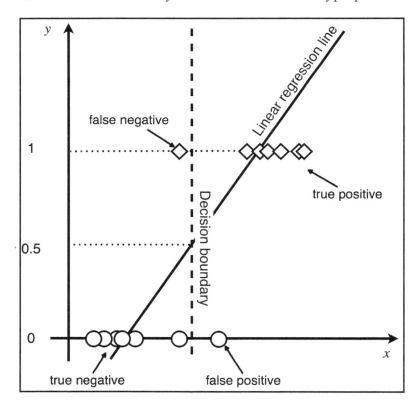

Figure 7.1: Linear classifier

Logistic regression

You can come up with a lot of problems a linear classifier has. One of them is that many datasets just cannot be separated properly by a straight line:

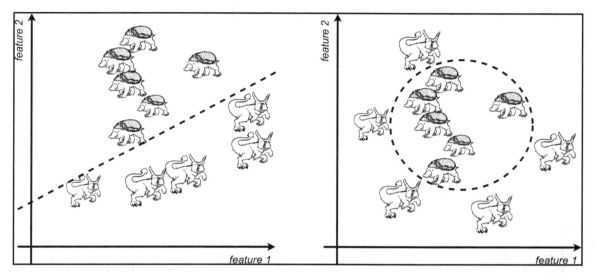

Figure 7.2: Linear separable (on the left) and nonlinear separable (on the right) data. The decision boundary as shown in the dashed line. Source: Mykola Sosnovshchenko.

Another problem is that a linear regression line can predict negative values or values greater than one for some samples even though we know for sure y should be either zero or one. To fix it, we need some function that takes values from [-∞, +∞] and output values in the range from zero to one. One such function is a logistic function. Please refer to the following formula and graph:

$$f(x) = \frac{1}{1 - e^{-x}}$$

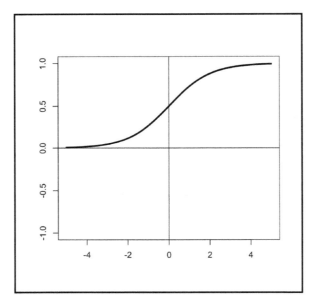

Figure 7.3: Logistic function

Remember that in linear regression, we had our hypothesis function defined as a linear transformation (dot product of vectors):

$$h_w(x) = w^T x$$

In a logistic regression, we add a nonlinear logistic transformation like this:

$$h_w(x) = f(w^T x) = \frac{1}{1 - e^{-w^T x}}$$

Logistic regression is used to estimate the probability of some event happening or not happening. In other words, it is a binary classification algorithm that outputs the probability of the sample belonging to one or another class. The typical example of logistic regression output looks like this: *There's a 0.95 chance the letter is spam, and 0.05 chance it's not.*

The output of the logistic regression is always in a range (0, 1). We still call this algorithm *regression*, despite using it for classification, because it produces a continuous output; however, this is the closest we can get to a discrete output using differential functions. Why do we want them to be differential? Because we want to use our good friend gradient descent to learn the parameter vector w.

Implementing logistic regression in Swift

The most important differences of this implementation from multiple linear regression are the following:

- Normalization is required only for feature matrix x, and not for the target vector y, because the output has range (0, 1)
- The hypothesis is different
- The cost function looks different, but the cost gradient remains the same

Again, we'll need some accelerate functions:

```
import Accelerate
```

The logistic regression class definition looks similar to multiple linear regression:

```
public class LogisticRegression {
public var weights: [Double]!

public init(normalization: Bool) {
    self.normalization = normalization
}

private(set) var normalization: Bool
private(set) var xMeanVec = [Double]()
private(set) var xStdVec = [Double]()
```

The prediction part of logistic regression

This is the code that implements hypotheses for one sample input and for a matrix of inputs:

```
public func predict(xVec: [Double]) -> Double {
    if normalization {
        let input = xVec
        let differenceVec = vecSubtract(input, xMeanVec)
        let normalizedInputVec = vecDivide(differenceVec, xStdVec)
        let h = hypothesis(xVec: [1.0]+normalizedInputVec)
        return h
    } else {
        return hypothesis(xVec: [1.0]+xVec)
    }
}

private func hypothesis(xVec: [Double]) -> Double {
    var result = 0.0
    vDSP_dotprD(xVec, 1, weights, 1, &result, vDSP_Length(xVec.count))
    return 1.0 / (1.0 + exp(-result))
}

public func predict(xMat: [[Double]]) -> [Double] {
    let rows = xMat.count
    precondition(rows > 0)
    let columns = xMat.first!.count
    precondition(columns > 0)
    if normalization {
        let flattenedNormalizedX = xMat.map{
            return vecDivide(vecSubtract($0, xMeanVec), xStdVec)
            }.reduce([], +)
        // Add a column of ones in front of the matrix.
        let basisExpanded = prependColumnOfOnes(matrix:
flattenedNormalizedX, rows: rows, columns: columns)
        let hVec = hypothesis(xMatFlattened: basisExpanded)
        return hVec
    } else {
        // Flatten and prepend a column of ones.
        let flattened = xMat.map{[1.0]+$0}.reduce([], +)
        return hypothesis(xMatFlattened: flattened)
    }
}

private func hypothesis(xMatFlattened: [Double]) -> [Double] {
    let matCount = xMatFlattened.count
    let featureCount = weights.count
```

```
    precondition(matCount > 0)
    let sampleCount = matCount/featureCount
    precondition(sampleCount*featureCount == matCount)
    let labelSize = 1
    var result = gemm(aMat: xMatFlattened, bMat: weights, rowsAC:
sampleCount, colsBC: labelSize, colsA_rowsB: featureCount)
    // -h
    vDSP_vnegD(result, 1, &result, 1, vDSP_Length(sampleCount))
    // exp(-h)
    // vForce function for double-precision exponent.
    var outputLength = Int32(sampleCount)
    vvexp(&result, result, &outputLength)
    // 1.0 + exp(-h)
    var one = 1.0
    vDSP_vsaddD(result, 1, &one, &result, 1, vDSP_Length(sampleCount))
    // 1.0 / (1.0 + exp(-h))
    vDSP_svdivD(&one, result, 1, &result, 1, vDSP_Length(sampleCount))
    return result
}
```

Training the logistic regression

The training part is also very similar to linear regression:

```
public func train(xMat: [[Double]], yVec: [Double], learningRate: Double,
maxSteps: Int) {
  precondition(maxSteps > 0, "The number of learning iterations should be
grater then 0.")
  let sampleCount = xMat.count
  precondition(sampleCount == yVec.count, "The number of samples in xMat
should be equal to the number of labels in yVec.")
  precondition(sampleCount > 0, "xMat should contain at least one sample.")
  precondition(xMat.first!.count > 0, "Samples should have at least one
feature.")
  let featureCount = xMat.first!.count
  let weightsCount = featureCount+1
  weights = [Double](repeating: 1.0, count: weightsCount)
  if normalization {
    // Flatten
    let flattenedXMat = xMat.reduce([], +)
    let (normalizedXMat, xMeanVec, xStdVec) = matNormalize(matrix:
flattenedXMat, rows: sampleCount, columns: featureCount)
    // Save means and std-s for prediction phase
    self.xMeanVec = xMeanVec
    self.xStdVec = xStdVec
    // Add first column of ones to matrix
```

```
    let designMatrix = prependColumnOfOnes(matrix: normalizedXMat, rows:
sampleCount, columns: featureCount)
    gradientDescent(xMatFlattened: designMatrix, yVec: yVec, α:
learningRate, maxSteps: maxSteps)
    } else {
        // Flatten and prepend a column of ones
        let flattenedXMat = xMat.map{[1.0]+$0}.reduce([], +)
        gradientDescent(xMatFlattened: flattenedXMat, yVec: yVec, α:
learningRate, maxSteps: maxSteps)
    }
}
```

Cost function

The cost function is something we can use to assess the prediction quality:

```
// cost(y, h) = -sum(y.*log(h)+(1-y).*log(1-h))/m
public func cost(trueVec: [Double], predictedVec: [Double]) -> Double {
    let count = trueVec.count
    // Calculate squared Euclidean distance.
    var result = 0.0
    var left = [Double](repeating: 0.0, count: count)
    var right = [Double](repeating: 0.0, count: count)
    // log(h)
    var outputLength = Int32(count)
    vvlog(&left, predictedVec, &outputLength)
    // -y.*log(h)
    left = vecMultiply(trueVec, left)
    // 1-y
    var minusOne = -1.0
    var oneMinusTrueVec = [Double](repeating: 0.0, count: count)
    vDSP_vsaddD(trueVec, 1, &minusOne, &oneMinusTrueVec, 1,
vDSP_Length(count))
    vDSP_vnegD(oneMinusTrueVec, 1, &oneMinusTrueVec, 1, vDSP_Length(count))
    // 1-h
    var oneMinusPredictedVec = [Double](repeating: 0.0, count: count)
    vDSP_vsaddD(predictedVec, 1, &minusOne, &oneMinusPredictedVec, 1,
vDSP_Length(count))
    vDSP_vnegD(oneMinusPredictedVec, 1, &oneMinusPredictedVec, 1,
vDSP_Length(count))
    // log(1-h)
    vvlog(&right, oneMinusPredictedVec, &outputLength)
    // (1-y).*log(1-h)
    right = vecMultiply(oneMinusTrueVec, right)
    // left+right
    let sum = vecAdd(left, right)
```

```
// sum()
vDSP_sveD(sum, 1, &result, vDSP_Length(count))
// Normalize by vector length.
result/=(Double(count))
return -result
}
```

The derivative of a `cost` function is something we use to adjust weights to minimize the `cost` function itself:

```
// x'*sum(h-y)
private func costGradient(trueVec: [Double], predictedVec: [Double],
xMatFlattened: [Double]) -> [Double] {
  let matCount = xMatFlattened.count
  let featureCount = weights.count
  precondition(matCount > 0)
  precondition(Double(matCount).truncatingRemainder(dividingBy:
Double(featureCount)) == 0)
  let sampleCount = trueVec.count
  precondition(sampleCount > 0)
  precondition(sampleCount*featureCount == matCount)
  let labelSize = 1
  let diffVec = vecSubtract(predictedVec, trueVec)
  // Normalize by vector length.
  let scaleBy = 1/Double(sampleCount)
  let result = gemm(aMat: xMatFlattened, bMat: diffVec, rowsAC:
featureCount, colsBC: labelSize, colsA_rowsB: sampleCount, transposeA:
true, α: scaleBy)
  return result
}

// alpha is a learning rate
private func gradientDescentStep(xMatFlattened: [Double], yVec: [Double],
α: Double) -> [Double] {
  // Calculate hypothesis predictions.
  let hVec = hypothesis(xMatFlattened: xMatFlattened)
  // Calculate gradient with respect to parameters.
  let gradient = costGradient(trueVec: yVec, predictedVec: hVec,
xMatFlattened: xMatFlattened)
  let featureCount = gradient.count
  // newWeights = weights - α*gradient
  var alpha = α
  var scaledGradient = [Double](repeating: 0.0, count: featureCount)
  vDSP_vsmulD(gradient, 1, &alpha, &scaledGradient, 1,
vDSP_Length(featureCount))
  let newWeights = vecSubtract(weights, scaledGradient)
  return newWeights
```

```
    }

    private func gradientDescent(xMatFlattened: [Double], yVec: [Double], α:
    Double, maxSteps: Int) {
      for _ in 0 ..< maxSteps {
        let newWeights = gradientDescentStep(xMatFlattened: xMatFlattened,
    yVec: yVec, α: α)
        if newWeights==weights {
          print("convergence")
          break
        } // convergence
        weights = newWeights
      }
    }
```

Predicting user intents

The problem: Apple's default Clock app, if opened from the app switcher menu (the one you see when swiping from the bottom of the screen upward), always shows the **Timer** tab. I personally use this app mostly for one reason every day—to set an alarm clock, which is in a different tab. By knowing the day of the week and time of the day, it's easy to make the app smarter (and less annoying) by opening the proper **Alarm** tab when needed and default tab otherwise. For this, we will need to collect historical records on what time we usually set an alarm on different days.

Let's formulate the task more precisely:

- Input data: The day, hour, and minute when the user had opened the application
- Expected output: The probability that the user wants to set up an alarm

The task is of binary classification, which makes logistic regression a perfect candidate for the solution.

Handling dates

The straightforward way to transform dates and time into numerical features is by replacing them with integers. For example, days of the week (assuming that Sunday is the first day) can be encoded as numbers from 0 to 6, and hours as integers from 0 to 23:

```
Monday, 11:45 pm, alarm tab → [1, 23, 45, 1]
Thursday, 1:15 am, alarm tab → [4, 1, 15, 1]
Saturday, 10:55 am, timer tab → [6, 10, 55, 0]
```

```
Tuesday, 5:30 pm, timer tab → [2, 17, 30, 0]
```

To explain why this is a bad approach, take a look at the following diagram. The samples 11:45 pm and 1:15 am are close to each other, but this will not be obvious to our model if we encode them in a straightforward way. We can fix this situation by projecting the day of the week (*d*) together with the hour (*h*) and minute (*m*) on the circle:

Parameter	Formula
dow_sin	$sin = (2\pi\frac{d}{7})$
dow_cos	$cos = (2\pi\frac{d}{7})$
time_sin	$cos(2\pi\frac{60h + m}{60 * 24})$
time_cos	$sin(2\pi\frac{60h + h}{60 * 24})$

The result of this transformation can be seen in the following diagram:

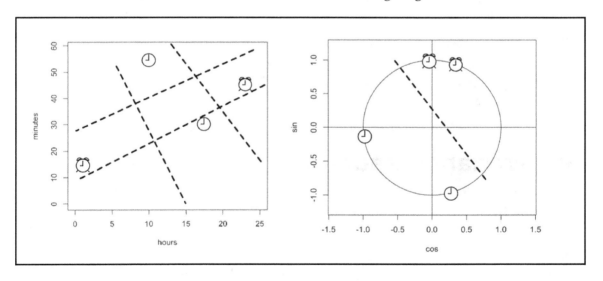

After the transformation, each sample in the dataset will contain four new features:

dow_sin	dow_cos	time_sin	time_cos	label
0.781831482	0.623489802	-0.065403129	0.997858	alert
-0.433883739	-0.900968868	0.321439465	0.946930129	alert
-0.781831482	0.623489802	0.279829014	-0.960049854	timer
0.974927912	-0.222520934	-0.991444861	-0.130526192	timer

Now these data points can be successfully separated by either the linear classifier or logistic regression.

Choosing the regression model for your problem

By now, you may feel overwhelmed by the number of models, regularization, and preprocessing techniques. No worries, there is a simple algorithm for choosing the model:

1. If your label is continuous—linear regression
2. If your label is binary—logistic regression
3. High dimensionality and multicollinearity—regularization methods (lasso, ridge, and ElasticNet)

Bias-variance trade-off

Errors in machine learning can be decomposed into two components: bias and variance. The difference between them is commonly explained using the shooting metaphor, as demonstrated in the following diagram. If you train a high-variance model on 10 different datasets, the results would be very different. If you train a high-bias model on 10 different datasets, you would get very similar results. In other words, high-bias models tend to underfit and high-variance models tend to overfit. Usually, the more parameters the model has the more it is prone to overfitting, but there are also differences between model classes: parametric models like linear and logistic regressions tend to be biased, while nonparametric models like KNN usually have a high variance:

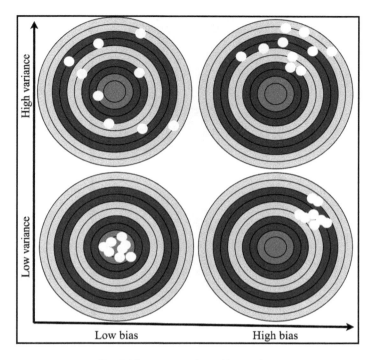

Figure 7.4: Two components of errors: bias and variance

Summary

In this chapter, we discussed how to turn linear regression into a classification algorithm. We also implemented logistic regression, an important classification algorithm.

Having gained an understanding of this will be of great use for us in the next chapter, where we will implement our first neural network.

8
Neural Networks

Just a decade ago, artificial neural networks (**NNs**) were considered by most researchers as an unpromising branch of computer science. But as computational power grew, and efficient algorithms to train NNs on GPUs were found, the situation changed dramatically. The latest discoveries in the field have achieved unprecedented results, such as tracking objects in video; synthesizing realistic speech, paintings, and music, automatic translation from one language to another; and extracting meaning from text, images, and video. NNs were rebranded as *deep learning* and they've set all kinds of records in computer vision and natural language processing, beating almost all other ML approaches over the last few years (2014-2018). Deep NNs caused a new machine learning boom, raising a wave of discussions and predictions about the artificial general intelligence forthcoming.

Now, there are already so many NN types that it's hard to keep track of them: convolutional, recurrent, recursive, autoencoders, generative adversarial, binary, with memory, with attention, and so on. New architectures and applications continue to appear almost every week, thanks to the growing community of enthusiasts all around the world who experiment with NNs, applying them to all possible kinds of tasks.

Here is a short list of what NNs are now doing more or less successfully:

- Coloring black and white photographs
- Drawing new Pokemon
- Writing scripts for advertisements
- Diagnosing cancer cells

Thanks to the breakthroughs in deep learning, we have come close to saying (though not yet loudly) that our computers can now fantasize, dream, and hallucinate. Today, researchers are working on NNs that can, on their own, design and train other NNs, write computer programs, help understand intracellular processes, and decipher forgotten scripts and the language of dolphins. Starting with this chapter, we will begin to plunge into deep learning.

In this chapter, we will cover the following topics:

- What are NNs, neurons, layers, and activation functions?
- What types of activation functions are there?
- How to train NNs: backpropagation, stochastic gradient descent
- What is deep learning?
- Which deep learning frameworks are best suited for iOS applications?
- Implementing a multilayer perceptron, and how to train it.

What are artificial NNs anyway?

The group of models that we call artificial NNs are universal approximation machines; in other words, the functions that can imitate the behavior of any other function of interest. Here, I mean functions in a more mathematical meaning, as opposed to computer science: functions that take a real-valued input vector and return a real-valued output vector. This definition holds true for feed-forward NNs, which we will be discussing in this chapter. In the following chapters, we'll see networks that map an input tensor (multidimensional array) to an output tensor, and also networks that take their own outputs as an input.

We can think of a NN as a graph and the neuron as a node in a directed acyclic graph. Each such node takes some input and produces some output. Modern NNs are only loosely inspired by the biological brain. If you want to know more about the biological prototype and its relation to NNs, check the *Seeing biological analogies* section.

Building the neuron

Considering that a biological neuron has an astonishingly complex structure (see *Figure 8.1*), how do we approach modeling it in our programs? Actually, most of this complexity is, so to say, at the hardware level. We can abstract it out and think of the neuron as a node in a graph, which takes one or more inputs and produces some output (sometimes called *activation*).

Wait, but doesn't that sound like something familiar? Yes, you are right: an artificial neuron is just a mathematical function.

The most common way to model the neuron is by using the weighted sum of inputs with the non-linearity function f:

$$y = f(w^T x + b)$$

Where w is a weights vector, x is an input vector, and b is a bias term. The y is a neuron's scalar output.

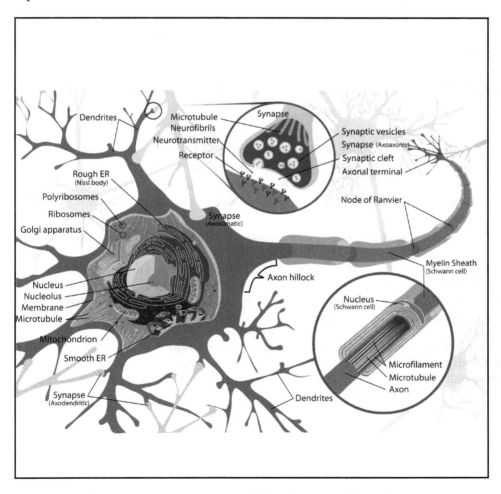

Figure 8.1: A typical motor neuron of a vertebrate. Public domain diagram from Wikimedia Commons

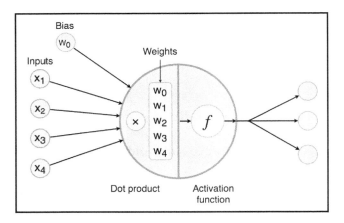

Figure 8.2: Artificial neuron diagram

A typical artificial neuron processes input in the following three steps, as demonstrated in the preceding diagram (*Figure 8.2*):

1. Take a weighted sum of inputs. Each neuron has a vector of weights of the same length as the number of inputs. Sometimes, one more weight is introduced as for bias term (always equal to one). The weighted sum of inputs is a dot product of the input vector and weight vector.
2. Pass the result through a non-linear function (synonyms: activation function, transfer function).
3. Pass the result of computations downstream to the next neurons.

The first step is a very familiar linear regression. If activation is a step function, this makes an individual neuron mathematically identical to a binary linear classifier. If you replace the step function with a logistic function, what you will get is a logistic regression. But now we call them neurons, and can assemble them into a network.

The learning of a neuron occurs when its input weight adjusts in such a way that the whole neuron produces better output. Again, this is the same as with a linear regression. To train a NN, we usually use a backpropagation algorithm, which is built on top of the familiar gradient descent.

Non-linearity function

An activation function maps the weighted input of a neuron into a real value to produce the neuron's output. Many of the NN's properties depend on the choice of activation function, including its ability to generalize, and the speed of the training process convergence. Usually, we want it to be differentiable, so we can optimize the whole network using the gradient descent. Most commonly used activation functions are non-linear: piecewise linear, or s-shaped (see *Table 8.1*). Nonlinear activation functions allow NNs to outperform other algorithms in many nontrivial tasks using only a few neurons. Oversimplifying, activation functions can be divided into two groups: step-like and rectifier-like (see *Figure 8.3*). Let's take a closer look at some examples:

Name	Formula	Derivative
Step function	$f(x) = \begin{cases} 0, \wedge x < 0 \\ 1, \wedge x \geq 0 \end{cases}$	$f'(x) = \begin{cases} 0, \wedge x \neq 0 \\ ?, \wedge x = 0 \end{cases}$
Logistic	$f(x) = \dfrac{1}{1 + e^{-x}}$	$f'(x) = f(x)(1 - f(x))$
Hyperbolic tangent	$f(x) = \dfrac{2}{1 + e^{-2x}} - 1$	$f'(x) = 1 - f(x)^2$
ReLU	$f(x) = \begin{cases} 0, \wedge x < 0 \\ x, \wedge x \geqslant 0 \end{cases}$	$f'(x) = \begin{cases} 0, \wedge x < 0 \\ 1, \wedge x \geqslant 0 \end{cases}$
Leaky ReLU	$f(x) = \begin{cases} ax, \wedge x < 0 \\ x, \wedge x \geq 0 \end{cases}$	$f'(x) = \begin{cases} a, \wedge x < 0 \\ 1, \wedge x \geq 0 \end{cases}$
Softplus	$f(x) = ln(1 + e^x)$	$f'(x) = \dfrac{1}{1 + e^{-x}}$
Maxout	$f(x) = \min_i x_i$	$\dfrac{\partial f}{\partial x_j} = \begin{cases} 1, \wedge j = \operatorname*{argmax}_i x_i \\ 0, \wedge j \neq \operatorname*{argmax}_i x_i \end{cases}$

Table 8.1: Commonly used activation functions

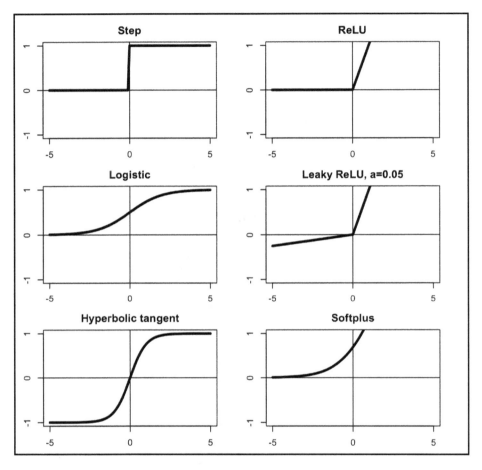

Figure 8.3: Plots of the common activation functions: step-like in the left column, and rectifier-like in the right column

Step-like activation functions

The heaviside step function (also known as **unit step function** or **threshold function**) outputs 0 for all values less than *zero*, and 1 for everything else. This is a natural choice to model a biological neuron, which produces an electrical impulse, *1*, or stays silent: *0*. Unfortunately, the function is not differentiable because of the discontinuity at *0*, which makes it impossible to train such networks using gradient descent algorithm. Each individual neuron in such a network is a mathematical equivalent of a binary linear classifier, hence such networks are unable to perform well on nonlinear tasks.

A **logistic (sigmoid) function** is a continuous approximation of a step function. The function squashes the input from range (-∞, +∞) to the range (*0, 1*). It allows NNs to be trained using gradient descent, but it also has two problems:

- Because of the sigmoid's shape, NNs that use it are prone to a **vanishing gradient problem**, which will be explained later (see the *Vanishing gradient problem* section).
- The output of the sigmoid is not zero-centered. This introduces undesirable zig-zagging behavior of the weights values during training, and the networks generally train slower.

With the sigmoid activation function, each neuron essentially performs the logistic regression.

Hyperbolic tangent (tanh) is a scaled logistic function, so the shape of the function is very similar but the range of its output is (*-1, 1*). This means that the tanh still suffers from the vanishing gradient, but at least its output is now zero-centered.

Rectifier-like activation functions

A rectifier is a piecewise linear function, which you hardly ever meet outside of the NNs context. This class of function was designed specifically to mitigate the problems and limitations of traditional step-like activation functions. A rectifier applies a simple thresholding: max(0, x). A neuron uses a rectifier is known as a **rectified linear unit** (**ReLU**).

Unlike sigmoids, a rectifier doesn't saturate at the upper end. This helps the neuron to tell apart a poor prediction from a very poor prediction, and update weights accordingly even in such a difficult situation. ReLU is also very cheap computationally: unlike sigmoids, which require exponentials, ReLU can be implemented as a thresholding operation. It also has been shown that a network of ReLUs can converge up to six times faster than one using sigmoids, so ReLU quickly gained popularity in the deep learning community after its invention.

ReLU has its own drawbacks, so several modifications were proposed to fix them:

- **Leaky ReLU**: Instead of *0* for all values, less than *0* and this activation returns a tiny fraction of an input (*0.01*, for example). The size of the fraction is determined by the constant α. Presumably, this should prevent ReLU from saturation at the bottom end, but in practice it usually doesn't help much.

- **Randomized ReLU**: α is random in some bounds. Randomization is a common way of NN regularization, which we will see later in this chapter.
- **Parametric ReLU (PReLU)**: α is a trainable parameter, which is adjusted through a gradient descent.
- **Softplus**: An approximation of a ReLU using exponentials. A derivative of this function is a sigmoid.
- **Maxout unit**: Combines both ReLU and leaky ReLU in one expression. In this way, it allows the maxout unit to have all ReLU benefits, namely linearity, with no saturation, but doesn't have the dying ReLU problem. The downside here is that the maxout unit has double the number of parameters in comparison to ReLU, so it's computationally more expensive.

Building the network

Individual neurons can be organized in a network (see *Figure 8.4*), usually by joining several neurons in parallel in a layer and then stacking layers on top of each other. Such a network is known as a **feed-forward NN** or a **multilayer perceptron (MLP)**. The first layer is an input layer, the last layer is an output layer, and all inner layers are known as *hidden layers*. If each neuron of one layer is connected to the all neurons in the next layer, such a network is called a **fully-connected NN**.

A fully-connected feed-forward multilayer perceptron with one type of activation (usually sigmoid) is a traditional (canonical) type of NN. It is mostly used for classification purposes. In the following chapters, we will discuss other types of NNs, but in this chapter we will stick to the MLP:

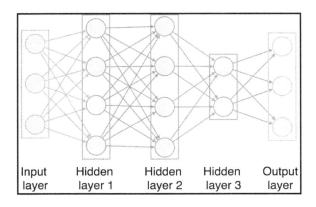

Figure 8.4: Fully-connected feed-forward NN with five layers

Building a neural layer in Swift

A fully-connected layer is easy to implement, because it can be expressed as two operations:

- A matrix multiplication between weights matrix W and input vector x.
- A point wise application of activation function f:

$$y = f(Wx + b)$$

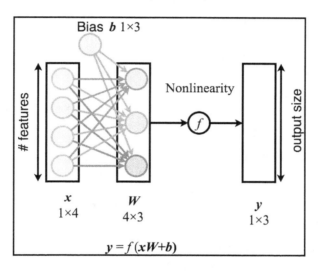

Figure 8.5: One layer in detail

In many frameworks, the two operations are separated so that matrix multiplication happens in the fully-connected layer and activation happens in the next nonlinearity layer. This is handy because in this way we can easily replace the weighted sum with convolution. In the next chapter, we will discuss convolutional NNs.

But for now, let's see how NNs can perform logical operations. One neuron is enough to model any logical gate, except XOR. This finding caused the first AI winter in the 1960s; however, XOR is trivial to a model having a network with two layers.

Using neurons to build logical functions

Among other obscured parts of iOS and macOS SDK, there is one interesting library called SIMD. It is an interface for direct access to vector instructions and vector types, which are mapped directly to the vector unit in the CPU, without the need to write an assembly code. You can reference vector and matrix types as well as linear algebra operators defined in this header right from your Swift code, starting from 2.0 version.

 The **universal approximation** theorem states that a simple NN with one hidden layer can approximate a wide variety of continuous functions if proper weights are found. This is also commonly rephrased as NNs as universal function approximators. However, the theorem doesn't tell if it's possible to find such proper weights.

To get access to those goodies, you need to `import simd` in Swift files, or `#include <simd/simd.h>` in C/C++/Objective-C files. GPU also has SIMD units in it, so you can import SIMD into your metal shader code as well.

 As per iOS 10.3/Xcode 8.2.1, some parts of C SIMD functionality are not available in the Swift version of it; for instance, logical and trigonometric operations. To see them, create Objective-C file, `#import <simd/simd.h>` and click *command*, click on the `simd.h` to go to the header files.

The part I like the most about the SIMD is that all vectors and matrices in it have size explicitly mentioned as a part of their type. For example, function `float 4()` returns the matrix of size 4 x 4. But it also makes SIMD inflexible because only matrices of sizes from 2 up to 4 are available.

Take a look at the SIMD playground for some examples of SIMD usage:

```
let firstVector = float4(1.0, 2.0, 3.0, 4.0)
let secondVector = firstVector
let dotProduct = dot(firstVector, secondVector)
```

The result is as follows:

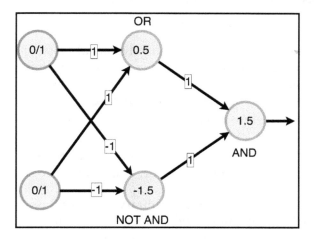

Figure 8.6: A NN implementing XOR function

To illustrate that SIMD can be used for ML algorithms, let's implement a simple XOR NN in SIMD:

```
func xor(_ a: Bool, _ b: Bool) -> Bool {
    let input = float2(Float(a), Float(b))

    let weights1 = float2(1.0, 1.0)
    let weights2 = float2(-1.0, -1.0)
    let matrixOfWeights1 = float2x2([weights1, weights2])
    let weightedSums = input * matrixOfWeights1

    let stepLayer = float2(0.5, -1.5)
    let secondLayerOutput = step(weightedSums, edge: stepLayer)
    let weights3 = float2(1.0, 1.0)
    let outputStep: Float = 1.5
    let weightedSum3 = reduce_add(secondLayerOutput * weights3)
    let result = weightedSum3 > outputStep
    return result
}
```

The good thing about SIMD is that it explicitly says to the CPU to calculate the dot product in one step, without looping over the vector but rather utilizing SIMD instructions.

Implementing layers in Swift

There are at least three options to consider when you want to implement a NN in Swift:

- Implement it in pure Swift (which may be useful mostly for the study purposes). A lot of implementations of different complexity and functionality can be found on the GitHub. It looks like every programmer at some stage of her/his life starts to write a NN library in her/his favourite programming language.
- Implement it using low-level acceleration libraries—Metal Performance Shaders, or BNNS.
- Implement it using some general-purpose NN framework—Keras, TensorFlow, PyTorch, and so on—and then convert it to Core ML format.

 The Metal Performance Shader library includes three types of activations for NNs: ReLU, sigmoid, and TanH (`MPSCNNNeuronReLU`, `MPSCNNNeuronSigmoid`, `MPSCNNNeuronTanH`). For more information refer to:
`https://developer.apple.com/reference/metalperformanceshaders`.

Training the network

The most common way to train NNs these days is with a backward propagation of errors algorithm, or backpropagation (often *backprop* for short). As we have seen already, individual neurons remind us of linear or logistic regression a lot, so it should not come as a surprise that backpropagation usually comes together with our old friend the gradient descent algorithm. NN training works in the following way:

- Forward pass—input is presented to the layer and the transformations are applied to it layer by layer until the prediction is outputted on the last layer.
- Loss computation—the prediction is compared to the ground truth, and an error value is calculated for each neuron of the output layer using the loss function J.
- The errors are then propagated backward (backpropagation), such that each neuron has an error associated to it, proportional to its contribution to the output.
- Weights (w) are updated using one step of gradient descent. The gradient of the loss function $\frac{\partial J}{\partial w}$ is calculated for each neuron, with respect to its weights using the error value. Then the usual gradient descent step happens as in linear regression.

Backpropagation is possible only if all the transformations in the forward propagation are differentiable (in the simplest case, dot products and activation functions) because it is essentially an application of a chain rule from calculus.

For further reading, go to `https://en.wikipedia.org/wiki/back propagation`.

Vanishing gradient problem

The sigmoid asymptotically approaches zero on the one end, and the *1* on another end. On those tails, the derivative of a function is very small. This is bad news for the backpropagation algorithm because these almost-zero values are killing the signal when it propagates through the network back to update weights.

The problem with dead neurons: if you initialize network weights at random, sigmoidal neurons with large weights would be dead (almost not transmitting the signal) from the very beginning.

Seeing biological analogies

Everyone has heard that artificial NNs mimic the way the brain works. This is actually far from the truth. What is true is that NNs as a field grew out of attempts to simulate how the brain works. The elementary unit of a brain is a neuron (a nerve cell). The human brain contains approximately 86 billion neurons. Neurons can generate electric potential (action potential) in its body. The neuron has branched projections of two types. One being short projections, known as dendrites (from Greek δενεδρον, tree). Usually, their function is to receive electrical impulses from other neurons. The other type is longer projections, known as axons (from Greek αξων, axis). Some neurons don't have axons, but no neurons have more than one. The function of the axon is to carry electrical impulses away from the neuron body to other cells.

By its axon, the neuron connects to the bodies (or to the dendrites) of other neurons and transmits electrical signals to them. Not all neurons transmit signals to other neurons; some of them excite muscles and glands.

Axons on their ends have structures called synapses—a connection to the cell body, or dendrite. To transmit a signal to the next neuron, the synapse emits chemical neuromediators (or rarely, electrical signals). There are about 1,014-1,015 synapses in the human brain. You can calculate yourself how much disk space is required to store such enormous amount of information. In our artificial brains, we have much fewer artificial neurons. Even the largest among the modern NNs are comparable rather to the brain of a jellyfish or a snail. However, number of neurons or synapses is not the whole story, as there are some animals whose brain contains more neurons than a human's. If you're interested in the topic, visit the Wikipedia page: `https://en.wikipedia.org/wiki/List_of_animals_by_number_of_neurons`.

Even though the concept of NNs was borrowed from biology, one should have a powerful imagination to see how a biological prototype is similar to modern artificial NNs. That's why some researchers believe that some other names, like *computational graphs*, are more appropriate. Biological terminology was once more popular in this domain, but now literally the only biological term that is widely used is *neuron*.

Basic neural network subroutines (BNNS)

BNNS is a submodule of Accelerate, containing convolution NN primitives optimized for running inference on CPU. It was introduced in iOS 10 and macOS 10.12. Note that it contains only functions for inference, not for training.

The motivation behind this library was to provide unified API for common routines, such that app developers wouldn't need to re-implement convolutions and other primitives from scratch every time (which is hard, as we have seen already in the chapter on CNNs). In a typical CNN, most energy is spent in the convolution layers. Fully connected layers are more expensive computationally, but usually CNNs contain one or a few of them at the very end so convolutions still consume about 70% of energy. That's why it's important to have highly-optimized convolution layers. Unlike MPS, CNN is available on iOS, macOS, tvOS, and even watchOS. So, if you want to run deep learning on a TV set or your watch (just because you can), this is your tool of choice.

Speaking more seriously, BNNS is useful when you're implementing NNs for devices without Metal Performance Shaders support (older iOS devices and all macOS devices for now). In all other cases, you still want to use MPS CNNs to harness GPU massive parallelism.

To check availability of Metal features, look through `https://developer.apple.com/metal/availability/`.

BNNS contains three types of layers: convolution, pooling, and fully-connected layers, and several activations: identity, rectified linear, leaky rectified linear, sigmoid, tanh, scaled tanh, and abs.

BNNS example

In the following example, input images are of size 224 x 224 x 64 and output images are of size 222 x 222 x 96. The dimensionality of convolution weights is 3 x 3 x 64 x 96. That's 5.45 billion floating-point operations (gigaFloPS). In a whole MNIST recognition network, it's about 1-2 trillion operations per forward pass.

BNNS is a part of Accelerate, so you need to import Accelerate to access the neural networks building blocks. The first thing you do is describing the input stack:

```
var inputStack = BNNSImageStackDescriptor(
    width: 224, height: 224, channels: 64,
    row_stride: 224, image_stride: 224*224,
    data_type: BNNSDataTypeFloat32,
    data_scale: 1.0, data_bias: 0.0)
```

Most of the parameters are self-evident; `row_stride` is an increment to the next row in pixels, `image_stride` is similarly increment to the next channel in pixels, and `data_type` is a type of storage.

The output stack should look similar:

```
var outputStack = BNNSImageStackDescriptor(
    width: 1, height: 10, channels: 1,
    row_stride: 1, image_stride: 10,
    data_type: BNNSDataTypeFloat32,
    data_scale: 1.0, data_bias: 0.0)
```

Now let's create a convolution layer. `BNNSConvolutionLayerParameters` contains the description of the convolution layer:

```
let activation = BNNSActivation(function: BNNSActivationFunctionIdentity,
alpha: 0, beta: 0)

var convolutionParameters = BNNSConvolutionLayerParameters(
    x_stride: 1, y_stride: 1,
    x_padding: 0, y_padding: 0,
```

```
k_width: 3, k_height: 3,
in_channels: 64, out_channels: 96,
weights: convolutionWeights,
bias: convolutionBias,
activation: activation)
```

k_width and k_height are kernel width and height respectively.

Creating the layer itself:

```
let convolutionLayer = BNNSFilterCreateConvolutionLayer(&inputStack,
&outputStack, &convolutionParameters, nil)
```

nil is for default BNNSFilterParameters.

Now you can use the filter and destroy it when it's not needed anymore by calling BNNSFilterDestroy(convolutionLayer).

Pooling layer:

```
// Describe pooling layer
BNNSPoolingLayerParameters pool = {
    .k_width = 3,
// kernel height
// kernel width
// X padding
// Y padding
    .k_height = 3,
    .x_padding = 1,
    .y_padding = 1,
    .x_stride = 2,
    .y_stride = 2,
    .in_channels = 64,
    .out_channels = 64,
    .pooling_function = BNNSPoolingFunctionMax  // pooling function
};
// Create pooling layer filter
BNNSFilter filter = BNNSFilterCreatePoolingLayer(
    &in_stack,      // BNNSImageStackDescriptor for input stack
    &out_stack,     // BNNSImageStackDescriptor for output stack
    &pool,          // BNNSPoolingLayerParameters
    NULL);          // BNNSFilterParameters (NULL = defaults)
// Use the filter ...
// Destroy filter
BNNSFilterDestroy(filter);

// Describe input vector
BNNSVectorDescriptor in_vec = {
```

```
        .size = 3000,
// size
// storage type
};
// Describe fully connected layer
BNNSFullyConnectedLayerParameters full = {
    .in_size = 3000,
    .out_size = 20000,
    .weights = {
        .data_type = BNNSDataTypeFloat16,
        .data = weights
// input vector size
// output vector size
// weights storage type
// pointer to weights data
} };
// Create fully connected layer filter
BNNSFilter filter = BNNSFilterCreateFullyConnectedLayer(
    &in_vec,        // BNNSVectorDescriptor for input vector
    &out_vec,       // BNNSVectorDescriptor for output vector
    &full,          // BNNSFullyConnectedLayerParameters
    NULL);          // BNNSFilterParameters (NULL = defaults)// Use the
filter ...
// Destroy filter
BNNSFilterDestroy(filter);
// Apply filter to one pair of (in,out)
int status = BNNSFilterApply(filter,
                                in,
out);
// BNNSFilter
// pointer to input data
// pointer to output data
// Apply filter to N pairs of (in,out)
int status = BNNSFilterApplyBatch(filter,
                                    20,
                                    in,
                                    3000,
                                    out,
                                    20000);
// BNNSFilter
// batch size (N)
// pointer to input data
// input stride (values)
// pointer to output data
// output stride (values)
```

Summary

In this chapter, we've become acquainted with artificial NNs and their main components. NNs are built from neurons that are usually organized in layers. A typical neuron performs a weighted sum of inputs and then applies a non-linear activation function on it to calculate its output. There are many different activation functions, but the most popular these days is ReLU and its modifications, due to their computational properties.

NNs are usually trained using the backpropagation algorithm, built on top of stochastic gradient descent. Feed-forward NNs with several layers are also known as multilayer perceptrons. MLPs can be used for classification tasks.

In the next chapter, we'll continue to discuss NNs, but this time we'll focus on convolution NNs, which are especially popular in the computer vision domain.

9
Convolutional Neural Networks

In this chapter, we are discussing the **convolutional neural networks (CNNs)**. At first we are going to discuss all components with examples in Swift just to develop an intuition about the algorithm and what is going on under the hood. However, in the real life you most likely will not develop CNN from scratch, because you will use some ready available and battle-tested deep learning framework.

So, in the second part of the chapter we will show a full development cycle of deep learning mobile application. We are going to take the photos of people's faces labeled with their emotions, train a CNN on a GPU workstation, and then integrate it into an iOS application using Keras, Vision, and Core ML frameworks.

To the end of this chapter you will have learned about:

- Affective computing
- Computer vision, its tasks, and its methods
- CNNs, their anatomy, and core concepts behind them
- Applications of CNNs in computer vision
- How to train CNNs using a GPU workstation and Keras
- Deep learning tricks: Regularization, data augmentation, and early stopping
- CNNs architectures
- How to convert a trained model to Core ML format for use in an iOS application
- How to detect faces and facial expressions in photos using CNNs and Vision framework

Understanding users emotions

While voice input is undoubtedly a useful feature, we all well know how the actual meaning of the sentence can be opposite to the literal one, depending on the speaker's intonation, facial expression, and context. Try this simple sentence: *Oh, really?* Depending on the conditions, this can mean: *I doubt, I didn't know, I'm impressed, I don't care, This is obvious,* and so on. The problem is that speech is not the only mode of conversation for human beings, and that's why much research is focused these days on *teaching* computers to understand (and also simulate) gestures, facial expressions, sentiments in a text, eye movements, sarcasm, and other affect manifestations. An interdisciplinary field that emerges around the question of emotional and compassionate AI is known as **affective computing**. It integrates knowledge from the computer and cognitive sciences, as well as psychology and robotics. The aim is the creation of computer systems that will adapt themselves to the user's emotional state, understand their mood, and simulate empathy. Back in 1995, in pre-smartphone epoch, the name of the field was coined by Rosalind Picard. In her technical report titled *Affective Computing* [2], she predicts that it will be especially relevant in the context of wearable devices. Using facial expression recognition in this chapter, we're going to introduce elements of affective intelligence into our mobile app. This can be used in a context of language understanding, or in a multitude of other ways from emoji recommendations to smart photo sorting.

Please note that affective computing is similar to the sentiment analysis, but is a more broad term: the former is interested in all kind of affects, their detection and simulation, and the latter is mostly concerned with the polarity of the text piece (positive/negative).

Introducing computer vision problems

In this book, we mentioned computer vision several times, but since this chapter is focused on this particular domain, we will look at it in more detail now. There are several practical tasks related to image and video processing, which are referred to as **computer vision domain**. While working on some computer vision task, it's important to know these names, to be able to find what you need in the vast ocean of computer vision publications:

- **Object recognition**: The same as classification. Assigning labels to the images. *This is a cat*. Age estimation. Facial expression recognition.
- **Object localization**: Finding frame of object in the image. *The cat is in this frame.*
- **Object detection**: Finding frames of objects in the image. *The cat is in this frame.*
- **Semantic segmentation**: Each point in the picture is assigned to one class. If the picture contains several cats, each cat's pixel would be assigned to the *cat* class.
- **Instance segmentation**: Each point in the picture is assigned to one instance of class. If the picture contains several cats, each cat's pixel would be assigned to the separate segment of *cat* class.
- **Pose estimation**: Determining the orientation of the object in the space.
- **Object tracking**: Analyzing the video to find the trajectory of the moving object.
- **Image segmentation**: Finding borders between different objects into an image. Background subtraction.
- 3D-scene restoration and depth estimation.
- Image search and retrieval.

Some common computer vision tasks, like **optical character recognition (OCR)**, consist of several steps; for example, *image segmentation → image recognition*:

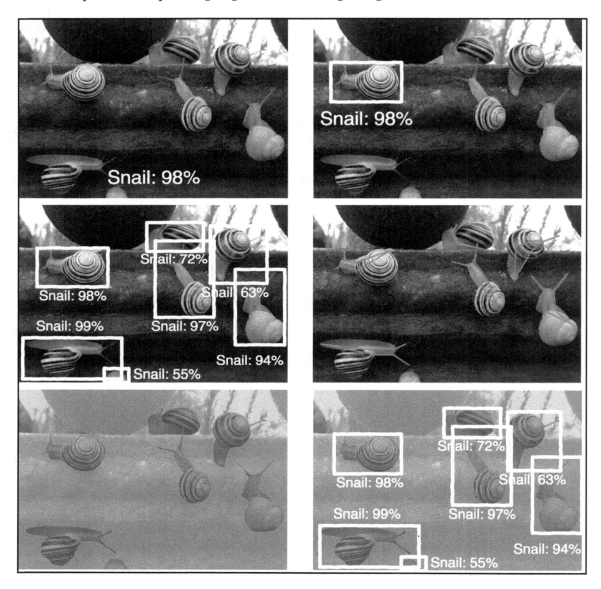

Figure 9.1: Popular computer vision tasks. Top row: recognition, localization. Middle row: object detection, pose estimation. Bottom row: semantic segmentation and instance segmentation

These tasks are recognized as hard problems, because of the variable factors: different camera position, lighting, object's occlusion, intra-class variability, changes in object shape, and so on. Many familiar machine learning algorithms found their unexpected applications in computer vision. For example, we have already seen that *k*-means can be used for image segmentation, and the extension of linear regression RANSAC for stitching photos into a panorama.

CNNs—historical background:

For many years, the progress in computer vision has been slow, arduous and involved a lot of domain expert knowledge, manual feature picking and model parameters tuning. Significant changes crept up unnoticed: In 2012, Alex Krizhevsky won the annual ImageNet image recognition competition, leaving the rest of the competitors far behind. For his classifier, he used then little known CNN (AlexNet architecture). What was even more surprising is the fact that CNNs were proposed at least as early as 1994, when Yan LeCunn published his LeNet5 architecture description for handwritten numbers recognition. But they were recognized impractical for most real-world tasks, because required almost eternity and tons of data to learn anything useful. The novelty was that Krizhevsky trained his network using graphics accelerators (GPUs) and not a CPU. Harnessing massive parallelism of these devices he reduced training time from weeks to hours. The result was sensational, and therefore the convolutional networks gained popularity very quickly in the community of researchers and practitioners.

Let's take a closer look at this type of neural network.

Introducing convolutional neural networks

CNNs, or ConvNets have gotten a lot of attention in the last few years, mainly due to their major successes in the domain of computer vision. They are at the core of most computer vision systems nowadays, including self-driving cars and large-scale photo classification systems.

In some sense, CNNs are very similar to multilayer perceptron, which we have discussed in the previous chapter. These networks also build from the layers, but unlike MLP, which usually has all layers similar to each other, CNNs usually include many layers of different types. And the most important type of the layer is (surprise, surprise) the convolutional layer. Modern CNNs can be really deep—hundreds of different layers. Nevertheless, you can still see the whole network as one differentiable function that takes some input (usually raw values of image pixels), and produces some output (for example, class probabilities: 0.8 cat, 0.2 dog).

Pooling operation

Pooling or subsampling is a simple operation of input size decreasing (*Figure 9.2*). If you have a black and white image, and you want to decrease its size, you can do it in the following way: chose a sliding window of size $n \times m$ and stride s. Go through the image, applying sliding window and shifting on the s pixels every time you want to move your window. At each position calculate an average (for average pooling) or maximum (for max pooling) and record this value into the destination matrix. Now, there are two common ways to handle borders of the image:

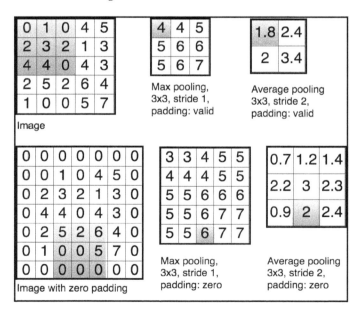

Figure 9.2. Pooling operation. Grey window in the source image corresponds to the grey cell in the destination image

The pooling is used in the CNNs to reduce the size of the data, as it travels down the network.

Convolution operation

Convolution is one of the most important operations in the image processing. Blurring, sharpening, edge detection, denoising, embossing and many other familiar operations in image editors are actually convolutions. It is similar to the pooling operation in some way, because it is also a sliding window operation, but instead of taking the average over the window, it performs element-wise multiplication by the kernel – matrix of size n × n and sums the result. The result of the operation depends on the kernel (also known as **convolution filter**) – a matrix, which is usually square, but not necessarily, see *Figure 9.3*. The notions of the stride and padding are the same as in the pooling case:

-25	0	0	0	0
0	-25	0	0	0
0	-25	25	0	0
0	0	0	25	0
0	0	0	0	25

-25	0	0	0	0
0	-25	0	0	0
0	-25	25	0	0
0	-25	25	25	0
0	-52	25	0	25

1	0	0	0	0
0	0	0	0	0
0	0	0	0	0
0	0	0	0	0
0	0	0	0	-1

1	0	0	0	1
1	-1	-1	-1	1
1	-1	-1	-1	1
1	-1	-1	-1	1
1	0	0	0	1

-1	0	0	1	1
-1	0	0	1	1
-1	0	0	1	1
-1	0	0	1	1
-1	0	0	1	1

Figure 9.3: Different convolution filters have different effects on the picture

Convolution operation works in the following way (see the following diagram):

- The convolution kernel (filter) slides over the image from left to right, and from top to bottom
- At each position, we calculate an element-wise product of filter and the patch of the image, which is covered by a filter on this step
- The elements of the resulting matrix are summed up
- The result of the convolution is a matrix composed of the sums at each position of the filter:

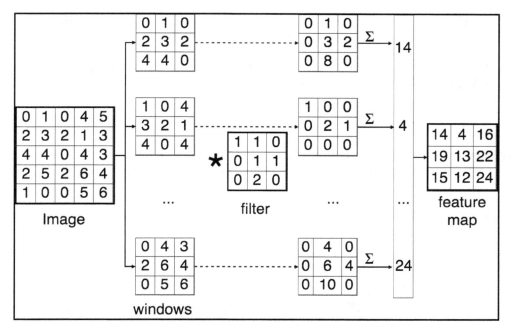

Figure 9.4: Convolution operation with 3 x 3 kernel, stride 1 and valid padding: : the source image is getting split into windows; each window is multiplied by filter elementwise; sum of the values into each of the windows

The algorithm looks simple at first glance, so you probably can come up with a Swift implementation similar to this one:

```
let input = ... //source image, 2D array
var output = ... //destination image, 2D array
for i in 0..<imageHeight {
    for j in 0..<imageWidth {
        var accumulator = 0;
        for ik in 0..<kernelHeight {
            for jk in 0..<kernelWidth {
                accumulator += kernel[ik][jk] *
                input[i+ik-kernelHeight/2][j+jk-kernelWidth/2]
            }
        }
        output[i][j] = accumulator;
    }
}
```

However, you really shouldn't implement your own convolution operation in production code. Here is a non-exhaustive list of problems that you'd have to deal with:

- Handle the edges of the image properly (see the following diagram)
- Handle stride—how much the kernel shifts after each step
- Handle integer overflow properly
- Optimize for speed

A good convolution implementation may require hundreds of lines of code (and even more). iOS SDK provides developers with several APIs that they can choose from, depending on their needs and goals:

- For image filtering:
    - `CIImageFilter` from Core Image framework
    - `vImage convolution` functions from accelerate framework, for instance `vImageConvolve_ARGB8888()`
- For running CNNs:
    - **For CPU execution**: BNNS convolution layer: `BNNSFilterCreateConvolutionLayer`
    - **For GPU execution**: `MPSCNNConvolution` class from Metal Performance Shaders framework

`vImage functions` is a recommended way for the processing of large images, or for repeating the operation many times in a row. To filter middle-sized images, it's more efficient to stick with CoreImage. When you implement CNNs, you usually want to use either the Metal or accelerate framework. This is something we will discuss in much detail in the `Chapter 11`, *Machine Learning Libraries*.

Check `Convolution.playground` in the supplementary code to see how different convolution filters produce different effects. Try your own filters, and see what happens. We are using the `vImageConvolve_ARGB8888()` function from the accelerate framework to apply filters.

The following is an example:

```
import Accelerate

let error = vImageConvolve_ARGB8888(&input, &output, nil, 0, 0, kernel,
kernelHeight, kernelWidth, Int32(divisor), nil, flags)
```

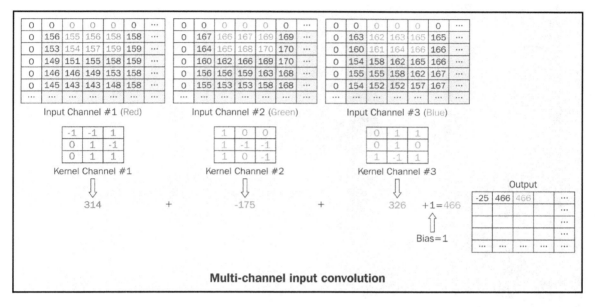

Figure 9.5: Multichannel convolution

Convolutions in CNNs

The first layer applies the filters to the input image, and sends the resulting feature matrices downstream. The next layers apply their filters to the input they get, extracting features from a higher and higher level (see *Figure 9.6 - 9.8*). In the task of image classification (or *object recognition*), CNNs gradually adjust the filters during the training to extract useful features from the picture. In this case, useful features are different patterns, like eyes, beaks, wheels, and so on:

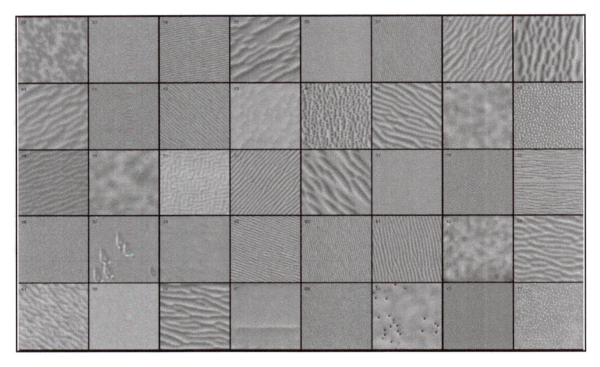

Figure 9.6: Each CNN layer learns a set of convolutional kernels. Here you see outputs of the different filters from the 2nd convolutional layer in the 2nd block of VGG 16

 The interesting thing is that convolution neural networks are used extensively outside of the computer vision domain; for instance, in natural language modeling and speech recognition. This is because of their capability to extract meaningful features from the raw data. There is no fundamental difference between extracting edges and corners from images, and syntactic features from texts.

Building the network

When you first encounter a variety of architectures of CNNs, you feel overwhelmed by the abundance of new terms, different layers, and their hyperparameters. In fact, at the moment, only a few architectures have found broad application, and the number of designs suitable for mobile development is even smaller.

There are five basic types of layers plus an input layer, which usually does nothing except passing data forward:

- **Input layer**: The first layer in the neural network. It does nothing, only takes the input and passes it downstream.
- **Convolution layers**: Where convolutions happen
- **Fully**: Connected or dense layers
- **Nonlinearity layers**: These are layers which apply activation functions to the output of the previous layer: sigmoid, ReLU, tanh, softmax and so on.
- **Pooling layers**: Downsample their input.
- **Regularization layers**: layers to fight an overfitting.

Modern deep learning frameworks contain much more different types of layers for all needs, but these are the most commonly used. In the following sections, we will discuss each type of layer in details. As CNNs are normally not trained on the mobile devices, but used for predictions only, we do not go into the details of the backpropagation in CNNs here. However, if you are interested in knowing more details, the NN Demo.playground in the supplementary materials of this chapter contains pure Swift implementation of CNN and all its classical layers. It also contains an implementation of stochastic gradient descent algorithm and several of its variants. Please refer to this playground for more technical details on the layer's gears and training algorithm. The playground is a Swift port of ConvNetJS library by Andrej Karpathy. It was developed solely for the study purposes, to demonstrate how CNNs work inside, not for the use in the real applications, and it does not utilize GPU or CPU acceleration. The original JS library can be found here: https://cs.stanford.edu/people/karpathy/convnetjs/

Input layer

This is a dummy layer; it does nothing in both forward and backward passes. We only use it to define the input tensor size.

Convolutional layer

In CNNs convolutions happen in the special layers, called **convolutional layers**. Each layer has an array of convolutional filters, which also can be seen as one 3D convolutional filter with width, height, and number of channels (or depth). In the first convolutional layer, we usually want to have 3 channels corresponding to the RGB channels of the input images:

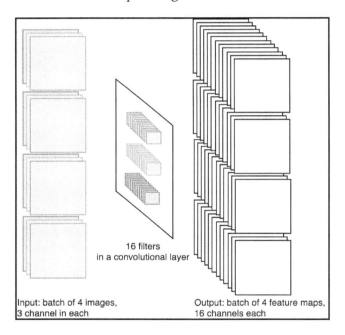

16 filters
in a convolutional layer

Input: batch of 4 images,
3 channel in each

Output: batch of 4 feature maps,
16 channels each

Figure 9.7: The first convolutional layer takes a batch of images as its input and outputs a batch of feature maps. The results of each of the 16 red, green and blue filters are being summed up to obtain the final feature map

The output of a convolution layer is called a **feature map**, because it shows where specific features are located in the input image. Note, that only the first convolutional layer takes an image as its input, all subsequent layers take outputs of their predecessors (feature maps) as their inputs. Those feature maps are stored as tensors.

Tensor in the context of deep learning is a multidimensional array. Neural network parameters, for example convolutional filters, stored as tensors and all data travels through a deep neural network in the form of tensors. 0-dimensional tensor is a scalar, 1D is a vector, 2D is a matrix, 3D sometimes called **volume**.

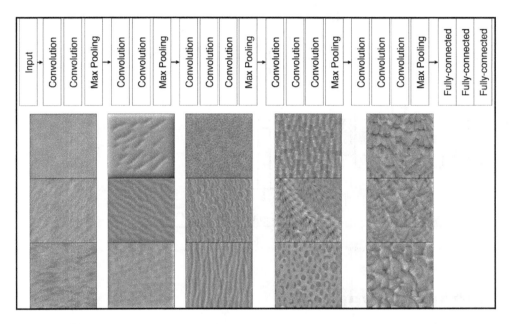

Figure 9.8: Each next layer in CNN extracts more abstract features, then the previous one. Example taken from the VGG-16 network.

Note, that for your production apps, you usually don't want to write your own convolutional layers in Swift, because you want to utilize the power of the GPU, so you normally use the existing deep learning libraries (see `Chapter 10`, *Natural Language Processing*) or implement custom layers in Metal or Accelerate (see `Chapter 11`, *Machine Learning Libraries*).

Fully-connected layers

Fully-collected layer is like one layer of a multilayer perceptron from the previous chapter, but without activation function. You can imagine it as a matrix of weights multiplied by an input or as a layer of artificial neurons (*Figure 9.9*):

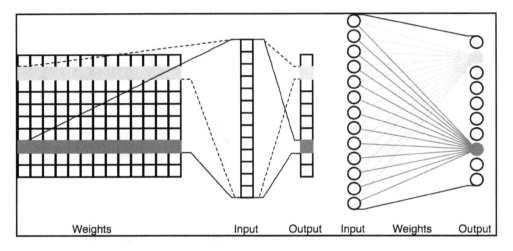

Figure 9.9: Two ways to represent a fully-connected layer: in a form of matrix-vector multiplication and in a form of a graph.

Nonlinearity layers

This are all kind of nonlinearities, that we've already discussed in the previous chapter: tanh, sigmoid, ReLU, and so on. You usually want to put them after a convolutional or a fully-connected layer.

Softmax is a generalization of a logistic function to vectors: while the logistic function squashes scalar values to be between 0 and 1, softmax squashes vectors so that its elements adds up to 1. In the statistics, probability of outcomes in discrete random distribution adds up to 1, so this function is really useful for the classification, where target variable is discrete.

Pooling layer

Pooling layer performs pooling operation. Put it after a convolutional layer, when you want to reduce the size of the tensor which will be passed to the next layer.

Regularization layers

Regularization layers intended to fight overfitting and increase the speed of training. Among popular regularization layers are dropout and batch normalization layers, because both techniques were shown to be very useful in practice.

Dropout

Dropout is a common way of regularization for deep neural networks. The idea is to turn off random neurons in the previous layer with some predefined probability on each step of the training. The neurons which were turned off are not trained during this step, but will be restored on the next one with the original weights. This technique prevents overfitting because it does not allow to train all the neurons on all the data.

Batch normalization

Small changes in the layer parameters affects all the following layer inputs, and the effect gets amplified with each next layer. This is especially problematic for the deep networks. The distribution of inputs to each layer changes during training, because parameters of the previous layer are being adjusted. This problem is known as **internal covariate shift**. Batch normalization technique was proposed in 2015 by Sergey Ioffe and Christian Szegedy from Google [1] to fix the problem. It allows normalizing layer inputs for each mini-batch as part of the network architecture. Batch normalization layer is usually inserted between the dot product and nonlinearity.

The benefits are as follows:

- You can use higher learning rate
- You can be less careful about weights initialization
- Works as regularization - no need for dropout
- Same model trains 14 times faster

Covariate shift:

The common problem in machine learning systems formally known as **covariate shift**: when the model is being deployed to the production environment, it appears, that the data distribution in it is different from the distribution of the training data. The name comes from the covariates, which are basically the same as features. By analogy, the notion of internal covariate shift was introduced: when in the neural network the distribution of input data to each layer is not stable, but changes significantly after each step of the SGD.

If both input and output distributions changes, this is known as **dataset shift**.

Loss functions

Loss function is a necessary part, because it is what we want to minimize during the training. You can find a few popular loss functions in the table:

Name	Formula	Usually used for
Mean squared error or L2-loss	$\mathcal{L}(y - \hat{y}) = \sum_{i=1}^{n}(y - \hat{y}_i)^2$	Regression
Mean absolute error or L1-loss	$\mathcal{L}(y - \hat{y}) = \sum_{i=1}^{n}|y - \hat{y}_i|$	Regression
Categorical cross entropy	$\mathcal{L}(y - \hat{y}) = -\sum_{i=1}^{n} y_i \log \hat{y}_i$	Softmax multiclass classification

Where y is a ground-truth vector and $\hat{y}$ is a vector of predictions of length n.

Training the network

Stochastic gradient descent (SGD) is an effective way of training deep neural networks. SGD seeks such parameters Θ of the network, which minimize the loss function $\mathcal{L}$.

$$\Theta = arg \min_{\Theta} \frac{1}{N} \sum_{i=1}^{N} \mathcal{L}(x_i, \Theta)$$

Where $x_{i......N}$ is a training dataset.

Training happens in steps. At every step, we choose a subset of our training set of size m (mini-batch) and use it to approximate loss function gradient with respect to parameters Θ:

$$\frac{1}{m} \frac{\partial \mathcal{L}(x_i, \Theta)}{\partial \Theta}$$

Mini-batch training advantages are as follows:

- Gradient of the loss function over a mini-batch is a better approximation of the gradient over the whole training set then calculated over only one sample
- Thanks to the GPU you can perform computations in parallel on every sample in the batch, which is faster, then processing them one-by-one

Training the CNN for facial expression recognition

For the demonstration of the CNNs we will implement a simple neural network for emotion recognition. We will use the dataset of face expressions `fer2013` from the ICML 2013 contest *Facial Expression Recognition Challenge* [1].

The dataset can be downloaded from the kaggle site:

`https://www.kaggle.com/c/challenges-in-representation-learning-facial-expression-recognition-challenge/data`

You will be asked to register and accept the terms and conditions.

The archive `fer2013.tar.gz` contains `fer2013.csv` with the dataset itself and some supplementary information files. The `.csv` file contains 35,887 samples, of which 28,709 marked as training set, 3,589 as public test, and 3,589 private test. There are three columns in the table: emotion, pixels and usage. Every sample is a grayscale 48 × 48 pixels face photo in a form of pixel array. The faces were cropped in an automatic way, so there are some false-positives in the dataset (non-faces and cartoon faces). Each face is labeled as belonging to one of the 7 classes. The distribution of emotions in the dataset is as follows:

Class id	0	1	2	3	4	5	6
Emotion	Angry	Disgust	Fear	Happy	Sad	Surprise	Neutral
Count	4953	547	5121	8989	6077	4002	6198

Environment setup

To train the deep CNN, you will need a computer with a CUDA-compatible GPU. I used an Ubuntu 16.x machine with NVidia GTX980 GPU for model training, and a macOS machine to convert the model to Core ML format. If you don't have CUDA-compatible GPU, you can try to train the model on CPU; but be aware that this will take a lot of time. Also, the trained model for this chapter is available in the supplementary materials, so if you prefer not to contribute to the global warming by retraining the model from scratch, it's also possible.

Here's a list of what should be installed on your system to train the network:

- Latest NVIDIA drivers
- CUDA 8.0
- cuDNN 5.1
- Python 2.7
- `tensorflow-gpu` (or TensorFlow for CPU-only mode)
- Keras
- Keras-viz
- Matplotlib, Pandas

Please, refer to the official sites for the installation instructions.

Deep learning frameworks

There are a plenty of deep learning toolkits and libraries for different kinds of platforms. For a long time, the three most popular of them were Theano (Python), Torch (Lua), and Caffe (C++). Somehow, Caffe became an industrial standard, while Theano and Torch were mostly used among researchers. I call these three libraries the first generation of deep learning frameworks. Most of the pre-trained neural networks that are available on the internet are still in Caffe format. They had their own problems, so the next generation of frameworks followed in several years. If the first generation was created mainly by efforts of individual researchers, the second generation was pushed by big IT companies. Today, apart from Apple, every internet giant has its own open source deep learning framework: Google has TensorFlow and Keras, Microsoft has CNTK, Facebook released Caffe 2, and Torch was reborn as PyTorch, thanks to Twitter and Facebook. Amazon has chosen MXNet as its deep learning framework of choice at AWS. Which one should you choose for your deep learning projects? At the moment, the best iOS support is provided by Caffe 2 and TensorFlow frameworks. With the release of Core ML we've also got an easy way to convert models trained in Caffe and Keras to Apple in `ml` model format. In this chapter, we're using Keras for our CNNs.

 A side note: Apple's Metal 2 also contains many primitives for building deep learning neural networks, but it's hard to call it a deep learning framework, most importantly because it doesn't support training neural networks.

Keras

Keras is a popular Python package for building the deep learning neural networks. It has a user-friendly syntax. It's easy and fast to prototype and build your deep models in it. It started as a facade for the Theano symbolic computation library, but over time, it has also developed a TensorFlow backend, and so finally became a part of TensorFlow. So now, TensorFlow is a default backend, but you still have an option to switch back to Theano. There are also work-in-progress projects of MXNet and CNTK backends.

Keras contains functions for pre-processing of most common data types: images, texts, and time series.

Core ML supports convolution and recurrent neural networks built in Keras.

 Official website of Keras: `https://keras.io/`

Loading the data

As usual, first we add some magic to display images inline in the Jupyter:

```
%matplotlib inline
```

We're using Pandas to handle our data:

```
import pandas
```

Please, visit the Kaggle site and download the dataset: `https://www.kaggle.com/c/challenges-in-representation-learning-facial-expression-recognition-challenge`

Load the dataset into the memory:

```
data = pandas.read_csv("fer2013/fer2013.csv")
```

Dataset consists of gray scale face photos encoded as pixel intensities. 48 x 48 gives 2304 pixels for each. Every image is marked according to the emotion on the face.

```
data.head()
  emotion  pixels    Usage
0  0    70 80 82 72 58 58 60 63 54 58 60 48 89 115 121...  Training
1  0   151 150 147 155 148 133 111 140 170 174 182 15...  Training
2  2   231 212 156 164 174 138 161 173 182 200 106 38...  Training
3  4    24 32 36 30 32 23 19 20 30 41 21 22 32 34 21 1...  Training
4  6    4 0 0 0 0 0 0 0 0 0 0 3 15 23 28 48 50 58 84...  Training
How many faces of each class do we have?

data.emotion.value_counts()
3    8989
6    6198
4    6077
2    5121
0    4953
```

```
5      4002
1       547
Name: emotion, dtype: int64
```

Here 0=Angry, 1=Disgust, 2=Fear, 3=Happy, 4=Sad, 5=Surprise, and 6=Neutral.

Let's remove `Disgust`, as we have too little samples for it:

```
data = data[data.emotion != 1]
data.loc[data.emotion > 1, "emotion"] -= 1
data.emotion.value_counts()
2      8989
5      6198
3      6077
1      5121
0      4953
4      4002
Name: emotion, dtype: int64
emotion_labels = ["Angry", "Fear", "Happy", "Sad", "Surprise", "Neutral"]
num_classes = 6
```

This is how samples are distributed among training and test. We'll be using training to train the model and everything else will go to test set:

```
data.Usage.value_counts()
Training       28273
PrivateTest     3534
PublicTest      3533
Name: Usage, dtype: int64
```

The size of images and the number of channels (depth):

```
from math import sqrt
depth = 1
height = int(sqrt(len(data.pixels[0].split())))
width = int(height)
height
48
```

Let's see some faces:

```
import numpy as np
import scipy.misc
from IPython.display import display
for i in xrange(0, 5):
    array = np.mat(data.pixels[i]).reshape(48, 48)
    image = scipy.misc.toimage(array, cmin=0.0)
    display(image)
```

```
        print(emotion_labels[data.emotion[i]])

   //Images are being shown in the notebook
```

Many faces have ambiguous expressions, so our neural network will have a hard time classifying them. For example, the first face looks surprised or sad, rather than angry, and the second face doesn't look angry at all. Nevertheless, this is the dataset we have. For the real application, I would recommend collecting more samples of higher resolution, and then annotating them such that every photo is annotated several times by different independent annotators. Then, remove all photos that were annotated ambiguously.

Splitting the data

Do not forget to split your data into training and test sets before training the model as shown in the following:

```
train_set = data[(data.Usage == 'Training')]
test_set = data[(data.Usage != 'Training')]
X_train = np.array(map(str.split, train_set.pixels), np.float32)
X_test = np.array(map(str.split, test_set.pixels), np.float32)
(X_train.shape, X_test.shape)
((28273, 2304), (7067, 2304))
48*48
2304
X_train = X_train.reshape(28273, 48, 48, 1)
X_test = X_test.reshape(7067, 48, 48, 1)
(X_train.shape, X_test.shape)
((28273, 48, 48, 1), (7067, 48, 48, 1))
num_train = X_train.shape[0]
num_test = X_test.shape[0]
(num_train, num_test)
(28273, 7067)
```

Converting labels to categorical:

```
from keras.utils import np_utils # utilities for one-hot encoding of ground
truth values
Using TensorFlow backend.
y_train = train_set.emotion
y_train = np_utils.to_categorical(y_train, num_classes)
y_test = test_set.emotion
y_test = np_utils.to_categorical(y_test, num_classes)
```

Data augmentation

In the deep learning applications, generally, the more data you have, the better. Deep neural networks usually have a lot of parameters, so on the small datasets they overfit easily. We can generate more training samples from the samples we already have by using the technique called **data augmentation**. The idea is to change samples at random. With the face photos, we could, for example, flip faces horizontally, shift them a bit, or add some rotations:

```
from keras.preprocessing.image import ImageDataGenerator
datagen = ImageDataGenerator(
    rotation_range=25,
    width_shift_range=0.2,
    height_shift_range=0.2,
    horizontal_flip=True)
```

Compute quantities required for featurewise normalization (std, mean, and principal components, if ZCA whitening is applied):

```
datagen.fit(X_train)
batch_size = 32
```

At each iteration, we will consider 32 training examples at once, in other words, our batch size is 32. Let's see our images after augmentation:

```
from matplotlib import pyplot
for X_batch, y_batch in datagen.flow(X_train, y_train, batch_size=9):
```

Creating a grid of 3 x 3 images:

```
    for i in range(0, 9):
        pyplot.axis('off')
        pyplot.subplot(330 + 1 + i)
        pyplot.imshow(X_batch[i].reshape(48, 48),
cmap=pyplot.get_cmap('gray'))
```

Showing the plot with images:

```
    pyplot.axis('off')
    pyplot.show()
    break

<Images>
```

Generators that provide samples during training:

```
train_flow = datagen.flow(X_train, y_train, batch_size=batch_size)
test_flow = datagen.flow(X_test, y_test)
```

Creating the network

Keras allows building the deep neural networks by adding new layers one by one. Note, that all layers should be familiar to you to this moment.

```
from keras.models import Sequential
from keras.layers import Activation, Dropout, Flatten, Dense,
BatchNormalization, Conv2D, MaxPool2D
model = Sequential()

model.add(Conv2D(16, (3, 3), padding='same', activation='relu',
input_shape=(height, width, depth)))
model.add(Conv2D(16, (3, 3), padding='same'))
model.add(BatchNormalization())
model.add(Activation('relu'))
model.add(MaxPool2D((2,2)))

model.add(Conv2D(32, (3, 3), padding='same', activation='relu'))
model.add(Conv2D(32, (3, 3), padding='same'))
model.add(BatchNormalization())
model.add(Activation('relu'))
model.add(MaxPool2D((2,2)))

model.add(Conv2D(64, (3, 3), padding='same', activation='relu'))
model.add(Conv2D(64, (3, 3), padding='same'))
model.add(BatchNormalization())
model.add(Activation('relu'))
model.add(MaxPool2D((2,2)))

model.add(Flatten())
model.add(Dense(128))
model.add(BatchNormalization())
model.add(Activation('relu'))
model.add(Dense(num_classes, activation='softmax'))
model.compile(loss='categorical_crossentropy',
              optimizer='rmsprop',
              metrics=['accuracy'])
```

The list of layers can be accessed via the `layers` property of the `model` object:

```
model.layers
[<keras.layers.convolutional.Conv2D at 0x7f53b5d12fd0>,
 <keras.layers.convolutional.Conv2D at 0x7f53b5ca2090>,
 <keras.layers.normalization.BatchNormalization at 0x7f53b5ca2a10>,
 <keras.layers.core.Activation at 0x7f53b5cbbe50>,
 <keras.layers.pooling.MaxPooling2D at 0x7f53b5c68ed0>,
 <keras.layers.convolutional.Conv2D at 0x7f53b5c68bd0>,
 <keras.layers.convolutional.Conv2D at 0x7f53b5c8b310>,
 <keras.layers.normalization.BatchNormalization at 0x7f53b5c3ad10>,
 <keras.layers.core.Activation at 0x7f53b5c0e790>,
 <keras.layers.pooling.MaxPooling2D at 0x7f53b5bd7c50>,
 <keras.layers.convolutional.Conv2D at 0x7f53b5bbf990>,
 <keras.layers.convolutional.Conv2D at 0x7f53b5bb1950>,
 <keras.layers.normalization.BatchNormalization at 0x7f53b5b845d0>,
 <keras.layers.core.Activation at 0x7f53b5b3f950>,
 <keras.layers.pooling.MaxPooling2D at 0x7f53b5b05610>,
 <keras.layers.core.Flatten at 0x7f53b5ae31d0>,
 <keras.layers.core.Dense at 0x7f53b5af35d0>,
 <keras.layers.normalization.BatchNormalization at 0x7f53b5ac6690>,
 <keras.layers.core.Activation at 0x7f53b5a85750>,
 <keras.layers.core.Dense at 0x7f53b5a2e910>]
model.summary()
```

```
Layer (type)                 Output Shape             Param #
=================================================================
conv2d_1 (Conv2D)            (None, 48, 48, 16)       160

conv2d_2 (Conv2D)            (None, 48, 48, 16)       2320

batch_normalization_1 (Batch (None, 48, 48, 16)       64

activation_1 (Activation)    (None, 48, 48, 16)       0

max_pooling2d_1 (MaxPooling2 (None, 24, 24, 16)       0

conv2d_3 (Conv2D)            (None, 24, 24, 32)       4640

conv2d_4 (Conv2D)            (None, 24, 24, 32)       9248

batch_normalization_2 (Batch (None, 24, 24, 32)       128

activation_2 (Activation)    (None, 24, 24, 32)       0

max_pooling2d_2 (MaxPooling2 (None, 12, 12, 32)       0
```

conv2d_5 (Conv2D)	(None, 12, 12, 64)	18496
conv2d_6 (Conv2D)	(None, 12, 12, 64)	36928
batch_normalization_3 (Batch	(None, 12, 12, 64)	256
activation_3 (Activation)	(None, 12, 12, 64)	0
max_pooling2d_3 (MaxPooling2	(None, 6, 6, 64)	0
flatten_1 (Flatten)	(None, 2304)	0
dense_1 (Dense)	(None, 128)	295040
batch_normalization_4 (Batch	(None, 128)	512
activation_4 (Activation)	(None, 128)	0
dense_2 (Dense)	(None, 6)	774

```
Total params: 368,566
Trainable params: 368,086
Non-trainable params: 480
```

Plotting the network structure

Perhaps, the more convenient way to explore the structure of the network is to draw a picture. Let's do that:

```
from IPython.display import SVG
from keras.utils.vis_utils import model_to_dot

SVG(model_to_dct(model, show_shapes=True).create(prog='dot', format='svg'))

from IPython.display import Image
from keras.utils import plot_model
plot_model(model, show_shapes=True, show_layer_names=True,
to_file='model.png')
```

See the *Figure 9.10* for the result.

Training the network

First, we have to define how long we want to train out network. One `epoch` is one full pass over the training set. The number of steps in the epoch depends on the batch size and the number of samples in the training set. Let's say we want to pass over the training set 100 times:

```
num_epochs = 100
```

Fit the model on batches with real-time data augmentation:

```
num_epochs = 100 # we iterate 200 times over the entire training set
history = model.fit_generator(train_flow,
                    steps_per_epoch=len(X_train) / batch_size,
                    epochs=num_epochs,
                    verbose=1,
                    validation_data=test_flow,
                    validation_steps=len(X_test) / batch_size)
Epoch 1/100
883/883 [==============================] - 15s - loss: 1.7065 - acc: 0.2836
- val_loss: 1.8536 - val_acc: 0.1822
Epoch 2/100
883/883 [==============================] - 14s - loss: 1.4980 - acc: 0.4008
- val_loss: 1.5688 - val_acc: 0.3891
...
883/883 [==============================] - 13s - loss: 0.9292 - acc: 0.6497
- val_loss: 1.1499 - val_acc: 0.5819
Epoch 100/100
883/883 [==============================] - 13s - loss: 0.9225 - acc: 0.6487
- val_loss: 1.0829 - val_acc: 0.6122
```

If the training goes fine, the loss values should decrease over the time as shown in the following image:

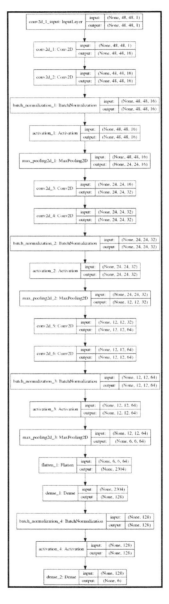

Figure 9.10: Neural network structure

Plotting loss

Loss values on training and validation sets allows to see, how our model improves over the time and decide when to stop training:

```
from matplotlib import pyplot as plt
history.history.keys()
['acc', 'loss', 'val_acc', 'val_loss'] plt.plot(history.history['loss'])
plt.plot(history.history['val_loss'])
plt.title('model loss')
plt.ylabel('loss')
plt.xlabel('epoch')
plt.legend(['train', 'test'], loc='upper left')
plt.show()
```

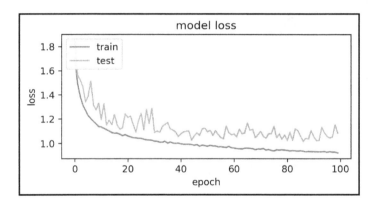

Figure 9.11: Loss on training and test sets over the training epochs

Making predictions

First, let's prepare data to make predictions about the images:

```
array = np.mat(data.pixels[1]).reshape(48, 48)
image = scipy.misc.toimage(array, cmin=0.0)
display(image)
print(emotion_labels[data.emotion[1]])

<Image>
```

Let us input an angry emotion image:

```
input_img = np.array(array).reshape(1,48,48,1)
```

Okay, we have an angry face. Now let's make prediction and check if the network can recognize it correctly:

```
prediction = model.predict(input_img)
print(prediction)
[[ 0.05708674  0.35863262  0.03299783  0.17862292  0.00069717  0.37196276]]
emotion_labels[prediction.argmax()]
'Neutral'
```

Note those array of 6 float numbers. These are probabilities of belonging to each class. In other words, the model predicts, that this face can be of an angry person only with the probability of 5%. The full table would look like this:

Angry	Fear	Happy	Sad	Surprise	Neutral
0.05708674	0.35863262	0.03299783	0.17862292	0.00069717	0.37196276

```
for i in xrange(1, 100):
    array = np.mat(data.pixels[i]).reshape(48, 48)
    image = scipy.misc.toimage(array, cmin=0.0)
    display(image)
    print(emotion_labels[data.emotion[i]])
    input_img = np.array(array).reshape(1,48,48,1)
    prediction = model.predict(input_img)
    print(emotion_labels[prediction.argmax()])
```

You will obtain the following result:

```
Angry
Neutral

Fear
Sad

Sad
Sad

Neutral
Neutral

Fear
Sad

Sad
Sad

Happy
Happy
```

```
Happy
Happy

Fear
Fear
```

Evaluating the trained model on the test set. The function reports the loss value and an accuracy as follows:

```
model.evaluate_generator(test_flow, steps=len(X_test) / batch_size)
[1.1285726155553546, 0.60696517426491459]
```

So, the final accuracy of our model is about 60%. Which is not that bad, considering how noisy is the dataset.

Saving the model in HDF5 format

Saving the model is really easy as shown in the following:

```
model.save('Emotions.h5')
```

Converting to Core ML format

The easiest way to use pre-trained CNN on iOS is by converting it to the Core ML format:

```
from keras.models import load_model
model = load_model('Emotions.h5')
coreml_model = convert(model,
                       image_input_names = 'image',
                       class_labels = emotion_labels)
...
coreml_model.save('Emotions.mlmodel')
```

Visualizing convolution filters

Debugging CNNs is notoriously difficult. One of the ways to check if the convolutional layers learned anything meaningful is to visualize their outputs using Keras-vis package:

```
from vis.utils import utils
from vis.visualization import import visualize_class_activation, get_num_filters
```

We have to convert grayscale images to `rgb` to use them with `keras-vis`:

```
def to_rgb(im):
    # I think this will be slow
    w, h = im.shape
    ret = np.empty((w, h, 3), dtype=np.uint8)
    ret[:, :, 0] = im
    ret[:, :, 1] = im
    ret[:, :, 2] = im
    return ret
```

Names of the layers we want to visualize (consult model structure for exact layer names):

```
layer_names = ['conv2d_1', 'conv2d_2',
               'conv2d_3', 'conv2d_4',
               'conv2d_5', 'conv2d_6']

layer_sizes = [(80, 20), (80, 20),
               (80, 40), (80, 40),
               (80, 80), (80, 80)]

stitched_figs = []

for (layer_name, layer_size) in zip(layer_names, layer_sizes):
    layer_idx = [idx for idx, layer in enumerate(model.layers) if
layer.name == layer_name][0]
```

Visualizing all filters in this layer:

```
filters = np.arange(get_num_filters(model.layers[layer_idx]))
```

Generating input image for each filter as shown in the following. Here `text` field is used to overlay `filter_value` on top of the image:

```
    vis_images = []
    for idx in filters:
        img = visualize_class_activation(model, layer_idx,
filter_indices=idx)
        vis_images.append(to_rgb(img.reshape(48,48)))
```

Generate stitched image palette with 8 cols as follows:

```
    stitched = utils.stitch_images(vis_images, cols=8)
    stitched_figs.append(stitched)
    plt.figure(figsize = layer_size)
    plt.axis('cff')
    plt.imshow(stitched, interpolation='nearest', aspect='auto')
    plt.title(layer_name)
```

```
plt.savefig(layer_name+"_filters.png", bbox_inches='tight')
plt.show()
```

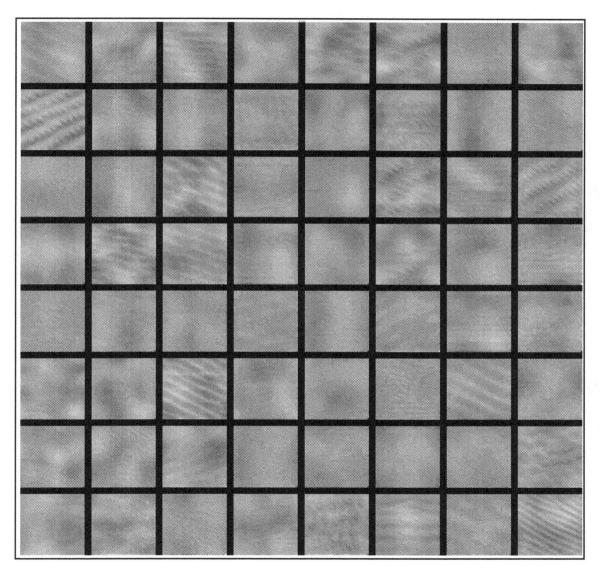

Figure 9.12: Convolution filters in the last convolution layer of our network

Deploying CNN to iOS

You need to drag-and-drop the Core ML file generated in the previous section into your project to start working with the model.

Imports:

```
import Foundation
import Vision
import AVFoundation
import UIKit
```

At first, let's define some data structures. An enumeration for possible classification results:

```
enum FaceExpressions: String {
  case angry = "angry"
  case anxious = "anxious"
  case neutral = "neutral"
  case happy = "happy"
  case sad = "sad"
}
```

An enum for errors of the classifier:

```
enum ClassifierError: Error {
  case unableToResizeBuffer
  case noResults
}
```

`Classifier` is a wrapper singleton for Core ML model:

```
class Classifier {
  public static let shared = Classifier()

  private let visionModel: VNCoreMLModel
  var visionRequests = [VNRequest]()
  var completion: ((_ label: [(FaceExpressions, Double)], _ error:
Error?)->())?

  private init() {
    guard let visionModel = try? VNCoreMLModel(for: Emotions().model) else {
    fatalError("Could not load model")
    }

    self.visionModel = visionModel

    let classificationRequest = VNCoreMLRequest(model: visionModel,
```

```
completionHandler: classificationResultHandler)
  classificationRequest.imageCropAndScaleOption = .centerCrop
  visionRequests = [classificationRequest]
  }
```

Function to run the network on inference:

```
public func classifyFace(image: CGImage, completion: @escaping (_ labels:
[(FaceExpressions, Double)], _ error: Error?)->()) {
  self.completion = completion
  let imageRequestHandler = VNImageRequestHandler(cgImage: image,
orientation: .up)
  do {
  try imageRequestHandler.perform(visionRequests)
  } catch {
  print(error)
  completion([], error)
  }
  }
```

This method will be called when the new classification result comes:

```
private func classificationResultHandler(request: VNRequest, error: Error?)
{
  if let error = error {
  print(error.localizedDescription)
  self.completion?([], error)
  return
  }
  guard let results = request.results as? [VNClassificationObservation] else
{
  print("No results")
  self.completion?([], ClassifierError.noResults)
  return
  }

  let sortedResults = results
  .sorted { $0.confidence > $1.confidence }
  .map{ (FaceExpressions(rawValue:$0.identifier)!, Double($0.confidence)) }

self.completion?(sortedResults, nil)
  print(sortedResults)
  }
}
```

We omit the UI part of the application here, please refer to the demo app for the full code.

Summary

In this chapter, we built a deep learning CNN, and trained it using Keras to recognize facial expressions on photos. Then we ported it for the mobile application using Core ML. The model can work in real time. We've also become acquainted with the Apple Vision framework.

CNNs are powerful tools that can be applied for many computer vision tasks, as well as for time-series prediction, natural language processing, and others. They are built around the concept of convolution—a mathematical operation that can be used for defining many types of image transformations. CNNs learn convolution filters in the similar manner as usual neural networks learn weights using the same stochastic gradient descent. Convolution requires less computations than usual matrix multiplications, which is why they can be effectively used on mobile devices. Apart from convolutional layers, CNNs usually include other types of layers like pooling, fully-connected, nonlinearity, regularization, and so on. Over the years, researchers proposed many CNN architectures for different purposes. Some of them were designed specifically to run on mobile devices; for example, SquizeNet, and MobileNets.

In the next chapter, we're going to explore the amazing world of human natural language. We're also going to use neural networks to build several chatbots with different personalities.

Bibliography

1. *Challenges in Representation Learning: A report on three machine learning contests*, I Goodfellow, D Erhan, PL Carrier, A Courville, M Mirza, B Hamner, W Cukierski, Y Tang, DH Lee, Y Zhou, C Ramaiah, F Feng, R Li, X Wang, D Athanasakis, J Shawe-Taylor, M Milakov, J Park, R Ionescu, M Popescu, C Grozea, J Bergstra, J Xie, L Romaszko, B Xu, Z Chuang, and Y. Bengio. arXiv 2013. Site of the competition http://deeplearning.net/icml2013-workshop-competition.
2. *Affective Computing*, Rosalind Picard. MIT Technical Report #32, 1995 http://affect.media.mit.edu/pdfs/95.picard.pdf.
3. Batch Normalization: Accelerating Deep Network Training by Reducing Internal Covariate Shift. Sergey Ioffe, Christian Szegedy, 2015.

10
Natural Language Processing

Language is an integral part of our daily life and a natural way of conveying ideas from person to person. But as easy it is for us to understand our native language, it is just as difficult for computers to process it. The internet changed the science of language forever because it allowed collecting huge volumes of text and audio records. The field of knowledge that arose at the intersection of linguistics, computer science, and machine learning was called **natural language processing** (**NLP**).

In this chapter, we will get acquainted with the basic concepts and applications of NLP, relevant in the context of mobile development. We will talk about the powerful tools provided by iOS and the macOS SDK for language processing. We also will learn about the theory of distributional semantics and vector representations of words as its embodiment. They will allow us to express the meaning of sentences in the computer's favorite format—in the form of numbers. Based on vector representations, we will build a chatbot from scratch to play a *Word Association* game.

In this chapter, we will cover the following topics:

- What is NLP?
- Python libraries—NLTK and Gensim
- iOS NLP tools—NSRegularExpression, NSDataDetector, NSLinguisticTagger, the Speech framework, and UIReferenceLibraryViewController
- macOS NLP tools—LatentSemanticMapping
- How to use tokenizers, lemmatization, and part-of-speech tagging
- What are vector word representations?

- How to generate word embeddings
- How to use the Word2Vec model on iOS
- How to build a chatbot from scratch

NLP in the mobile development world

Usually, NLP specialists deal with big amounts of raw text organized in **linguistics corpuses**. The algorithms in this domain are resource-consuming and often contain many hand-crafted heuristics. All this doesn't look like a good match for mobile applications, where each megabyte or frame per second is important. Despite these obstacles, NLP is widely used on mobile platforms, usually in tight integration with the server-side backend for heavy computations. Here is a list of some common NLP features that can be found in many mobile applications:

- Chatbots
- Spam filtering
- Automated translation
- Sentiment analysis
- Speech-to-text and text-to-speech
- Automatic spelling and grammar correction
- Automatic completion
- Keyboard suggestions

Until recently, all but the last two tasks were done on the server side, but as mobile computational power grows, more apps tend to do processing (at least partially) locally on the client. When we talk about NLP on a mobile device, in most cases, it is about processing private user information: messages, letters, notes, and similar texts. So the security issue here is particularly acute. By eliminating the server from our schema, we significantly reduce the risk of leaking user data. In this chapter, in addition to discussing common tricks and popular NLP tools, we will look at the solutions Apple provides in iOS SDK. Further, continuing our conversation on neural networks, we will teach six chatbots to play a *Word Association* game. Each chatbot will have its individuality and will run on the device. Each of the models on average will not exceed 3 MB.

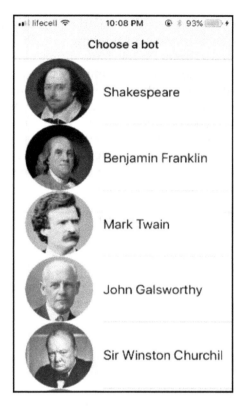

Figure 10.1: Every chatbot in our application will have its own individuality

Word Association game

Many of us may have played this game as kids. The rules are very simple:

- You say the word:

```
do while(true) {
```

- I say the first association to your word that came to my mind
- You give an association to my association:

```
}
```

For example, Dog → Cat → Pet → Toy → Baby → Girl → Wedding → Funeral. In the game, people reveal their life experience and way of thinking to each other; maybe that's why we could play it for hours as kids. Different people have different associations with the same word, and associations often head towards a completely unexpected direction. Psychologists have been studying associative series for more than a century, hoping to find in them the key to the mysteries of consciousness and the subconscious. Can you code a game AI to play like that? Perhaps you think you will need a manually composed database of associations. But what if you want your AI to have several personalities? Thanks to machine learning, this is definitely possible and you even don't need to compose the database manually. In the following screenshot, you can see the results of two games with two characters, Mark Twain and Benjamin Franklin:

Figure 10.2: Playing a Word Association game with historical personalities

If you haven't got the idea of the game, visit Wikipedia to get a more thorough explanation of the game there: `https://en.wikipedia.org/wiki/Word_Association`.

Python NLP libraries

The two Python libraries that we're going to use in this chapter are **natural language toolkit** (**NLTK**) and Gensim. We will use the first one for text preprocessing and the second one for training or machine learning models. To install them, activate your Python virtual environment:

```
> cd ~
> virtualenv swift-ml-book
```

And run `pip install`:

```
> pip install -U nltk gensim
```

Official sites:

- NLTK, `http://www.nltk.org/`
- Gensim, `https://radimrehurek.com/gensim/`

 Other popular libraries for NLP in Python:

- TextBlob, `https://textblob.readthedocs.io/en/dev/`
- Stanford's CoreNLP, `https://stanfordnlp.github.io/CoreNLP/`
- SpaCy, `https://spacy.io/`

Textual corpuses

For our NLP experiments, we need some reasonably big texts. I used the complete works of classical writers and statesmen from the Gutenberg project because they are in the public domain, but you can find your own texts and train models on them. If you want to use the same texts as I did, I included them in the supplementary material for this chapter under the `Corpuses` folder. There should be five of them: Benjamin Franklin, John Galsworthy, Mark Twain, William Shakespeare, and Winston Churchill. Create a new Jupyter notebook and load Mark Twain's corpus as one long string:

```
import zipfile
zip_ref = zipfile.ZipFile('Corpuses.zip', 'r')
zip_ref.extractall('')
zip_ref.close()
In [1]:
```

```
import codecs
In [2]:
one_long_string = ""
with codecs.open('Corpuses/MarkTwain.txt', 'r', 'utf-8-sig') as text_file:
    one_long_string = text_file.read()
In [3]:
one_long_string[99000:99900]
Out[3]:
u"size, very elegantly wrought and dressed in the fancifulrncostumes of two
centuries ago. The design was a history of something or somebody, but none
of us were learned enough to read the story. The old father, reposing under
a stone close by, dated 1686, might have told usrnif he could have risen.
But he didn't.rnrnAs we came down through the town we encountered a squad
of little donkeysrnready saddled for use. The saddles were peculiar, to say
the least.rnThey consisted of a sort of saw-buck with a small mattress on
it, andrnthis furniture covered about half the donkey. There were no
stirrups,rnbut really such supports were not needed--to use such a saddle
was thernnext thing to riding a dinner table--there was ample support clear
out tornone's knee joints. A pack of ragged Portuguese muleteers crowded
aroundrnus, offering their beasts at half a dollar an hour--more rascality
to"
```

Common NLP approaches and subtasks

Most programmers are familiar with the simplest way of processing natural language: regular expressions. There are many regular expression implementations for different programming languages that differ in small details. Because of these details, the same regular expression on various platforms can produce different results or not work at all. The two most popular standards are POSIX and Perl. The Foundation framework, however, contains its own version of regular expressions, based on the ICU C++ library. It is an extension of the POSIX standard for Unicode strings.

Why are we even talking about regular expressions here? Regular expressions are a great example of what NLP specialists call heuristics—manually written rules, ad hoc solutions, and describing a complex structure in such a way that all exceptions and variations are taken into account. Sophisticated heuristics require deep domain expertise to build. Only when we are not able to capture all the complexity using heuristics will we go for machine learning. Heuristics are fragile and costly to build, but not necessarily something wrong; unlike machine learning, they are deterministic and easy to test.

Heuristics and machine learning are the two arms that wield NLP. Big NLP tasks usually consist of smaller ones. To perform a grammar correction, you must split your text into sentences, split sentences into words, determine the parts of speech in those sentences, and so on. In our text corpus preprocessing, we will go through several such tasks: sentence tokenization, word tokenization, lemmatization, and stop words removal.

Tokenization

Tokens in linguistics are different from the authorization tokens were used to. They are linguistic units: words are tokens, numbers and punctuation marks are tokens, and sentences are tokens. In other words, they are discrete pieces of information or meaning. Tokenization is a process of splitting text into **lexical tokens**. Sentence tokenizers split texts into sentences, and word tokenizers split them further into separate words, punctuation marks, and so on. This task may seem simple (**there is a regexp for that!**), but this impression is deceptive. Here are a few problems to consider:

- How to tokenize words with a hyphen or an apostrophe, for example, *New York-based* or *you're*?
- How to tokenize web addresses and emails, for example, `My_mail@examplewebsite.com`?
- What to do with emoji and kaomoji? (´ ˚ □ ˚)ʸ ~**ᴸ−ᴸ**!
- What to do with languages in which gluing several words into one long word is the norm? An example is the German *siebenhundertsiebenundsiebzigtausendsiebenhundertsiebenundsiebzig*. This is the number 777,777 by the way.
- What to do with languages that do not use spaces at all (Chinese and Thai)?

Fortunately, there are many tokenizer implementations for different languages, including the NLTK Python library and Apple `NSLinguisticTagger`:

```
In [4]:
from nltk import word_tokenize, sent_tokenize
In [5]:
sentences = sent_tokenize(one_long_string)
del(one_long_string)
In [6]:
sentences[200:205]
Out[6]:
[u'Ah, if I had only known then that he was only a common mortal, and
thatrnhis mission had nothing more overpowering about it than the
collecting ofrnseeds and uncommon yams and extraordinary cabbages and
```

peculiar bullfrogsrnfor that poor, useless, innocent, mildewed old fossil the SmithsonianrnInstitute, I would have felt so much relieved.',
 u'During that memorable month I basked in the happiness of being for oncernin my life drifting with the tide of a great popular movement.',
 u'Everybodyrnwas going to Europe--I, too, was going to Europe.',
 u'Everybody was going tornthe famous Paris Exposition--I, too, was going to the Paris Exposition.',
 u'The steamship lines were carrying Americans out of the various ports ofrnthe country at the rate of four or five thousand a week in the aggregate.']

```
In [7]:
tokenized_sentences = map(word_tokenize, sentences)
del(sentences)
In [8]:
print(tokenized_sentences[200:205])
```

[[u'Ah', u',', u'if', u'I', u'had', u'only', u'known', u'then', u'that', u'he', u'was', u'only', u'a', u'common', u'mortal', u',', u'and', u'that', u'his', u'mission', u'had', u'nothing', u'more', u'overpowering', u'about', u'it', u'than', u'the', u'collecting', u'of', u'seeds', u'and', u'uncommon', u'yams', u'and', u'extraordinary', u'cabbages', u'and', u'peculiar', u'bullfrogs', u'for', u'that', u'poor', u',', u'useless', u',', u'innocent', u',', u'mildewed', u'old', u'fossil', u'the', u'Smithsonian', u'Institute', u',', u'I', u'would', u'have', u'felt', u'so', u'much', u'relieved', u'.'], [u'During', u'that', u'memorable', u'month', u'I', u'basked', u'in', u'the', u'happiness', u'of', u'being', u'for', u'once', u'in', u'my', u'life', u'drifting', u'with', u'the', u'tide', u'of', u'a', u'great', u'popular', u'movement', u'.'], [u'Everybody', u'was', u'going', u'to', u'Europe', u'--', u'I', u',', u'too', u',', u'was', u'going', u'to', u'Europe', u'.'], [u'Everybody', u'was', u'going', u'to', u'the', u'famous', u'Paris', u'Exposition', u'--', u'I', u',', u'too', u',', u'was', u'going', u'to', u'the', u'Paris', u'Exposition', u'.'], [u'The', u'steamship', u'lines', u'were', u'carrying', u'Americans', u'out', u'of', u'the', u'various', u'ports', u'of', u'the', u'country', u'at', u'the', u'rate', u'of', u'four', u'or', u'five', u'thousand', u'a', u'week', u'in', u'the', u'aggregate', u'.']]

```
In [9]:
from nltk import download
In [10]:
download('stopwords')
[nltk_data] Downloading package stopwords to
[nltk_data]     /Users/Oleksandr/nltk_data...
[nltk_data]   Package stopwords is already up-to-date!
Out[10]:
True
In [11]:
from nltk.stem import WordNetLemmatizer
In [12]:
wordnet_lemmatizer = WordNetLemmatizer()
```

```
In [13]:
lemmatized_sentences = map(lambda sentence:
map(wordnet_lemmatizer.lemmatize, sentence), tokenized_sentences)
In [14]:
print(lemmatized_sentences[200:205])
[[u'Ah', u',', u'if', u'I', u'had', u'only', u'known', u'then', u'that',
u'he', u'wa', u'only', u'a', u'common', u'mortal', u',', u'and', u'that',
u'his', u'mission', u'had', u'nothing', u'more', u'overpowering', u'about',
u'it', u'than', u'the', u'collecting', u'of', u'seed', u'and', u'uncommon',
u'yam', u'and', u'extraordinary', u'cabbage', u'and', u'peculiar',
u'bullfrog', u'for', u'that', u'poor', u',', u'useless', u',', u'innocent',
u',', u'mildewed', u'old', u'fossil', u'the', u'Smithsonian', u'Institute',
u',', u'I', u'would', u'have', u'felt', u'so', u'much', u'relieved', u'.'],
[u'During', u'that', u'memorable', u'month', u'I', u'basked', u'in',
u'the', u'happiness', u'of', u'being', u'for', u'once', u'in', u'my',
u'life', u'drifting', u'with', u'the', u'tide', u'of', u'a', u'great',
u'popular', u'movement', u'.'], [u'Everybody', u'wa', u'going', u'to',
u'Europe', u'--', u'I', u',', u'too', u',', u'wa', u'going', u'to',
u'Europe', u'.'], [u'Everybody', u'wa', u'going', u'to', u'the', u'famous',
u'Paris', u'Exposition', u'--', u'I', u',', u'too', u',', u'wa', u'going',
u'to', u'the', u'Paris', u'Exposition', u'.'], [u'The', u'steamship',
u'line', u'were', u'carrying', u'Americans', u'out', u'of', u'the',
u'various', u'port', u'of', u'the', u'country', u'at', u'the', u'rate',
u'of', u'four', u'or', u'five', u'thousand', u'a', u'week', u'in', u'the',
u'aggregate', u'.']]
In [15]:
del(tokenized_sentences)
```

Stemming

Stemming is the process of reducing words to their stems. The idea here is that related words can usually be reduced to a common stem.

For example: (**whit**e, **whit**ening, **whit**ish, **whit**er) → **whit**.

This can be used, for instance, to expand user queries. But some cases can be tricky, consider the English *man* and *men*, the Irish *bhean* = *woman* and *mnà* = *women*, or the even more extreme English *am, is, are, was, were,* and *been*. There are several popular stemmers for English.

Lemmatization

This is a more advanced approach than stemming. Instead of reducing words to stems, lemmatizers match every word to its *lemma*, the form in a dictionary. This is especially useful for languages such as Polish, where one verb can easily have 220 different grammatical forms, mostly with different spellings: `http://wsjp.pl/do_druku.php?id_hasla=34745id_znaczenia=0`.

The problem here is homonyms.

Part-of-speech (POS) tagging

NLTK uses a pre-trained machine learning model (averaged perceptron) for POS tagging. The task is especially hard for English because, unlike many other languages, the same word can play the role of different parts of speech depending on the context:

```
In [16]:
from nltk import download
In [17]:
download('averaged_perceptron_tagger')
[nltk_data] Downloading package averaged_perceptron_tagger to
[nltk_data]     /Users/Oleksandr/nltk_data...
[nltk_data]   Package averaged_perceptron_tagger is already up-to-
[nltk_data]       date!
Out[17]:
True
In [18]:
from nltk import pos_tag, pos_tag_sents
In [19]:
pos_tag(word_tokenize('Cats, cat, Cat, and "The Cats"'))
Out[19]:
[('Cats', 'NNS'),
 (',', ','),
 ('cat', 'NN'),
 (',', ','),
 ('Cat', 'NNP'),
 (',', ','),
 ('and', 'CC'),
 ('``', '``'),
 ('The', 'DT'),
 ('Cats', 'NNP'),
 ("''", "''")]
In [20]:
pos_sentences = pos_tag_sents(lemmatized_sentences)
```

```
del(lemmatized_sentences)
In [21]:
print(pos_sentences[200:205])
[[(u'Ah', 'NNP'), (u',', ','), (u'if', 'IN'), (u'I', 'PRP'), (u'had',
'VBD'), (u'only', 'RB'), (u'known', 'VBN'), (u'then', 'RB'), (u'that',
'IN'), (u'he', 'PRP'), (u'wa', 'VBZ'), (u'only', 'RB'), (u'a', 'DT'),
(u'common', 'JJ'), (u'mortal', 'NN'), (u',', ','), (u'and', 'CC'),
(u'that', 'IN'), (u'his', 'PRP$'), (u'mission', 'NN'), (u'had', 'VBD'),
(u'nothing', 'NN'), (u'more', 'RBR'), (u'overpowering', 'VBG'), (u'about',
'IN'), (u'it', 'PRP'), (u'than', 'IN'), (u'the', 'DT'), (u'collecting',
'NN'), (u'of', 'IN'), (u'seed', 'NN'), (u'and', 'CC'), (u'uncommon', 'JJ'),
(u'yam', 'NN'), (u'and', 'CC'), (u'extraordinary', 'JJ'), (u'cabbage',
'NN'), (u'and', 'CC'), (u'peculiar', 'JJ'), (u'bullfrog', 'NN'), (u'for',
'IN'), (u'that', 'DT'), (u'poor', 'JJ'), (u',', ','), (u'useless', 'JJ'),
(u',', ','), (u'innocent', 'JJ'), (u',', ','), (u'mildewed', 'VBD'),
(u'old', 'JJ'), (u'fossil', 'NN'), (u'the', 'DT'), (u'Smithscnian', 'NNP'),
(u'Institute', 'NNP'), (u',', ','), (u'I', 'PRP'), (u'would', 'MD'),
(u'have', 'VB'), (u'felt', 'VBN'), (u'so', 'RB'), (u'much', 'JJ'),
(u'relieved', 'NN'), (u'.', '.')], [(u'During', 'IN'), (u'that', 'DT'),
(u'memorable', 'JJ'), (u'month', 'NN'), (u'I', 'PRP'), (u'basked', 'VBD'),
(u'in', 'IN'), (u'the', 'DT'), (u'happiness', 'NN'), (u'of', 'IN'),
(u'being', 'VBG'), (u'for', 'IN'), (u'once', 'RB'), (u'in', 'IN'), (u'my',
'PRP$'), (u'life', 'NN'), (u'drifting', 'VBG'), (u'with', 'IN'), (u'the',
'DT'), (u'tide', 'NN'), (u'of', 'IN'), (u'a', 'DT'), (u'great', 'JJ'),
(u'popular', 'JJ'), (u'movement', 'NN'), (u'.', '.')], [(u'Everybody',
'NN'), (u'wa', 'VBZ'), (u'going', 'VBG'), (u'to', 'TO'), (u'Europe',
'NNP'), (u'--', ':'), (u'I', 'PRP'), (u',', ','), (u'too', 'RB'), (u',',
','), (u'wa', 'VBZ'), (u'going', 'VBG'), (u'to', 'TO'), (u'Europe', 'NNP'),
(u'.', '.')], [(u'Everybody', 'NN'), (u'wa', 'VBZ'), (u'going', 'VBG'),
(u'to', 'TO'), (u'the', 'DT'), (u'famous', 'JJ'), (u'Paris', 'NNP'),
(u'Exposition', 'NNP'), (u'--', ':'), (u'I', 'PRP'), (u',', ','), (u'too',
'RB'), (u',', ','), (u'wa', 'VBZ'), (u'going', 'VBG'), (u'to', 'TO'),
(u'the', 'DT'), (u'Paris', 'NNP'), (u'Exposition', 'NNP'), (u'.', '.')],
[(u'The', 'DT'), (u'steamship', 'NN'), (u'line', 'NN'), (u'were', 'VBD'),
(u'carrying', 'VBG'), (u'Americans', 'NNPS'), (u'out', 'IN'), (u'of',
'IN'), (u'the', 'DT'), (u'various', 'JJ'), (u'port', 'NN'), (u'of', 'IN'),
(u'the', 'DT'), (u'country', 'NN'), (u'at', 'IN'), (u'the', 'DT'),
(u'rate', 'NN'), (u'of', 'IN'), (u'four', 'CD'), (u'or', 'CC'), (u'five',
'CD'), (u'thousand', 'NNS'), (u'a', 'DT'), (u'week', 'NN'), (u'in', 'IN'),
(u'the', 'DT'), (u'aggregate', 'NN'), (u'.', '.')]]
In [22]:
download('tagsets')
[nltk_data] Downloading package tagsets to
[nltk_data]     /Users/Oleksandr/nltk_data...
[nltk_data]   Package tagsets is already up-to-date!
Out[22]:
True
In [23]:
```

```
from nltk.help import upenn_tagset
In [24]:
upenn_tagset()
```

You can find the full list of tags in the notebook or in the NLTK documentation: https://www.ling.upenn.edu/courses/Fall_2003/ling001/penn_treebank_pos.html. Here I'm only recounting the POS important for our goal with some examples.

Adjectives:

```
JJ: adjective or numeral, ordinal
third ill-mannered pre-war regrettable oiled calamitous first
JJR: adjective, comparative
JJS: adjective, superlative
```

Nouns:

```
NN: noun, common, singular or mass
common-carrier cabbage knuckle-duster Casino afghan shed
NNP: noun, proper, singular
Conchita Escobar Kreisler Sawyer CTCA Shannon A.K.C. Liverpool
NNPS: noun, proper, plural
Americans Americas Anarcho-Syndicalists Andalusians Andes
NNS: noun, common, plural
```

Adverbs:

```
RB: adverb
occasionally unabatingly maddeningly adventurously swiftly
RBR: adverb, comparative
RBS: adverb, superlative
```

Interjections:

```
UH: interjection
Goodbye Wow Hey Oops amen huh uh anyways honey man baby hush
```

Verbs:

```
VB: verb, base form
ask assemble assess assign assume avoid bake balkanize begin
VBD: verb, past tense
VBG: verb, present participle or gerund
VBN: verb, past participle
VBP: verb, present tense, not 3rd person singular
VBZ: verb, present tense, 3rd person singular
```

Named entity recognition (NER)

Note the (u'Paris', 'NNP'), (u'Exposition', 'NNP'), (u'Americans, NNPS). NNP stands for proper noun, NNPS proper noun plural. We need to get rid of all capital letters from non-proper nouns and from all punctuation marks and numbers:

```
In [25]:
# tags_to_delete = ['$', "''", "(", ")", ",", "--", ".", ":", "CC"]
tags_to_not_lowercase = set(['NNP', 'NNPS'])
tags_to_preserve = set(['JJ', 'JJR', 'JJS', 'NN', 'NNP', 'NNPS', 'NNS',
'RB', 'RBR', 'RBS','UH', 'VB', 'VBD', 'VBG', 'VBN', 'VBP', 'VBZ'])
In [26]:
print(pos_sentences[203])
[(u'Everybody', 'NN'), (u'wa', 'VBZ'), (u'going', 'VBG'), (u'to', 'TO'),
(u'the', 'DT'), (u'famous', 'JJ'), (u'Paris', 'NNP'), (u'Exposition',
'NNP'), (u'--', ':'), (u'I', 'PRP'), (u',', ','), (u'too', 'RB'), (u',',
','), (u'wa', 'VBZ'), (u'going', 'VBG'), (u'to', 'TO'), (u'the', 'DT'),
(u'Paris', 'NNP'), (u'Exposition', 'NNP'), (u'.', '.')]
In [27]:
def carefully_lowercase(words):
    return [(word.lower(), pos) if pos not in tags_to_not_lowercase else
(word, pos)
            for (word, pos) in words]
In [28]:
def filter_meaningful(words):
    return [word for (word, pos) in words if pos in tags_to_preserve]
In [29]:
res = map(carefully_lowercase, pos_sentences[203:205])
print(res)
[[(u'everybody', 'NN'), (u'wa', 'VBZ'), (u'going', 'VBG'), (u'to', 'TO'),
(u'the', 'DT'), (u'famous', 'JJ'), (u'Paris', 'NNP'), (u'Exposition',
'NNP'), (u'--', ':'), (u'i', 'PRP'), (u',', ','), (u'too', 'RB'), (u',',
','), (u'wa', 'VBZ'), (u'going', 'VBG'), (u'to', 'TO'), (u'the', 'DT'),
(u'Paris', 'NNP'), (u'Exposition', 'NNP'), (u'.', '.')], [(u'the', 'DT'),
(u'steamship', 'NN'), (u'line', 'NN'), (u'were', 'VBD'), (u'carrying',
'VBG'), (u'Americans', 'NNPS'), (u'out', 'IN'), (u'of', 'IN'), (u'the',
'DT'), (u'various', 'JJ'), (u'port', 'NN'), (u'of', 'IN'), (u'the', 'DT'),
(u'country', 'NN'), (u'at', 'IN'), (u'the', 'DT'), (u'rate', 'NN'), (u'of',
'IN'), (u'four', 'CD'), (u'or', 'CC'), (u'five', 'CD'), (u'thousand',
'NNS'), (u'a', 'DT'), (u'week', 'NN'), (u'in', 'IN'), (u'the', 'DT'),
(u'aggregate', 'NN'), (u'.', '.')]]
In [30]:
filtered = map(filter_meaningful, res)
del(res)
print(filtered)
[[u'everybody', u'wa', u'going', u'famous', u'Paris', u'Exposition',
u'too', u'wa', u'going', u'Paris', u'Exposition'], [u'steamship', u'line',
```

```
u'were', u'carrying', u'Americans', u'various', u'port', u'country',
u'rate', u'thousand', u'week', u'aggregate']]
In [31]:
lowercased_pos_sentences = map(carefully_lowercase,  pos_sentences)
del(pos_sentences)
```

Removing stop words and punctuation

Stop words are all those words that don't add much information to the sentence. For example, the last sentence can be shortened to: *stop words don't add useful information sentence*. And despite the fact that it doesn't look like a proper English sentence, you'd likely understand the meaning if you heard it somewhere. That's why in many cases we can make our models simpler by simply ignoring these words. Stop words are usually the most common words in natural texts. For English, a list of them can be found in `nltk.corpus.stopwords`:

```
In [32]:
sentences_to_train_on = map(lambda words: [word for (word, pos) in words],
lowercased_pos_sentences)
In [33]:
print(sentences_to_train_on[203:205])
[[u'everybody', u'wa', u'going', u'to', u'the', u'famous', u'Paris',
u'Exposition', u'--', u'i', u',', u'too', u',', u'wa', u'going', u'to',
u'the', u'Paris', u'Exposition', u'.'], [u'the', u'steamship', u'line',
u'were', u'carrying', u'Americans', u'out', u'of', u'the', u'various',
u'port', u'of', u'the', u'country', u'at', u'the', u'rate', u'of', u'four',
u'or', u'five', u'thousand', u'a', u'week', u'in', u'the', u'aggregate',
u'.']]
In [34]:
import itertools
In [35]:
filtered = map(filter_meaningful, lowercased_pos_sentences)
flatten = list(itertools.chain(*filtered))
words_to_keep = set(flatten)
In [36]:
del(filtered, flatten, lowercased_pos_sentences)
In [37]:
from nltk.corpus import stopwords
import string
In [38]:
stop_words = set(stopwords.words('english') + list(string.punctuation) +
['wa'])
```

Distributional semantics hypothesis

It's difficult to say what it means "to understand meaning of a text", but everyone will say that people can do this, and computers do not. Natural language understanding is one of the tough problems in Artificial Intelligence. How to capture the semantics of the sentence

Traditionally there were two opposite approaches to the problem. The first one goes like this: start from the definitions of separate words, hard-code the relations between them, and write down the sentence structures. If you are persistent enough, hopefully you will end up with a complex model that will incorporate enough expert knowledge to parse some natural questions and produce meaningful answers. And then, you'll find out that for a new language, you need to start everything over.

That's why many researchers turned to the opposite approach: statistical methods. Here, we start from a big amount of textual data and allow the computer to figure out the meaning of the text. The hypothesis of **distributional semantics** assumes that the meaning of a specific word in a sentence is not defined by the word itself but rather by all contexts in which that word appears. Wikipedia gives a more formal wording:

> *"Linguistic items with similar distributions have similar meanings."*

Now hold on tight! In the following sections, we're going to discuss an algorithm that can blow your mind. When I first came across it, I spent nights experimenting with it. I was feeding different texts into it, starting from the movie reviews dataset and finishing with the New Testament in ancient Greek and the undeciphered Voynich manuscript. It felt just like some craze or magic. The algorithm was able to capture the meanings of the words and whole sentences from raw texts, even in long-dead languages. This was the first time for me that computers seemingly crossed the line between *crunching megabytes of texts* and *understanding the meaning of text written by humans and for humans.*

Word vector representations

Distributional semantics represents words as vectors in the space of senses. The vectors corresponding to the words with similar meanings should be close to each other in this space. How to build such vectors is not a simple question, however. The simplest approach to take is to start from one-hot vectors for the words, but then the vectors will be both sparse and giant, each one of the same length as the number of words in the vocabulary. That's why we use dimensionality reduction with autoencoder-like architecture.

Autoencoder neural networks

Autoencoder is a neural network whose goal is to produce an output identical to an input. For example, if you pass a picture into it, it should return the same picture on the other end. This seems... not complicated! But the trick is the special architecture—its inner layers have fewer neurons than input and output layers, usually with some extreme bottleneck in the middle. The layer before the bottleneck is called encoder and the layer after it is called **decoder network**. The encoder converts the input into some inner representation and the decoder then restores the data to its original form. During training, the network must figure out how to compress the input data most effectively and then un-compress it with the least possible information loss. This architecture can also be employed to train neural networks, which change input data in a way we want them to. For example, autoencoders have been successfully used to remove noise from images.

Autoencoder neural networks are an example of so-called **representation learning**. It is something between supervised and unsupervised learning.

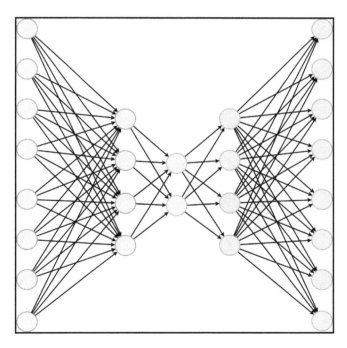

Figure 10.3: Autoencoder architecture

The blue layers are the encoder part, the **yellow layer** in the middle is a bottleneck, and the **green layers** are the decoder. The network in the picture is a fully connected network (every neuron of one layer is connected to every neuron in the next layer); however, this is not the only option for autoencoders.

Word2Vec

Word2Vec is an efficient algorithm for word embeddings generation based on neural networks. It was originally described by Mikolov et al. in *Distributed Representations of Words and Phrases and their Compositionality* (2013). The original C implementation in the form of a command-line application is available at `https://code.google.com/archive/p/word2vec/`.

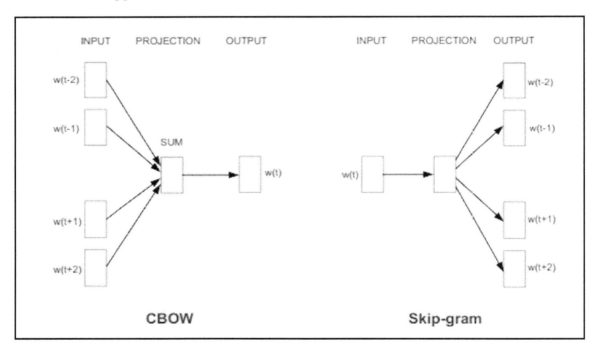

Figure 10.4: Architecture of Word2Vec

Word2Vec is often referred to as an instance of deep learning, but the architecture is actually quite shallow: only three layers in depth. This misconception is likely related to its wide adoption for enhancing productivity of deep networks in NLP. The Word2Vec architecture is similar to an autoencoder. The input of the neural network is a sufficiently big text corpus, and the output is a list of vectors (arrays of numbers), one vector for each word in the corpus. The algorithm uses the context of each word to encode in those vectors information about co-occurrences of words. As a result, the vectors have some peculiar properties; the vectors of words with similar meaning are also close to each other. While we can't mathematically calculate the precise distance between word meanings, we can calculate the similarity of two vectors without any problems. That's why algorithms that turn words into vectors are so important. For example, using the cosine similarity metric, we can find the words closest to cat:

- Bird: 0.760521
- Cow: 0.766533
- Dog: 0.831517
- Rat: 0.748557
- Blonde: 0.763721
- Pig: 0.751001
- Goat: 0.798104
- Hamster: 0.768635
- Bee: 0.774112
- Llama: 0.747295

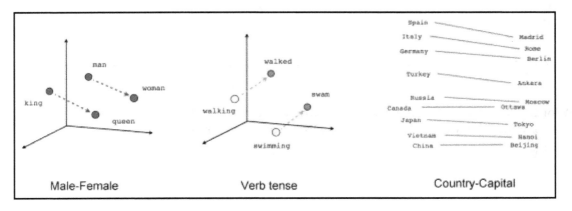

Figure 10.5: Examples of relationships between words that can be captured using Word2Vec

You can add, substract, and project vectors. Interestingly, these operations have some quite meaningful results, for example, *king-men+woman=queen, dog-men+woman=cat* and so on. By the way, as you can see from the last example, an algorithm captures all our stereotypes quite precisely.

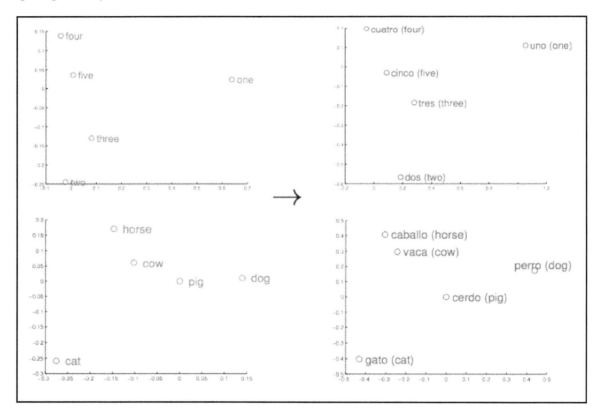

Figure 10.6: The distribution of words into vector spaces is similar among different languages

Word2Vec can be used not only with natural text but also with any sequence of discrete states, where context matters: playlists, DNA, source codes, and so on.

Word2Vec in Gensim

There is no point in running Word2Vec on an iOS device: in the app, we need only the vectors it generates. For running Word2Vec, we will use the Python NLP package gensim. This library is popular for topic modeling and contains a fast Word2Vec implementation with a nice API. We don't want to load large corpuses of text on a mobile phone and don't want to train Word2vec on the iOS device, so we will learn a vector representation using the Gensim Python library. Then, we will do some preprocessing (remove everything except nouns) and plug this database into our iOS application:

```
In [39]:
import gensim
In [40]:
def trim_rule(word, count, min_count):
    if word not in words_to_keep or word in stop_words:
        return gensim.utils.RULE_DISCARD
    else:
        return gensim.utils.RULE_DEFAULT
In [41]:
model = gensim.models.Word2Vec(sentences_to_train_on, min_count=15,
trim_rule=trim_rule)
```

Vector space properties

"The Hatter opened his eyes very wide on hearing this; but all he SAID was, 'Why is a raven like a writing-desk?'
'Come, we shall have some fun now!' thought Alice. 'I'm glad they've begun asking riddles. - I believe I can guess that,' she added aloud.
'Do you mean that you think you can find out the answer to it?' said the March Hare."

– Lewis Carroll, *Alice in a Wonderland*

Why is a raven like a writing desk? With the help of distributive semantic and vector word representations, finally we can help Alice to solve Hatter's riddle (in a mathematically precise way):

```
In [42]:
model.most_similar('house', topn=5)
Out[42]:
[(u'camp', 0.8188982009887695),
 (u'cabin', 0.8176383972167969),
 (u'town', 0.7998955845832825),
```

```
    (u'room', 0.7963996529579163),
    (u'street', 0.7951667308807373)]
In [43]:
model.most_similar('America', topn=5)
Out[43]:
[(u'India', 0.8678370714187622),
    (u'Europe', 0.8501001596450806),
    (u'number', 0.8464810848236084),
    (u'member', 0.8352445363998413),
    (u'date', 0.8332008123397827)]
In [44]:
model.most_similar('water', topn=5)
Out[44]:
[(u'bottom', 0.9041773676872253),
    (u'sand', 0.9032160639762878),
    (u'mud', 0.8798269033432007),
    (u'level', 0.8781479597091675),
    (u'rock', 0.8766734600067139)]
In [45]:
model.most_similar('money', topn=5)
Out[45]:
[(u'pay', 0.8744806051254272),
    (u'sell', 0.8554744720458984),
    (u'stock', 0.8477637767791748),
    (u'bill', 0.8445131182670593),
    (u'buy', 0.8271161913871765)]
In [46]:
model.most_similar('cat', topn=5)
Out[46]:
[(u'dog', 0.836624026298523),
    (u'wear', 0.8159085512161255),
    (u'cow', 0.7607206106185913),
    (u'like', 0.7499277591705322),
    (u'bird', 0.7386394739151001)]
```

iOS application

To use vectors in an iOS application, we must export them in a binary format:

```
In [47]:
model.wv.save_word2vec_format(fname='MarkTwain.bin', binary=True)
```

This binary contains words and their embedding vectors, all of the same length. The original implementation of Word2Vec was written in C, so I took it and adapted the code for our purpose—to parse the binary file and find closest words to the one that we specify.

Chatbot anatomy

Most chatbots look like reincarnations of console applications: you have a predefined set of commands and the bot produces an output for every command of yours. Someone even joked that Linux includes an awesome chatbot called **console**. But they don't always have to be that way. Let's see how we can make them more interesting. A typical chatbot consists of one or several input streams, a brain, and output streams. Inputs can be a keyboard, voice recognition, or set of predefined phrases. The brain is a sort of algorithm for transforming input into output. In our example, the brain will be based on word embeddings. Output streams also may be different, such as text, speech, search results (like Siri does), and so on.

Voice input

The code is as follows:

```
SFSpeechRecognizer
class func requestAuthorization(_ handler: @escaping
(SFSpeechRecognizerAuthorizationStatus) -> Swift.Void)

import Speech

class VoiceRecognizer: NSObject, SFSpeechRecognizerDelegate {
static var shared = VoiceRecognizer()

private let speechRecognizer = SFSpeechRecognizer(locale:
Locale(identifier: "en-US"))!
private var recognitionRequest: SFSpeechAudioBufferRecognitionRequest?
private var recognitionTask: SFSpeechRecognitionTask?
private let audioEngine = AVAudioEngine()

public var isListening: Bool {
    return audioEngine.isRunning
}

public func stopListening() {
    self.audioEngine.stop()
    self.recognitionRequest?.endAudio()
}

public func startListening(gotResult: @escaping (String)->(), end:
@escaping ()->()) {
    speechRecognizer.delegate = self
```

Cancel the previous task if it's running:

```
if let recognitionTask = recognitionTask {
    recognitionTask.cancel()
    self.recognitionTask = nil
}
do {
    let audioSession = AVAudioSession.sharedInstance()
    try audioSession.setCategory(AVAudioSessionCategoryRecord)
    try audioSession.setMode(AVAudioSessionModeMeasurement)
    try audioSession.setActive(true, with: .notifyOthersOnDeactivation)
} catch {
    print(error)
}
recognitionRequest = SFSpeechAudioBufferRecognitionRequest()
let inputNode = audioEngine.inputNode
guard let recognitionRequest = recognitionRequest else {
fatalError("Unable to created a SFSpeechAudioBufferRecogniticnRequest
object") }
```

Configure the request so that the results are returned before audio recording is finished:

```
recognitionRequest.shouldReportPartialResults = false
```

Create a recognition task. Store the recognition task as a property, to be able to cancel it if needed:

```
recognitionTask = speechRecognizer.recognitionTask(with:
recognitionRequest) { [weak self] result, error in
    guard let `self` = self else { return }
    var isFinal = false
    if let result = result {
        let string = result.bestTranscription.formattedString
        gotResult(string)
        isFinal = result.isFinal
    }
    if error != nil || isFinal {
        self.audioEngine.stop()
        inputNode.removeTap(onBus: 0)
        self.recognitionRequest = nil
        self.recognitionTask = nil
        end()
    }
}
let recordingFormat = inputNode.outputFormat(forBus: 0)
inputNode.installTap(onBus: 0, bufferSize: 1024, format:
recordingFormat) { (buffer: AVAudioPCMBuffer, when: AVAudioTime) in
    self.recognitionRequest?.append(buffer)
```

```
    }
    audioEngine.prepare()
    do {
        try audioEngine.start()
    } catch {
        print(error)
    }
}
}
```

NSLinguisticTagger and friends

`NSLinguisticTagger` is an all-in-one class for language detection, tokenization,
lemmatization, part-of-speech tagging, named entity recognition and so on. The API is in
the traditions of Objective-C: You have to create an instance of the class with some options,
then assign it with a string to analyze, and then iterate through tags that it had found using
`enumerateTags()` method. For each tag, it returns `NSRange` object which is somewhat
inconvenient to use in Swift, so we have to add some utility functions to convert them to
Swift ranges:

```
extension String {
func range(from nsRange: NSRange) -> Range<String.Index>? {
    guard
        let from16 = utf16.index(utf16.startIndex, offsetBy:
nsRange.location, limitedBy: utf16.endIndex),
        let to16 = utf16.index(utf16.startIndex, offsetBy: nsRange.location
+ nsRange.length, limitedBy: utf16.endIndex),
        let from = from16.samePosition(in: self),
        let to = to16.samePosition(in: self)
        else { return nil }
    return from ..< to
}
}

struct NLPPreprocessor {

static func preprocess(inputString: String, errorCallback:
(NLPPreprocessorError)->()) -> [String] {

    let languageDetector = NSLinguisticTagger(tagSchemes: [.language],
options: 0)
    languageDetector.string = inputString
    let language = languageDetector.dominantLanguage

    if language != "en" {
```

```
        errorCallback(.nonEnglishLanguage)
        return []
    }
```

This is a workaround to make NSLinguisticTagger's lemmatizer work with short sentences:

```
    let string = inputString + ". Hello, world!"
    let tagSchemes: [NSLinguisticTagScheme] = [.tokenType, .lemma,
.lexicalClass]
    let options = NSLinguisticTagger.Options.omitPunctuation.rawValue |
NSLinguisticTagger.Options.omitWhitespace.rawValue
    let tagger = NSLinguisticTagger(tagSchemes:
NSLinguisticTagger.availableTagSchemes(forLanguage: "en"), options:
Int(options))
    tagger.string = string
    let range = NSRange(location: 0, length: string.utf16.count)
    var resultTokens = [String?]()
    let queryOptions = NSLinguisticTagger.Options(rawValue: options)
```

Using POS tagger to remove all word types that are not playable:

```
    let posToPreserve: Set<NSLinguisticTag> = Set([.noun, .verb,
.adjective, .adverb, .interjection, .idiom, .otherWord])
    for scheme in tagSchemes {
        var i = 0
        tagger.enumerateTags(in: range, scheme: scheme, options:
queryOptions)
        { (tag, range1, _, _) in
            defer { i+=1 }
            guard let tag = tag else {
                // Preserve total count of tokens.
                if scheme == .tokenType { resultTokens.append(nil) }
                return
            }
            switch scheme {
            case .tokenType:
```

Save only words while keeping the total count of tokens:

```
            let token = string.substring(with: string.range(from:
range1)!)
            if tag == .word {
                resultTokens.append(token)
            } else {
                resultTokens.append(nil)
            }
            case .lemma:
```

If a word has a lemma, save it:

```
                resultTokens[i] = tag.rawValue
            case .lexicalClass:
                // Using POS tagger to remove all word types that are not
playable.
                if !posToPreserve.contains(tag) {
                    resultTokens[i] = nil
                }
            default:
                break
            }
        }
    }
```

This is again a workaround to make NSLinguisticTagger's lemmatizer work with short sentences:

```
    var result = resultTokens.flatMap{$0}
    print(result)
    result.removeLast()
    result.removeLast()
    return result
}
}
```

Word2Vec on iOS

The original implementation is written in C, so I added a simple Objective-C wrapper:

```
@interface W2VDistance : NSObject

- (void)loadBinaryVectorFile:(NSURL * _Nonnull) fileURL
                        error:(NSError *_Nullable* _Nullable) error;

- (NSDictionary <NSString *, NSNumber *>  *
_Nullable)closestToWord:(NSString * _Nonnull) word
numberOfClosest:(NSNumber * _Nullable) numberOfClosest;

- (NSDictionary <NSString *, NSNumber *>  *
_Nullable)analogyToPhrase:(NSString * _Nonnull) phrase
numberOfClosest:(NSNumber * _Nullable) numberOfClosest;

@end
private func getW2VAnalogy(sentence: String) -> String? {
guard let words = word2VecProvider?.analogy(toPhrase: sentence,
```

```
numberOfClosest: 1)?.keys else {
    return nil
}
return Array(words).last
}

private func getW2VWord(word: String) -> String? {
guard let words = word2VecProvider?.closest(toWord: word, numberOfClosest:
1)?.keys else {
    return nil
}
return Array(words).last
}
```

Text-to-speech output

The code is as follows:

```
import Speech

class SpeechSynthesizer: NSObject, AVSpeechSynthesizerDelegate {
static var shared = SpeechSynthesizer()

private var synthesizer = AVSpeechSynthesizer()
var voice = AVSpeechSynthesisVoice(language: "en-US")

public func prepare() {
    let dummyUtterance = AVSpeechUtterance(string: " ")
    dummyUtterance.voice = AVSpeechSynthesisVoice(language: "en-US")
    synthesizer.speak(dummyUtterance)
}

public func speakAloud(word: String) {
    if synthesizer.isSpeaking {
        synthesizer.stopSpeaking(at: .immediate)
    }
    let utterance = AVSpeechUtterance(string: word)
    utterance.rate = 0.4
    utterance.preUtteranceDelay = 0.1;
    utterance.postUtteranceDelay = 0.1;
    utterance.voice = self.voice
    synthesizer.speak(utterance)
}

public func speechSynthesizer(_ synthesizer: AVSpeechSynthesizer, didStart
utterance: AVSpeechUtterance) {
```

```
}

public func speechSynthesizer(_ synthesizer: AVSpeechSynthesizer, didFinish
utterance: AVSpeechUtterance) {
}

public func speechSynthesizer(_ synthesizer: AVSpeechSynthesizer, didCancel
utterance: AVSpeechUtterance) {
}
}
```

UIReferenceLibraryViewController

The code is as follows:

```
let hasDefinition =
UIReferenceLibraryViewController.dictionaryHasDefinition(forTerm: term)
if hasDefinition {
    let referenceController = UIReferenceLibraryViewController(term: term)
navigationController?.pushViewController(referenceController, animated:
true)
}
```

Figure 10.7: Reference library view controller user interface

Putting it all together

The code is as follows:

```
private func recognitionEnded() {
recordButton.isEnabled = true
recordButton.setTitle("Listen", for: [])
let result = self.recognitionResult

let words: [String]
if allLowercase {
    words = result.split(separator: "
").map(String.init).map{$0.lowercased()}
} else {
    words = NLPPreprocessor.preprocess(inputString: result) { error in
        messages.append(result)
        messages.append("This doesn't look like English.")
        reloadTable()
    }
}

let wordCount = words.count

var stringToPassToW2V: String
var stringToShowInUI: String
switch wordCount {
case 1:
    stringToPassToW2V = String(words.last!)
    stringToShowInUI = String(words.last!)
case 2:
    let wordPair = Array(words.suffix(2))
    stringToPassToW2V = "(wordPair[0]) (wordPair[1])"
    stringToShowInUI = "(wordPair[0]) - (wordPair[1])"
case 3...:
    let wordTriplet = Array(words.suffix(3))
    stringToPassToW2V = "(wordTriplet[0]) (wordTriplet[1])
(wordTriplet[2])"
    stringToShowInUI = "(wordTriplet[0]) - (wordTriplet[1]) +
(wordTriplet[2])"
default:
    print("Warning: wrong number of input words.")
    return
}
print(stringToPassToW2V)
messages.append(stringToShowInUI)
reloadTable()
```

```
DispatchQueue.main.async() { [weak self] in
    guard let `self` = self else { return }
    var response: String?
    if wordCount > 1 {
        response = self.getW2VAnalogy(sentence:
stringToPassToW2V)?.capitalized
    } else {
        response = self.getW2VWord(word: stringToPassToW2V)?.capitalized
    }
    if response?.isEmpty ?? true || response == "``" {
        response = "I don't know this word."
    }
//              SpeechSynthesizer.shared.speakAloud(word: response!)
    self.messages.append(response!)
    self.reloadTable()
    print(response!)
}
}

private func gotNewWord(string: String) {
recognitionResult = string
}
```

Word2Vec friends and relatives

GloVE, Lexvec FastText.

One popular alternative to word2vec is GloVe (Global Vectors).

Doc2Vec - Efficient Vector Representation for Documents Through Corruption.

https://openreview.net/pdf?id=B1Igu2ogg

https://github.com/mchen24/iclr2017

Both models learn geometrical encodings (vectors) of words from their co-occurrence information (how frequently they appear together in large text corpora). They differ in that word2vec is a "predictive" model, whereas GloVe is a "count-based" model. See this paper for more on the distinctions between these two approaches: http://clic.cimec.unitn.it/ marco

Predictive models learn their vectors in order to improve their predictive ability of Loss(target word | context words; Vectors), that is, the loss of predicting the target words from the context words given the vector representations. In Word2Vec, this is cast as a feed-forward neural network and optimized as such using SGD, and so on.

Count-based models learn their vectors by essentially doing dimensionality reduction on the co-occurrence counts matrix. They first construct a large matrix of (words x context) co-occurrence information, that is, for each "word" (the rows), you count how frequently we see this word in some "context" (the columns) in a large corpus. The number of "contexts" is of course large, since it is essentially combinatorial in size. So then they factorize this matrix to yield a lower-dimensional (word x features) matrix, where each row now yields a vector representation for each word. In general, this is done by minimizing a "reconstruction loss" which tries to find the lower-dimensional representations which can explain most of the variance in the high-dimensional data. In the specific case of GloVe, the counts matrix is preprocessed by normalizing the counts and log-smoothing them. This turns out to be A Good Thing in terms of the quality of the learned representations.

However, as pointed out, when we control for all the training hyper-parameters, the embeddings generated using the two methods tend to perform very similarly in downstream NLP tasks. The additional benefits of GloVe over word2vec is that it is easier to parallelize the implementation which means it's easier to train over more data, which, with these models, is always A Good Thing.

Another related technique is latent semantic analysis. macOS SDK includes its implementation as Latent Semantic Mapping framework. LSM algorithm takes text documents (a lot of them), calculates term frequency vectors, and reduces the dimensionality of the obtained vector space. Having such space, you can then determine the topic of previously unseen documents, or calculate, how similar two documents are. Latent semantic mapping powers Junk Mail Filter, Parental Controls, Kanji Text Input, and Help in macOS. You can use it to improve such features as document search, sorting, filtering, classification and retrieval.

macOS includes command line tool lsm:

```
https://developer.apple.com/legacy/library/documentation/Darwin/Reference/
ManPages/man1/lsm.1.html
```

```
http://www.extinguishedscholar.com/wpglob/?p=297
```

```
https://en.wikipedia.org/wiki/Latent_semantic_analysis
```

Watch WWDC 2011 session *Latent Semantic Mapping: Exposing the Meaning behind Words and Documents* for more details of the API and algorithm as well as for general useful advices on doing machine learning:

```
https://developer.apple.com/videos/play/wwdc2011/136/
```

Where to go from here?

Word embeddings are such an elegant idea that they immediately became an indispensable part of many applications in NLP and other domains. Here are several possible directions for your further exploration:

- You can easily transform the *Word Association* game into a question-answer system by replacing vectors of words with vectors of sentences. The simplest way to get the sentence vectors is by adding all the word vectors together. Interestingly, such sentence vectors still keep the semantics, so you can use them to find similar sentences.
- Using clustering on embedding vectors, you can separate words, sentences, and documents into groups by similarity.
- As we have mentioned, Word2Vec vectors are popular as parts of the more complex NLP pipelines. For example, you can feed them into a neural network or some other machine learning algorithm. In this way, you can train a classifier for pieces of text, for example, to recognize text sentiments or topics.
- Word2Vec itself is just a compression algorithm; it doesn't know anything about languages or people. You can run it on anything similar to natural text and get equally good results: Code2Vec, Logs2Vec, Playlist2Vec, and so on.

Summary

For developing applications that can understand voice or text input, we use techniques from the natural language processing domain. We have just seen several widely used ways to preprocess texts: tokenization, stop words removal, stemming, lemmatization, POS tagging, and named entity recognition.

Word embedding algorithms, and mainly Word2Vec, draw inspiration from the distributive semantics hypothesis, which states that the meaning of the word is defined by its context. Using an autoencoder-like neural network, we learn fixed-size vectors for each word in a text corpus. Effectively, this neural network captures the context of the word and encodes it in the corresponding vector. Then, using linear algebra operations with those vectors, we can discover different interesting relationships between words. For example, it allows us to find semantically close words (cosine similarity between vectors).

In the next section of the book, we are going to dig deeper into some practical questions of machine learning. We will start with an overview of existing iOS-compatible machine learning libraries.

11
Machine Learning Libraries

This chapter is an overview of existing iOS-compatible libraries for machine learning. We will look at important general-purpose machine learning libraries, frameworks, and APIs, as well as some domain-specific libraries.

In this chapter, we will cover the following topics:

- What third-party ML libraries and APIs are available for iOS developers
- Overview of some existing Swift-compatible ML libraries and their features
- How to use non-Swift libraries in Swift iOS project
- What low-level acceleration libraries are available for iOS

Machine learning and AI APIs

When adding artificial intelligence to your application, it's not always necessary to write something from scratch, or even use a library. Many cloud providers offer data processing and analysis as a service. Almost all internet giants provide machine learning in the cloud in some form. In addition, plenty of smaller players are present in the market, and they often provide services of comparable quality at a similar cost. The greatest drawback of such small companies is that they tend to be rapidly acquired by major players. After that, their services are being merged with the services of the big companies (at best), or just being closed (at worst).

The range of such services is constantly growing and changing, so I do not see much point in a detailed consideration of these services in this book. I provide a list of services here that have not disappeared during the last year, and are unlikely to vanish in the coming year:

- **Amazon Machine Learning** provides general-purpose machine learning. Go to: `https://aws.amazon.com/documentation/machine-learning/`.
- **Google Cloud Platform** provides general-purpose machine learning, computer vision, NLP, speech recognition, text translation, and so on. Go to: `https://cloud.google.com/products/machine-learning/`.
- **IBM Watson** services include NLP, text to speech, speech to text, computer vision, and data analytics. Go to: `http://www.ibm.com/watson/developercloud/`.
- **Microsoft Cognitive Services** include computer vision, speech recognition, NLP, search, bot framework, and others. Go to: `https://www.microsoft.com/cognitive-services/en-us/apis`.
- **Microsoft Azure Machine Learning** is a cloud-based engine for training and deploying your own models. Go to: `https://azure.microsoft.com/en-us/services/machine-learning/`.
- **Wit.ai** (acquired by Facebook) provides speech recognition and intents understanding. Go to: `https://wit.ai/`.

Libraries

As iOS developers, we are primarily interested in compatible high-performance libraries with a low memory footprint. Swift is a relatively young programming language, so the libraries for machine learning written in it are mostly amateur attempts. However, several more professional and actively growing Swift machine learning packages already exist.

Still, it would be unwise to neglect libraries written in other iOS-compatible languages such as Objective-C, C, C ++, Lua, and JavaScript, because often they are much more mature and have a broad community. Several reliable cross-platform libraries are worth mentioning in this context.

Importing C libraries into your Swift code is straightforward: you can read about C-Swift interoperability at Apple's Developer portal. Technically, C++ libraries are not compatible with Swift, but you can bridge them via Objective-C so that no C++ or Objective-C++ headers are visible to Swift. Fortunately, Objective C integrates with C++ smoothly.

Lua can be compiled as a standalone C library and can be included in the project. You can use JavaScript libraries with the help of the `CoreJavaScript` framework from iOS SDK.

General-purpose machine learning libraries

In the following comparison tables, I have included around twenty libraries for machine learning. I considered such characteristics as the language of implementation and interface, the availability and type of acceleration, license type, ongoing development status, and compatibility with popular package managers. Later in this chapter, we will look at the unique features of each library in more detail.

Table 2.1: Comparison of general-purpose machine learning libraries for iOS (part 1):

Library	Language	Algorithms
AIToolbox	Swift	LinReg, LogReg, GMM, MDP, SVM, NN, PCA, k-means, genetic algorithms, DL: LSTM, CNN.
BrainCore	Swift	DL: FF, LSTM.
Caffe, Caffe2, MXNet, TensorFlow, tiny-dnn	C++	DL.
dlib	C++	Bayesian networks, SVMs, regressions, structured prediction, DL, clustering and other unsupervised, semi-supervised, reinforcement learning, feature selection.
FANN	C	NNs.
LearnKit	ObjC	Anomaly detection, collaborative filtering, decision trees, random forest, k-means, kNN, regressions, naive Bayes, NNs, PCA, SVMs.
MLKit	Swift	Regressions, genetic algorithms, k-means, NN.
multilinear-math	Swift	Multilinear PCA, multilinear subspace learning, LinReg, LogReg, FF NN.
OpenCV (`ml` module)	C++	Normal Bayes, kNN, SVM, decision trees, boosting, gradient boosted trees, random trees, extremely randomized trees, expectation-maximization, NN, hierarchical clustering.

Shark	C++	Supervised: Linear discriminant analysis, LinReg, SVMs, FF and recurrent NNs, radial basis function networks, regularization networks, Gaussian processes, kNN, decision trees, random forests. Unsupervised: PCA, RBM, hierarchical clustering, evolutionary algorithms.
Swix	Swift	SVM, kNN, PCA.
Torch	Lua	DL.
YCML	ObjC	LinReg, SVM, extreme learning machines, forward selection, kernel process regression, binary RBM, feature learning, ranking, and others.

Table 2.2: Comparison of general-purpose machine learning libraries for iOS (part 2):

Library	Acceleration	License	Development	Package Manager
AIToolbox	Accelerate, Metal	Apache-2.0	Active	-
BrainCore	Metal	MIT	Inactive	CocoaPods, Carthage
Caffe	-/CUDA	BSD-2-Clause	Active	hunter
Caffe2	Metal/NNPack	Custom, BSD-like	Active	CocoaPods
dlib	-	Boost	Active	hunter
FANN	-	LGPL	Inactive	CocoaPods
LearnKit	Accelerate	MIT	Active	-
MLKit	-	MIT	Active	Carthage
multilinear-math	Metal	Apache	Active	Swift Package Manager
MXNet	-/ CUDA, OpenMP,	Apache-2.0	Active	-
OpenCV (ml module)	Accelerate/ CUDA, OpenCL, and others	BSD-3-Clause	Active	CocoaPods, hunter

Shark	-	GPL-3.0	Inactive	CocoaPods
Swix	Accelerate, OpenCV	MIT	Inactive	-
TensorFlow	?/ CUDA	Apache-2.0	Active	-
tiny-dnn	-/CUDA, OpenCL, OpenMP, and others	BSD-3-Clause	Active	hunter
Torch	-/ CUDA, OpenCL	BSD-3-Clause	Active	-
YCML	Accelerate	GPL-3.0	Active	-

The following is the list of abbreviations:

- **Convolution neural networks (CNN)**
- **Deep learning (DL)**
- **Feed-forward (FF)**
- **Gaussian mixture model (GMM)**
- **K-nearest neighbors (KNN)**
- **Linear regression (LinReg)**
- **Logistic regression (LogReg)**
- **Long short-term memory (LSTM)**
- **Markov decision process (MDP)**
- **Neural network (NN)**
- **Principal components analysis (PCA)**
- **Support vector machine (SVM)**

Package managers

- Carthage: https://github.com/Carthage/Carthage
- CocoaPods: https://cocoapods.org/
- Hunter: https://github.com/ruslo/hunter
- Swift Package Manager: https://swift.org/package-manager/

AIToolbox

The Swift library contains multiple machine learning models. They are compatible with both iOS and macOS. All models are implemented as separate classes with unified interfaces, so you can replace one model with another in your code with minimal effort. Some models support saving to `plist` files and loading from such files. The Accelerate framework is used throughout the library to boost the speed of calculations.

For regression tasks, you can choose between linear, nonlinear, and SVM regression. Linear regression supports regularization. The SVM model here is a port of the `libSVM` library initially written in C and can also be used for classification. Other classification algorithms include logistic regression and neural networks. Several types of nonlinearities for neural network layers are present (including convolutions). Your network can be a simple feedforward or recurrent (including LSTM) network, or can combine both types of layers. The Metal framework is used to accelerate neural networks. You can train your networks online or in batch mode.

Unsupervised learning algorithms implemented in the AIToolbox are PCA, K-means, and Gaussian mixture model. MDP can be used for reinforcement learning. Other AI primitives and algorithms present in the library include graphs and trees, alpha-beta algorithms, genetic algorithms, and constraint propagation.

The library also provides handy classes for plotting descendants from UIView and NSView. There are several modes of plotting such as those to represent functions, classification or regression data, and classification areas. There are also classes for model validation or hyperparameter tuning, like k-fold validation.

GitHub repository: `https://github.com/KevinCoble/AIToolbox`

BrainCore

This Swift library provides feedforward and recurrent neural networks. Several types of layers are present, including the inner product layer, the linear rectifier (ReLU) layer, the sigmoid layer, the RNN and LSTM layer and the L2 loss layer. BrainCore uses Metal acceleration for both training and inference stages. The definition of a new neural network looks very clear because of some pleasant syntactic sugar:

```
let net = Net.build {
    [dataLayer1, dataLayer2] => lstmLayer
    lstmLayer =>> ipLayer1 => reluLayer1 => sinkLayer1
    lstmLayer =>> ipLayer2 => reluLayer2 => sinkLayer2
}
```

The library can be used on both iOS and macOS. It uses the Upsurge mathematical library as a dependency. It is available via CocoaPods or Carthage.

GitHub repository: `https://github.com/aleph7/BrainCore`

Caffe

Caffe is one of the most popular deep learning frameworks. It is written in C++.

From the official site:

> *"Caffe is a deep learning framework made with expression, speed, and modularity in mind. It is developed by the Berkeley Vision and Learning Center (BVLC) and by community contributors."*

The library is primarily targeted at Linux and macOS X but unofficial Android, iOS, and Windows ports are also compatible. Caffe supports CUDA acceleration but can also be executed on the CPU alone. On iOS, it uses only CPU. The interfaces include C++, command line, Python, and MATLAB. Caffe provides recurrent and convolutional neural networks. To define a network, you need to describe its structure in a `config` file in a special format.

ModelZoo contains many pre-trained Caffe models. Unlike MXNet, Torch, and TensorFlow, it doesn't have automatic differentiation features.

Official site: http://caffe.berkeleyvision.org
iOS port from the BrainCore author: https://github.com/aleph7/caffe

Caffe2

Caffe2 is a mobile-first deep learning library from Facebook, and started as an attempt to refactor the original Caffe framework. It uses Metal for computation acceleration on the iOS and provides more flexibility than Caffe. For example, it includes recurrent neural networks.

Official site: https://caffe2.ai/

dlib

dlib is a mature C++ machine learning library with a big community. It includes many advanced ML algorithms that are not present in any other iOS-compatible libraries. It also contains different useful additions, like metaprogramming, compression algorithms, and functions for digital signal and image processing. Porting dlib to iOS is relatively straightforward—you need to delete UI and HTTP-related files and then you'll be able to compile it for iOS.

Official site: http://dlib.net/

FANN

The **FANN** (Fast Artificial Neural Network) library is a C implementation of multilayer neural networks. It includes different types of training (backpropagation, evolving topology) and different activation functions. Trained networks can be saved and loaded from file. It is well documented and has bindings to many programming languages. To connect it to your iOS project, use CocoaPods.

Official site: `http://leenissen.dk/fann/wp/`

LearnKit

LearnKit is a Cocoa framework written in Objective-C for machine learning. It currently runs on top of the Accelerate framework on iOS and OS X. It supports a big variety of algorithms.

GitHub repository: `https://github.com/mattrajca/LearnKit`

MLKit

MLKit provides several regression algorithms: linear, polynomial and ridge regression (+ L2 regularization), lasso regression, k-means, genetic algorithms, and simple neural networks. It also includes classes for data splitting and k-fold model validation. MLKit uses the Upsurge mathematical library as a dependency.

GitHub repository: `https://github.com/Somnibyte/MLKit`

Multilinear-math

The name refers to the tensor operations that this library provides. It also contains a set of machine learning and AI primitives. Its algorithms include principal component analysis, multilinear subspace learning algorithms for dimensionality reduction, linear and logistic regression, stochastic gradient descent, feedforward neural networks, sigmoid, ReLU, Softplus activation functions, and regularizations.

It also provides a Swift interface to the Accelerate framework and LAPACK, including vector and matrix operations, eigen decomposition, and SVD. On top of that, it implements the `MultidimensionData` protocol to work with multidimensional data.

GitHub
repository: `https://github.com/vincentherrmann/multilinear-math`

MXNet

Quote from the official site:

"MXNet is a deep learning framework designed for both efficiency and flexibility."

MXNet is compatible with Linux, macOS, Windows, Android, iOS, and JavaScript. Its interfaces include C++, Python, Julia, Matlab, JavaScript, Go, R, and Scala. MXNet supports automatic differentiation and acceleration using OpenMP and CUDA. MXNet is well documented and has a long list of tutorials and examples at its official site. The official site hosts its own Model Zoo with pre-trained neural networks. You can also convert pre-trained Caffe models using the `caffe_converter` tool.

Official site: `http://mxnet.readthedocs.org/en/latest/`

Shark

Shark is written in C++. It provides methods for linear and nonlinear optimization (evolutionary and gradient-based algorithms), SVMs and neural networks, regression algorithms, decision trees, random forests, and a wide range of unsupervised learning algorithms. An older version of Shark is available on CocoaPod.

Official
site: `http://image.diku.dk/shark/sphinx_pages/build/html/index.htm`
`l`
CocoaPods: `https://cocoapods.org/pods/Shark-SDK`

TensorFlow

TensorFlow is a library for numerical computation from Google. It is widely used for deep learning and more traditional statistical learning. The library architecture is built around data flow graphs. The TensorFlow website states that:

> *"Nodes in the graph represent mathematical operations, while the graph edges represent the multidimensional data arrays (tensors) communicated between them. The flexible architecture allows you to deploy computation to one or more CPUs or GPUs in a desktop, server, or mobile device with a single API."*

The library is so well documented that you can learn ML from scratch using only TensorFlow. The official site includes tons of tutorials, video courses, example apps for different platforms (including iOS), and pre-trained models. Two officially supported APIs are in Python and C++ (limited). It supports acceleration on CUDA GPUs and automatic differentiation. You can convert pre-trained Caffe models using the `caffe-tensorflow` tool.

 Official site: `http://www.tensorflow.org/`

tiny-dnn

tiny-dnn is a header-only convolutional neural network framework written in C++.

The following is an example of neural network creation from the official documentation:

```
network<sequential> net;
// add layers
net << conv<tan_h>(32, 32, 5, 1, 6)   // in:32x32x1, 5x5conv, 6fmaps
    << ave_pool<tan_h>(28, 28, 6, 2)  // in:28x28x6, 2x2pooling
    << fc<tan_h>(14 * 14 * 6, 120)    // in:14x14x6, out:120
    << fc<identity>(120, 10);         // in:120,     out:10
```

You can train your models or you can convert pre-trained Caffe models using the `caffe_converter` tool. It supports a handful of acceleration types. OpenCV is a dependency for iOS. You can find an iOS example on tiny-dnn's GitHub repository.

GitHub repository: `https://github.com/tiny-dnn/tiny-dnn`

Torch

Torch is a framework for scientific computations with wide support for machine learning written in Lua. It is one of the most popular deep learning frameworks. Its supported platforms are Linux, macOS, Windows, Android, and iOS, and it also supports acceleration with CUDA and OpenCL (partially). There are numerous third-party packages that introduce additional capabilities to Torch. Autograd introduces automatic differentiation, `nn` package allows construct neural networks from simple building blocks, the `rnn` package provides recurrent neural networks, and iTorch provides interoperability with IPython Notebook. The Caffe model can be loaded using the `loadcaffe` package. Its library is well documented and easy to install.

The main problem for Swift developers will be the Lua language itself, because its paradigm is quite different from Swift's one; however, there are libraries that introduce strong typing and functional capabilities to Lua to make life less painful.

Official site: `http://torch.ch/`
Unofficial iOS port: `https://github.com/clementfarabet/torch-ios`

YCML

YCML is a machine learning framework for Objective-C and Swift (macOS and iOS).

From the documentation at official site: `http://yconst.com/software/ycml/`:

> *"The following algorithms are currently available: Gradient Descent Backpropagation, Resilient Backpropagation (RProp), Extreme Learning Machines (ELM), Forward Selection using Orthogonal Least Squares (for RBF Net), also with the PRESS statistic, Binary Restricted Boltzmann Machines (CD & PCD, Untested!). YCML also contains some optimization algorithms as support for deriving predictive models, although they can be used for any kind of problem: Gradient Descent (Single-Objective, Unconstrained), RProp Gradient Descent (Single-Objective, Unconstrained), NSGA-II (Multi-Objective, Constrained)."*

Inference-only libraries

With the release of iOS 11, several popular machine learning frameworks became compatible with it on the model level. You can build and train your models with these frameworks, then export them in a framework-specific format and convert them to the CoreML format for future integration with your app. Such models have fixed parameters and can be used only for inference. As Xcode generates a separate Swift class for each of those models, there is no way to replace or update them in the runtime. The main usage area for such models are different pattern-recognizing applications, like *count your calories by taking a photo*. At the time of writing this book (iOS 11 Beta), CoreML is compatible with the following libraries and models:

- **Caffe 1.0**: Neural networks
- **Keras 1.2.2**: Neural networks
- **libSVM 3.22**: SVM
- **scikit-learn 0.18.1**: Tree ensembles, generalized linear models, SVM, feature engineering, and pipelines
- **XGBoost 0.6**: Gradient-boosted trees

All these libraries are long-standing industrial standards.

 Check the official package documentation for the latest information: http://pythonhosted.org/coremltools/

There were also several attempts to implement deep inference on top of the Metal framework prior to Core ML's release:

- DeepLearningKit
- Espresso
- Forge
- Bender

Forge and Bender are still active, because they provide more flexible and clean API than MPS CNN Graph. They will likely become obsolete in the near future, as Apple keeps adding more and more features to Metal Performance Shaders.

Keras

Keras is a popular Python package for building deep learning neural networks. It has a user-friendly syntax. It's easy and fast to prototype and build your deep models in. It started as a facade for the Theano symbolic computation library, but with time, it also got a TensorFlow backend and finally became a part of TensorFlow. So now, TensorFlow is a default backend, but you still have an option to switch back to Theano. There are also work-in-progress projects on MXNet and CNTK backends.

Keras contains functions for pre-processing most common data types, which include images, texts, and time series.

CoreML supports convolution and recurrent neural networks built in Keras.

 Website: `https://keras.io/`

LibSVM

Classification, regression, distribution estimation, and anomaly detection, for more information refer to: `https://www.csie.ntu.edu.tw/~cjlin/libsvm/`.

Scikit-learn

You'll be familiar with this library if you have read the previous chapters. It contains a large set of general-purpose learners and data preprocessing methods. Its documentation is awesome.

CoreML supports random forests, generalized linear models, and data built in scikit-learn. For more information refer to: `http://scikit-learn.org/`.

XGBoost

When I started writing this book, I didn't expect to write about this tool. Why? Because this is a heavy artillery of machine learning contests. XGBoost is a production standard in many areas, but it is very resource consuming during the training phase: all your gigabytes will be consumed in the blink of an eye. That's why it is mainly used on servers and clusters of servers for web-ranking and other heavy-lifting tasks. It is also a tool that's considered to be a silver bullet for winning a Kaggle machine learning competition (if it's not about computer vision). CoreML supports gradient-boosting decision trees trained in XGBoost. For more information refer to: `https://xgboost.readthedocs.io/en/latest/`.

NLP libraries

In this section we will discuss the various NLP libraries:

Word2Vec

This is the original C implementation of the Word2Vec algorithm. It works on iOS, but consumes a significant amount of memory. It was released under the Apache 2.0 license.

Google repository: `https://code.google.com/p/word2vec/`

Twitter text

Parsing tweets is a common task in NLP. Tweets usually contain some unusual language (like usernames), they mention headers, hashtags, cashtags, and so on. Twitter provides an Objective-C API for tweet processing. This has nothing to do with machine learning per se, but it is still a useful tool for data preprocessing.

GitHub repository: `https://github.com/twitter/twitter-text`

Speech recognition

In this section, we will discuss the frequently used libraries for speech recognition.

TLSphinx

From the documentation:

> *"TLSphinx is a Swift wrapper around Pocketsphinx, a portable library, that allow an application to perform speech recognition without the audio ever leaving the device."*

It was released under the MIT license.

 GitHub repository: `https://github.com/tryolabs/TLSphinx`

OpenEars

This free iOS library provides speech recognition and text-to-speech for Chinese, French, Spanish, English, Dutch, Italian, and German languages. The models were released under different licenses, with some of them being commercially-friendly. It has an Objective-C and Swift APIs. Paid plugins are available.

 Official site: `http://www.politepix.com/openears/`

Computer vision

Under this section let us look at few computer vision libraries in detail:

OpenCV

OpenCV is a library of computer vision algorithms, image processing, and general-purpose numerical algorithms. It is implemented in C/C++ but has interfaces for Python, Java, Ruby, Matlab, Lua, and other languages. It can be freely used for academic and commercial purposes because it is distributed under the BSD license.

Since OpenCV 3.1, there is a DNN module and in OpenCV 3.3, the module has been promoted to `opencv_contrib`.

Official site: `http://opencv.org`
Additional OpenCV modules: `https://github.com/opencv/opencv_contrib`
Demo Swift app using
OpenCV: `https://github.com/foundry/OpenCVSwiftStitch`

CCV

ccv is another C++ computer vision library for iOS, macOS, Android, Linux FreeBSD, and Windows. It is distributed under the BSD three-clause license.

From the official site:

"One core concept of ccv development is application driven. Thus, ccv ends up implementing a handful state-of-art algorithms. It includes a close to state-of-the-art image classifier, a state-of-the-art frontal face detector, reasonable collection of object detectors for pedestrians and cars, a useful text detection algorithm, a long-term general object tracking algorithm, and the long-standing feature point extraction algorithm."

Official site: `http://libccv.org/`

OpenFace

OpenFace is a state-of-the-art open source library that deals with faces. It includes algorithms for facial landmark detection, eye gaze estimation, head pose estimation, and facial action unit recognition.

GitHub repository: https://github.com/TadasBaltrusaitis/OpenFace
Unofficial iOS port: https://github.com/FaceAR/OpenFaceIOS

Tesseract

Tesseract is an open source tool for **optical character recognition** (OCR) written in C++. It has bindings to many programming languages, including two for Objective-C. You can use it to train your own model or you can use one of the community-trained models (including Ancient Greek, Latin, Hebrew, Farsi, and Polish). The latest version of Tesseract uses the LSTM neural network for character recognition. The library is available under the Apache-2.0 license.

GitHub repository: https://github.com/tesseract-ocr/tesseract

Low-level subroutine libraries

Some libraries are not doing machine learning on their own, but provide important low-level primitives for it. An example of such a library is Apple BNNS. It is a part of the Accelerate framework which provides highly optimized subroutines for convolutional neural networks. We'll discuss it in much detail in Chapter 10, *Natural Language Processing*. In the following section, we'll list some third-party libraries of its kind.

Eigen

Eigen is a C++ template library implementing linear algebra primitives and related algorithms. It is under the LGPL3+ license. Many popular computationally-heavy projects (TensorFlow, for instance) rely on it for matrix and vector operations.

 Official site: `eigen.tuxfamily.org`

fmincg-c

fmincg-c conjugates gradient implementation in C. It uses OpenCL to process algorithms faster. There are some examples written in Python.

 GitHub repository: `https://github.com/gautambhatrcb/fmincg-c`

IntuneFeatures

Audio feature extraction. The IntuneFeatures framework contains code to generate features from audio files and feature labels from the respective MIDI files. It currently supports these features: Log-scale spectrum power estimate by bands, spectrum power flux, peak power, peak power flux, and peak locations.

The `CompileFeatures` command line app takes audio and MIDI files as input and generates HDF5 databases with the features and the labels. These HDF5 files can then be used to train a neural network for transcription or related tasks.

 GitHub repository: `https://github.com/venturemedia/intune-features`

SigmaSwiftStatistics

This library is a collection of functions that perform statistical calculations in Swift. It can be used in Swift apps for Apple devices and in open source Swift programs on other platforms.

GitHub
repository: https://github.com/evgenyneu/SigmaSwiftStatistics

STEM

STEM is a Swift Tensor library for machine learning in some way similar to Torch. It provides tensors, operations on them, random tensors generation, computational graphs, and optimization.

GitHub repository: https://github.com/abeschneider/stem

Swix

Swix is an attempt to implement the NumPy mathematical library in Swift. It wraps OpenCV for some machine learning algorithms and provides Swift API with the Accelerate framework.

GitHub repository: https://github.com/scottsievert/swix

LibXtract

LibXtract is a simple, portable, lightweight library of audio feature extraction functions. The purpose of the library is to provide a relatively exhaustive set of feature extraction primitives that are designed to be 'cascaded' to create extraction hierarchies.

For example, variance, average deviation, skewness, and kurtosis all require the mean of the input vector to be precomputed. However, rather than compute the mean and inside of each function, it is expected that the mean will be passed in as an argument. This means that if the user wishes to use all of these features, the mean is calculated only once, and then passed to any functions that require it.

This philosophy of **cascading** features is followed throughout the library; for example, with features that operate on the magnitude spectrum of a signal vector (for example, irregularity). The magnitude spectrum is not calculated inside the respective function; instead, a pointer to the first element in an array containing the magnitude spectrum is passed in as an argument.

Hopefully this not only makes the library more efficient when computing a large number of features, but also makes it more flexible because extraction functions can be combined arbitrarily (one can take the irregularity of the Mel Frequency Cepstral Coefficients, for example).

A complete list of features can be found by viewing the header files, or reading the doxygen documentation, available with this package.

 GitHub repository: https://github.com/jamiebullock/LibXtract.

libLBFGS

GitHub repository: https://github.com/chokkan/liblbfgs

L-BFGS method of numerical optimization.

NNPACK

NNPACK is an Acceleration package for neural networks on multi-core CPUs. Caffe2, tiny-dnn, and MXNet support NNPACK acceleration. Prisma uses this library in the mobile app to boost performance.

 GitHub repository: `https://github.com/Maratyszcza/NNPACK`.

Upsurge

Upsurge is a SIMD-accelerated Swift library. It is a math utility for matrices, tensors, operators, and functions from the Accelerate framework, much like convolution. Matrix operations are its strength.

 GitHub repository: `https://github.com/aleph7/Upsurge`.

YCMatrix

YCMatrix is a Matrix operations Objective-C library. It is essentially a wrapper around the Accelerate framework. YCML uses it for all computation accelerations.

 GitHub repository: `https://github.com/yconst/YCMatrix`.

Choosing a deep learning framework

Choosing the correct deep learning framework is important to get the optimal speed and model size you desire. There are several things to consider—overhead, added by the library, GPU acceleration, do you need training or inference only?, in which framework existing solutions were implemented.

You should understand that you don't always need GPU acceleration. Sometimes, SIMD/Accelerate is more than enough to implement neural networks that do inference in real-time.

Sometimes, you have to consider whether the calculations are going to be done on the client side, on the server side, or if they will be balanced between both. Try to do benchmarks with an extreme number of records, and test them with different devices.

Summary

In this chapter, we learned about iOS compatible machine learning libraries and their features. We discussed five major deep learning frameworks: Caffe, TensorFlow, MXNet, and Torch, and so on. We also mentioned several smaller deep learning libraries and tools to convert deep learning models from one format to another. Among general purpose machine learning libraries, the most feature-rich and mature are AIToolbox, dlib, Shark, and YCML. NLP libraries for iOS are rare and restricted in their capabilities.

In addition to native iOS speech recognition and text-to-speech, there are several free and commercial libraries that provide the same functionality.

If you have some common computer vision tasks, you can find the appropriate algorithms in OpenCV or ccv libraries. OCR and all kinds of face-related tasks can also be performed using the open source toolchain. There are also several low-level libraries for linear algebra operations, tensors, and optimization that you can use to accelerate your ML algorithms.

12
Optimizing Neural Networks for Mobile Devices

Modern convolutional neural networks can be huge. For example, the pre-trained ResNet family network can be from 100 to 1,000 layers deep, and take from 138 MB to 0.5 GB in Torch data format. To deploy them to mobile or embedded devices can be problematic, especially if your app requires several models for different tasks. Also, CNNs are computationally heavy, and in some settings (for example, real-time video analysis) can drain device battery in no time. Actually, much faster than it took to write this chapter's intro. But why are they so big, and why do they consume so much energy? And how do we fix it without sacrificing accuracy?

As we've already discussed the speed optimization in the previous chapter, we are concentrating on the memory consumption in this chapter. We specifically focus on the deep learning neural networks, but we also give several general recommendations applicable to other kinds of machine learning models.

In this chapter, we will cover the following topics:

- Why compress the models?
- General recommendations for machine learning models compression
- Why deep neural networks are big
- What factors influence the size of a neural network?
- What parts of a neural network are the heaviest?
- Methods for model size reduction—parameter number reduction, pruning, trained quantization, and Huffman coding
- Compact CNN architectures

Delivering perfect user experience

According to the iTunes Connect Developer Guide, the total uncompressed size of the app should be less than 4 GB (as of December 15, 2017); however, this applies only to the binary itself, while asset files can take as much space as the disk capacity allows. There is also a limit on app size for the cellular download, as stated on the Apple Developer site (`https://developer.apple.com/news/?id=09192017b`):

> *"We've increased the cellular download limit from 100 MB to 150 MB, letting customers download more apps from the App Store over their cellular network."*

The simple conclusion is that you'd better store you model parameters as on-demand resources, or download them from your server after the app is already installed; but this is only one half of the problem. The other half is that you really don't want your app to take a lot of space and consume tons of traffic, because this is a bad user experience.

We can attack the problem from several directions (from the easiest to the most complex):

- Use standard lossless compression algorithms
- Choose the compact architectures
- Prevent models from growing too big
- Use lossy compression techniques—remove unimportant model parts

The first approach is only a half-measure, because you will still have to decompress your model in runtime. In the last case, we usually talk about reducing the number of the model's parameters, effectively reducing its capacity, and subsequently, accuracy.

Calculating the size of a convolutional neural network

Let's take some well-known CNN, say VGG16, and see in detail how exactly the memory is being spent. You can print the summary of it using Keras:

```
from keras.applications import VGG16
model = VGG16()
print(model.summary())
```

The network consists of 13 2D-convolutional layers (with 3×3 filters, stride 1 and pad 1) and 3 fully connected layers ("Dense"). Plus, there are an input layer, 5 max-pooling layers and a flatten layer, which do not hold parameters.

Layer	Output shape	Data memory	Parameters	Number of parameters
InputLayer	224×224×3	150528	0	0
Conv2D	224×224×64	3211264	3×3×3×64+64	1792
Conv2D	224×224×64	3211264	3×3×64×64+64	36928
MaxPool2D	112×112×64	802816	0	0
Conv2D	112×112×128	1605632	3×3×64×128+128	73856
Conv2D	112×112×128	1605632	3×3×128×128+128	147584
MaxPool2D	56×56×128	401408	0	0
Conv2D	56×56×256	802816	3×3×128×256+256	295168
Conv2D	56×56×256	802816	3×3×256×256+256	590080
Conv2D	56×56×256	802816	3×3×256×256+256	590080
MaxPool2D	28×28×256	200704	0	0
Conv2D	28×28×512	401408	3×3×256×512+512	1180160
Conv2D	28×28×512	401408	3×3×512×512+512	2359808
Conv2D	28×28×512	401408	3×3×512×512+512	2359808
MaxPool2D	14×14×512	100352	0	0
Conv2D	14×14×512	100352	3×3×512×512+512	2359808
Conv2D	14×14×512	100352	3×3×512×512+512	2359808
Conv2D	14×14×512	100352	3×3×512×512+512	2359808
MaxPool2D	7×7×512	25088	0	0
Flatten	25088	0	0	0
Dense	4096	4096	7×7×512×4096+4096	102764544
Dense	4096	4096	4097×4096	16781312
Dense	1000	1000	4097×1000	4097000

Total memory for data: Batch_size × 15,237,608 ≈ 15 M

???Total memory: Batch_size × 24M 5; 4 bytes ≈ 93 MB

Reference:

```
http://cs231n.github.io/convolutional-networks/#case
https://datascience.stackexchange.com/questions/17286/cnn-memory-consumption
```

Total parameters: 138,357,544≈138M

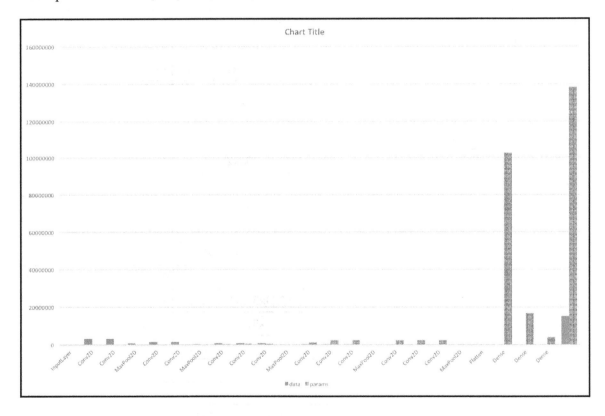

Lossless compression

A typical neural network contains a significant amount of redundant information. This enables us to apply both lossless and lossy compression to them, and often achieve fairly good results.

Huffman encoding is a type of compression that is commonly referred to in research papers concerning CNN compression. You can also use Apple compression or Facebook `zstd` libraries, which deliver state-of-the-art compression. Apple compression contains four compression algorithms (three common and one Apple-specific):

- LZ4 is the fastest of the four.
- ZLIB is standard zip archiving.
- LZMA is slower but delivers the best compression.
- LZFSE is a bit faster and delivers slightly better compression than ZLIB. It is optimized for the Apple hardware to be energy efficient.

Here is a code snippet for you to compress data using the LZFSE algorithm from the compression library, and decompress it back. You can find the full code in the `Compression.playground`:

```
import Compression
let data = ...
```

`sourceSize` holds the size of the data before compression:

```
let sourceSize = data.count
```

Allocating the buffer for the results of compression... we allocate it with the original (non-compressed) size:

```
let compressedBuffer = UnsafeMutablePointer<UInt8>.allocate(capacity:
sourceSize)
```

`compression_encode_buffer()` is the function used to compress your data. It takes the input and output buffers, their sizes, and the type of compression algorithm (`COMPRESSION_LZFSE`) and returns the size of compressed data:

```
var compressedSize: Int = 0
data.withUnsafeBytes { (sourceBuffer: UnsafePointer<UInt8>) in
compressedSize = compression_encode_buffer(compressedBuffer, sourceSize,
sourceBuffer, sourceSize, nil, COMPRESSION_LZFSE)
}
```

The `compressedSize` variable holds the size after compression.

Now, to the decompression. Here's how to allocate a buffer of appropriate size for uncompressed data:

```
var uncompressedBuffer = UnsafeMutablePointer<UInt8>.allocate(capacity:
sourceSize)
```

Again, the `compression_decode_buffer()` function returns the true size of the uncompressed data:

```
let uncompressedSize = compression_decode_buffer(uncompressedBuffer,
sourceSize, compressedBuffer, compressedSize, nil, COMPRESSION_LZFSE)
```

Converting the buffer to a normal data object:

```
let uncompressedData = Data(bytes: uncompressedBuffer, count:
uncompressedSize)
```

`uncompressedData.count` should be equal to the initial `sourceSize`.

For lossless compression to be effective, your network needs to have a lot of repetitive elements in its structure. This can be achieved using weights quantization of precision reduction (see the next section).

Apple lzfse compression library:

- `https://github.com/lzfse/lzfse`
- `https://developer.apple.com/reference/compression/data_compression`

Facebook zstd compression library:

- `https://github.com/facebook/zstd`
- `https://github.com/omniprog/SwiftZSTD`

Compact CNN architectures

During the inference, the whole neural network should be loaded into the memory, so as mobile developers we are especially interested in the small architectures, which consume as little memory as possible. Small neural networks also allow to reduce the bandwidth consumption when downloaded from the network.

Several architectures designed to reduce the size of convolutional neural networks have been proposed recently. We will discuss in brief several most known of them.

SqueezeNet

The architecture was proposed by Iandola et al. in 2017 for use in autonomous cars. As the baseline, researchers took the AlexNet architecture. This network takes 240 MB of memory, which is pretty much the equivalent of mobile devices. SqueezeNet has 50x fewer parameters, and achieves the same level of accuracy on the ImageNet dataset. Using additional compression, its size can be reduced to about 0.5 MB.

SqueezeNet is built from the fire modules. The objective was to create a neural network with a small number of parameters, but preserving the competitive level of accuracy. It was done with the following approaches:

- Reduce the network size by replacing the 3 x 3 filters with 1 x 1 filters. Here, by replacing the 3 x 3 filter with a 1 x 1 filter, we have an instant reduction in the number of parameters by 9x.
- Reduce the number of inputs for the remaining 3 x 3 filters. Here, the number of parameters are reduced by merely reducing the number of filters.
- Downsample late in the architecture for the convolution layers to have a larger activation map. To improve the classification accuracy, the authors of SqueezeNet decreased the stride with later convolution layers, and therefore created a larger activation/feature map.

 The original paper can be found here:
https://arxiv.org/abs/1602.07360.

MobileNets

MobileNets is a class of efficient CNNs targeted to mobile and embedded applications. It was proposed by the Google research team in *MobileNets: Efficient Convolutional Neural Networks for Mobile Vision Applications*, 2017. In comparison to the traditional CNN, it has much less parameters, and requires much less computation of the learning and prediction process. This makes it faster and lighter, preserving the predictions accuracy at the same time. The main innovation was the introduction of depth-wise separable convolutions: `http://machinethink.net/blog/googles-mobile-net-architecture-on-iphone/`.

 The original paper can be found here: `https://arxiv.org/abs/1704.04861`.

ShuffleNet

ShuffleNet architecture was proposed in 2017 by the research team from Face++ (Megvii Inc.). It is targeted on mobile devices with limited computation power (for example, 10 - 150 MFLOPs). In comparison to the classical CNN, ShuffleNet has less parameters and performs less computations, because it uses pointwise group convolution and channel shuffle; for instance, it works 13x faster than AlexNet. The accuracy remains the same: on ImageNet, it even performs slightly better (top-1 error metric) than MobileNet.

 The original paper can be found here: `https://arxiv.org/abs/1707.01083`.

CondenseNet

CondenseNet was proposed by Gao Huang, Shichen Liu, Laurens van der Maaten, and Kilian Q. Weinberger. It reaches unprecedented levels of efficiency by combining dense connectivity between layers with a mechanism to remove unused connections, and therefore enables reuse of features within the network. CondenseNet is believed to be much more efficient than the state-of-the-art compact convolutional networks, such as MobileNets and ShuffleNets.

Refer to this: *CondenseNet: An Efficient DenseNet using Learned Group Convolutions*, Gao Huang, Shichen Liu, Laurens van der Maaten, Kilian Q. Weinberger, November 25, 2017: `https://arxiv.org/abs/1711.09224`.

Preventing a neural network from growing big

To leverage cutting-edge deep learning networks on mobile platforms, it becomes extremely important to effectively tune the learning of a network such that we can do the most with the least resources. The implementation of the neural network for OCR by the Google Translate team is an interesting one to understand the few thumb rules to circumvent the network from growing too big.

Following are excerpts from the press release from Google, found at: `https://translate.googleblog.com/2015/07/how-google-translate-squeezes-deep.html`:

"We needed to develop a very small neural net, and put severe limits on how much we tried to teach it-in essence, put an upper bound on the density of information it handles. The challenge here was in creating the most effective training data. Since we're generating our own training data, we put a lot of effort into including just the right data and nothing more. For instance, we want to be able to recognize a letter with a small amount of rotation, but not too much. If we overdo the rotation, the neural network will use too much of its information density on unimportant things. So we put effort into making tools that would give us a fast iteration time and good visualizations. Inside of a few minutes, we can change the algorithms for generating training data, generate it, retrain, and visualize. From there we can look at what kind of letters are failing and why. At one point, we were warping our training data too much, and '$' started to be recognized as 'S'. We were able to quickly identify that and adjust the warping parameters to fix the problem. (Good, 2015)"

Here are the key takeaways from the above notes:

- Limit the learning capacity by limiting the variations within the training data.
- Effective training data can be created by augmenting only a small rotation in the images. Larger rotations would result in increased learning, and therefore increased size.
- Extensively leverage visualization to quickly fix incorrect results from the network.

What general rules can we derive from these revelations?

- Put an upper bound for the model size. This will limit the capacity of your model.
- Create the most effective training data and make the task of you network as simple as possible. For example, if neural network is recognizing the characters in the photo, add to the dataset letters rotated just a bit, but don't make it to learn characters flipped upside-down or mirrored. If you are creating your dataset by data augmentation, put efforts in keeping the dataset clean, so the network is not learning anything except things it needs to know.
- Which characters you can neglect? For example, you can let the network recognize "5" and "S" as the same character and handle the problem on the level of the dictionary.
- Be sure to visualize, what is going on inside of your network, and in which places it has problems. What characters it confuses the most often?

Lossy compression

All lossy methods of compression involve a potential problem: when you lose part of the information from your model, you should check how it performs after this. Retraining on the compressed model will help to adapt the network to the new constraints.

Network optimization techniques include:

- **Weight quantization**: Change computation precision. For example, the model can be trained in full precision (float32) and then compressed to int8. This improves the performance significantly.
- Weight pruning
- Weight decomposition
- Low rank approximation. Good approach for CPU.
- **Knowledge distillation**: Train a smaller model to predict an output of the bigger one.
- Dynamic memory allocation
- Layer and tensor fusion. The idea is to combine successive layers into one. This reduces the memory needed to store intermediate results.

At the moment, each of them has its own pros and cons, but no doubts, that more perfect techniques will be proposed in the closest future.

- **Kernel auto-tuning**: Optimizes execution time by choosing the best data layer and best parallel algorithms for the target Jetson, Tesla, or DrivePX GPU platform
- **Dynamic tensor memory**: Reduces memory footprint and improves memory reuse by allocating memory for each tensor only for the duration of its usage
- **Multi-stream execution**: Scales to multiple input streams, by processing them in parallel using the same model and weights

Optimizing for inference

Get rid of elements of a graph that are only used for back propagation, and are useless for inference.

For example, batch normalization layers can be merged with the preceding convolution layers into one layer, because both convolution and batch normalization are linear operations.

Network pruning

The general idea behind this method is that not all weights in the neural network are equally important. So, we can reduce the size of the network by throwing out unimportant weights. Technically, this can be done in the following way:

1. Train a large network:
   - Leverage any previously trained network, say, VGG16, and retrain only the fully connected layers
2. Rank the filters, or create a sparse network based on a criteria:
   - We could rank each filter by using any feasible criteria (say, Taylor Criteria), and pruning the lowest-ranking filters, or alternatively, replace all the values less than a certain threshold, with zeros resulting in a sparse network
3. Fine tune and repeat:
   - Perform several iterations of training on the sparse network

The tricky question here is how to decide which networks are not important enough. This can be solved in the same way as we usually choose our hyperparameters: check several thresholds, and compare the quality metrics of the resulting networks.

Be sure to perform several rounds of training on the pruned model to allow it to fix the damage you caused.

Weights quantization

To 8 bits or less.

Weights quantization allows to decrease the size of the model, but at expense of prediction accuracy. In any case, it requires the same amount of memory during the runtime. For quantization any general purpose clustering algorithm can be used, for example, k-means.

Standard clustering algorithms applied to the weights. By this we replace all this floating-points numbers with a few bits, representing its cluster. 1 floating point per cluster. Retrain again.

```
https://petewarden.com/2016/05/03/how-to-quantize-neural-networks-with-
tensorflow/
```

```
https://github.com/tensorflow/tensorflow/tree/master/tensorflow/contrib/
quantization
```

Reducing precision

Another simple approach to reduce the size of the network is to directly convert weights from double/float data type to another with lower memory size, or to a fixed precision. This (almost) doesn't affect quality of predictions, but allows to reduce the size of the model up to four times.

Reducing precision of the network is exclusively focused only after the training is complete. Previously, attempts to train a network with lower precision data types have been experimented, and the results indicated difficulties in handling the back propagation and gradients.

Once the network is trained, we could right away replace double by float, or even better, by fixed precision. For example, in the trained neural network, you have double weights like this:

```
0.954929658551372
```

It's highly unlikely that the neural network encodes something meaningful in all those numbers after the point. So, if you drop most of them, converting to float, nothing changes: 0.9549297. The neural networks are stable enough to deal with that kind of insignificant change. But even now, it looks like precision is too big. So, we can round it even more; for example, to 0.9550000. This will not decrease the size of a model in the memory, because weights are still float numbers; but it does reduce the size of your IPA binaries, because archiving can be more efficient. Also, compressed models will take less space on the disk.

Other approaches

Another popular approach to reduce the size of a neural network is via SVD. SVD is applied to pre-adjusted neural networks, and therefore reduces the number of parameters in the network. After reducing the number of parameters, an unconventional **backpropagation** algorithm is used to train the models restructured by SVD, which has lower time complexity than the conventional BP algorithm. Experimental results have shown almost 2x improved speed with zero loss in accuracy, and around 4x improvement with minor loss in accuracy.

Additional reading: you can explore several other approaches adopted by tech giants for the mobile platform:

- https://handong1587.github.io/deep_learning/2015/10/09/acceleration-model-compression.html
- https://research.googleblog.com/2017/02/on-device-machine-intelligence.html
- https://www.slideshare.net/embeddedvision/tensorflow-enabling-mobile-and-embedded-machine-intelligence-a-presentation-from-google

Facebook's approach in Caffe2

During the developer conference, Facebook had recently announced their approach to render cutting-edge art work on images and videos on the phone, while effectively leveraging the computing resources with a highly mobile-optimized deep neural network. The overall approach can be studied using the following visual (https://developers. facebook.com/videos/f8-2017/delivering-real-time-ai-in-the-palm-of-your-hand/):

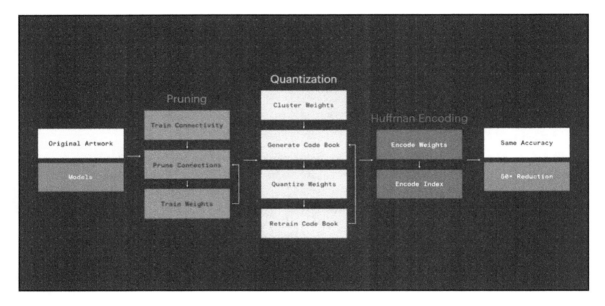

Figure 12.1: Facebook pipeline for compressing neural networks

Facebook used the following pipeline in their applications to achieve 50x size reduction, preserving the accuracy:

- Pruning
- Quantization
- Huffmann encoding, or standard general-purpose compression algorithms

Knowledge distillation

Knowledge distillation—you train your model to predict the logits of a more complex model. Use the large model's output as the ground truth to train the small model.

Additional reading:

- https://arxiv.org/abs/1503.02531
- https://www.slideshare.net/AlexanderKorbonits/distilling-dark-knowledge-from-neural-networks
- https://github.com/chengshengchan/model_compression/blob/master/teacher-student.py

Tools

The following are the tool is used for lossy compression:

TensorFlow compression tools

An example of the network compression

You can find suitable examples of the network compression at the following address:

https://github.com/caffe2/caffe2/issues/472

Summary

There are several ways in which we can achieve appropriate size for deep neural network deployment on mobile platforms. So far, the most popular are choosing the compact architecture, and lossy compression: quantization, pruning, and others. Make sure to check your network's accuracy hasn't degraded after the compression was applied.

Bibliography

1. O. Good, *How Google Translate squeezes deep learning onto a phone*, July 29, 2015:
   `https://research.googleblog.com/2015/07/how-google-translate-squeezes-deep.html`
2. Y. LeCun, J. S. Denker, S. A. Solla, R. E. Howard, and L. D. Jackel. *Optimal Brain Damage*. In NIPS, volume 2, pages 598–605, 1989

13
Best Practices

"The purpose of a storyteller is not to tell you how to think, but to give you questions to think upon."

– Brandon Sanderson, The Way of Kings

Imagine the field of AI as a huge national park. In previous chapters, we guided you along several exciting trails and showed you the most interesting sights for mobile developers. But there is still so much more that is unexplored. So, in this chapter, we want to provide you with a map of the common paths, from idea to production. We've outlined dangerous zones and left notes on solo hiking best practices! We also want to point out several interesting directions for your future exploration.

In this chapter, we will discuss the following topics:

- The path from idea to production
- Common pitfalls in machine learning projects also known as machine learning gremlins
- Machine learning best practices
- Recommended study resources

Mobile machine learning project life cycle

When developing a mobile machine learning product, you typically go through several stages:

- Preparatory stage

- Prototype creation
- Porting to a mobile platform or deployment of the trained model
- Production

Depending on your situation, your route may be shorter or longer; but usually, if you have skipped some stage, it just means that someone else did it for you. In the following explanation, we are omitting all the steps that are common to all kinds of mobile app projects and focusing only on the steps specific to machine learning.

Preparatory stage

This is the stage where you basically decide what you will do. There can be two possible outcomes for this stage: you have a plan on how to proceed, or you decide that you will not proceed:

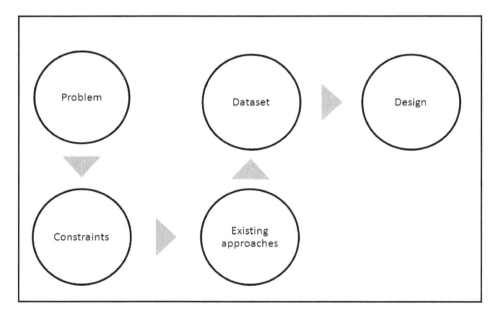

Figure 13.1: Preparatory stage map

Formulate the problem

If you can solve your problem without machine learning, don't use it. If the task can be solved with traditional programming techniques, congratulations! You don't need machine learning! Furthermore if your problem is of the kind where you can't allow errors, do not use machine learning.

For the start of your machine learning project, it is necessary to reduce a real-world problem to a machine learning task. Machine learning algorithms were developed by mathematicians and mostly tested on neat data in a controlled environment. You are fine if you can define your problem in terms of some existing machine learning approach: classification, regression, clustering, and so on. But to date, there are many problems that can't be easily adapted to the common machine learning blueprints. Among them are problems that require common sense reasoning and context understanding.

Define the constraints

It is easy to get lost in the variety of AI approaches. There is a set of constraints that will help you to focus and identify the optimal path to the solution. By answering the following questions to yourself, you will narrow the scope of your exploration significantly; or maybe, in some cases, you will conclude that the task is impossible (which is better to figure out at an earlier stage than a later one):

- What data can you use?
- What data should you not use?
- What should be the input and the output of your model?
- What is your desired accuracy or other measure of success? Remember that a machine learning algorithm will not be 100% accurate.
- Should the model be able to train on the target platform?
- How interpretable should your model be? Is it okay if your model is a black box?
- How much disk space and memory can your model consume in the training and inference stages? For example, the model shouldn't take more than 15 MB of disk space and more than 30 MB of RAM during inference.
- How fast should (or rather how slow can) the training and the inference be?
- What is your programming language and target platform?

Research the existing approaches

The key question here is, *how do other people solve similar problems?*

Can you use native iOS SDK to solve your problem? For example, if you want to detect people's faces in photos, you don't need to train your own neural network or Haar cascade. Just use the Vision framework instead. In other words, do not reinvent the wheel. Look for ready solutions that can work on the device or server side. For the most common daily tasks, you will find something appropriate.

Expanding the range of searches, perform a literature review. Even if you've not found ready solutions, you at least will get useful insights into the approaches and the domain specifics. The sites that will be handy at this stage are arXiv, Google Scholar, and GitHub. When you are done, you will have a clear understanding of classical and state-of-the-art approaches to the problem.

Even if you do not find a good enough solution, you will probably find a baseline solution to compare your future models with.

Research the data

If you have not found an existing solution and want to train your own algorithm, you will need a dataset.

Here, several scenarios are possible:

- You are feeling lucky, and you have found an existing dataset. The potential problem is that you may not be the only lucky person and your approach can be copied by others. There can also be licensing issues or other related problems.
- You collect or generate your own dataset.
- In the case of supervised learning, your dataset should be labeled. Hand-labeling is a laborious task, so it is often outsourced to some third-party services, such as Amazon Mechanical Turk.

Calculate how much will it cost to label your data in terms of time and money.

Another important thing to mention is that you should have a clear understanding of how the data was collected. This is important because the way of collecting data for model training can be significantly different from the way the same data will be collected in your app, and this will influence the results of your model's work. For example, if all the faces in the dataset were collected using a professional camera with perfect lighting conditions on a white background, do not expect your face recognition model to perform equally well on a mobile phone when the user has a bright window behind his/her back.

The question you should ask yourself is, "If I were a machine learning algorithm, would I be able to perform well, having this data?" If the data is insufficient, no algorithm will save the day. Remember that more data beats the better algorithm.

Make design choices

When you have a clear understanding of the goals, constraints, competing solutions, and your data, you can start with defining the technical specifics for your future model. The following questions should be answered before you implement your model:

- Is this a supervised or unsupervised learning problem? Classification or clustering? Discriminative or generative model?
- What is the measurement of success? What is your baseline solution and what are your benchmarks? How do you select the best model? In other words, what is the set of metrics that defines the best model?
- What is your strategy of model quality evaluation? Accuracy, precision-recall, cross-validation, or something else? This depends mostly on what costs more in your application domain: false positives or false negatives. Choose the quality metrics and set clear goals; for instance, precision shouldn't be less than 80%.
- Can the model be trained once and then do inference on all the devices or do you need to train a separate model for each client?
- Is data from one user enough for your model to operate or do you need to aggregate data from many users? This question will help you realize whether you need to put your model on server side.
- What is more important for you: accuracy or interpretability? For a classification problem, in the first case, you may want to go with neural networks or ensembles; in the second, you may want to go with decision trees or Naive Bayes.

- Do you need a probabilistic estimate? And just yes/no or 42% chance of yes and 58% chance of no?
- How do you clean your data? How do you choose good features?
- How do you split your data into training and test sets? 50/50? 90/10?
- Do you want your model to incorporate new data incrementally (online learning) or retrain the model on a whole bunch of data from time to time (batch learning)? Can your training data become outdated? How often does the environment in which your model operates change? Should it adapt or not?

Prototype creation

It is important to understand the difference between tools for prototyping and production, because very different requirements are imposed on the instruments during these two stages. Choosing the right tools for the right tasks will save you a lot of time.

During the prototyping phase, you want to be able to test your hypotheses and conduct experiments quickly. That is why it is reasonable to choose a flexible programming language within the reach of the environment, such as Python or R. You also want to have tools for data visualization and model debugging. This is something that the Swift ecosystem is still weak at. The matters of model size, speed, and stability may be secondary during prototyping (which doesn't mean that you should put them at the back of your mind). But when you are preparing your solution for production, you see those problems face to face, and in most cases, you have to rely on native, highly optimized libraries. In the search for a universal solution, you risk ending up with tools that work equally badly for both prototyping and production.

Implementing machine learning algorithms from scratch is a non-trivial task. Therefore, if it is possible, choose portable libraries (TensorFlow or OpenCV) or algorithms you know are already implemented for iOS. Otherwise, you will have to spend additional resources to reproduce algorithms written in Python on iOS:

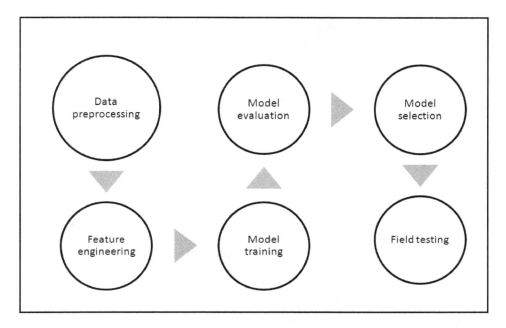

Figure 13.2: Prototype creation map

Data preprocessing

Start from simple data preprocessing. Be aware that usually data preparation takes 80% of a project's time. Maintain a clean repository with your data and tidy your data up. Remember, **garbage in, garbage out (GIGO)**!

Split the work into more or less independent chunks. Let's say you are writing an app for reading medical device indications via a phone camera to simplify nurses' work.

Write down separate chunks of work, their inputs, and outputs. In this way, you'll see which of them depend on each other and this also helps understand how to test each step. Table shows examples:

Serial number	Step	Input	Output
1	Device type recognition	Image	Device type
2	Device screen detection	Image	Vertices of a screen quadrilateral (points)
3	Perspective correction	Vertices of a quadrilateral, screen image	Screen image with the corrected perspective
4	Screen layout segmentation	Screen image, device type	Several images containing different elements of layout
5	Image preprocessing for OCR	Noisy images	Clean images
6	OCR	Images	Noisy text
7	Validation	Noisy text	Clean text

The data preprocessing pipeline should be documented. For example, if you are subtracting the mean and dividing your data by the standard deviation, when training your model, don't forget to write down exact values of the mean and standard deviation. This is a common problem with pre-trained neural networks on the internet. When authors forget to mention the preprocessing steps, the models became effectively useless.

For a classification task, dataset preprocessing usually includes engineering of informative features, class balancing, and missed values imputation. In the case of supervised learning, do not forget to split your dataset into three parts for the next stage: training set (most of your samples), test set, and validation set.

Model training, evaluation, and selection

Usually, it is better to start from simple and classical models because sometimes the simplest model performs the best. But this is just a rule of thumb, not a law of nature.

Every machine learning algorithm embodies some assumptions or prior knowledge about the data: KNN assumes that similar examples are of the same class, linear regression assumes linear dependencies and normally distributed errors, many models assume independence or limited dependencies between features or samples, and so on. This helps them to generalize behind the training data successfully. All these assumptions work only because the samples are not distributed uniformly across the space of all possible inputs, and there is something we can call pattern in the data. The task of the machine learner engineer/researcher is to know his data well enough to be able to make grounded assumptions about it. He chooses the algorithms based on those assumptions. What helps in practice is to ask yourself, "If I were in the place of my algorithm, would I be able to generalize well with such features, number of samples, and assumptions?" Think! What kind of knowledge do you have about the data? If you understand what precondition should be fulfilled for the sample to fall in one or another class (such as "if it has four paws, then this is a cat, but if it has..." then decision tree is your choice. If the similarity between instances is something that is quite well understood, then go for distance-based algorithms. If there is a lot of information about probabilistic dependencies in your data, try probabilistic graphical models.

The typical procedure for choosing the best model is as follows:

- Choose a set of models that look appropriate for your task. For example, for classification, this can be: KNN, logistic regression, decision tree, neural network, and so on.
- Use the training set to train your models and test set to validate their accuracy; adjust their hyperparameters (number of neighbors for KNN, number of decision tree splits, and number and types of layers for NN).
- When you have a set of trained models, choose the best among them using the validation set.

Once again, from the dataset perspective:

- **Training set**: To train all your models.
- **Test set**: To evaluate your models during the training phase, while you're still adjusting different hyperparameters.
- **Validation set**: To measure the ultimate accuracy. This one should be kept separate from the other two until the final choice between the set of models has been made.

The last one is important because you can overfit to both training and test sets by adjusting hyperparameters multiple times.

We do not recommend using ensembles of models on mobile devices as they usually take a lot of resources. Before you decide to go with one, check whether the same performance can or can't be reached if you put the same amount of effort in data collection, cleansing, and feature engineering.

Work iteratively; try one set of algorithms and features, then another. Keep records about the results of each iteration. Set seeds for random number generators in order to be able to reproduce your own results later.

All your business problem formulation ultimately converges to one question, "What loss function you are optimizing?" It is important to remember that learning is the process of adjusting the model to the data in a way that minimizes the loss function. So, if the loss function was chosen carelessly, the results can be far from what your real goals are.

Field testing

This is an important stage because it reveals the biases you have in your training data, the user's perception of your product, and other potential pain points. Try to check the model in the most realistic scenarios and conditions. Suppose you are developing a voice assistant. How will it work:

- On a noisy street when the wind is blowing?
- When a child is crying in the background?
- When some music is playing?
- When the user is not a native speaker or is getting emotional or drunk? Well, those may be the users who need your assistance the most!
- In all of these cases together?

If your solution is security-related, how good is it in the event of an active attack by an adversary? How easy is it to unlock your touch ID with the help of an orange, or cheat your face recognition by presenting it with a photo?

Having all those observations, you then go back and update your dataset and models accordingly.

Porting or deployment for a mobile platform

The next logical step is deploying your solution on a mobile platform (or platforms). Here, you have several considerations:

- Model memory consumption
- Data memory consumption
- Training speed (if you need on-device training)
- Inference speed
- Disk space consumption
- Battery consumption

You can profile all of this using Xcode instruments.

 For information on Swift code speed optimization check out this guide: *Writing High-Performance Swift Code*, at: `https://github.com/apple/ swift/blob/master/docs/OptimizationTips.rst`.

If your application includes several pre-trained models, for example, neural artistic style filters, you can use on-demand resources to store those models on the App Store and download them only when they are needed, not in the process of app installation. The On-Demand Resources Guide explains:

"On-demand resources are app contents that are hosted on the App Store and are separate from the related app bundle that you download. They enable smaller app bundles, faster downloads, and richer app content. The app requests sets of on-demand resources, and the operating system manages downloading and storage. ...
The resources can be of any type supported by bundles except for executable code."

As of spring 2017, App Store allows you to store up to 20 GB of on-demand resources. You also can define which resources will be purged when the OS hits the limit of disk space.

You can find more details about this technology and how to adopt it in your application here: `https://developer.apple.com/library/content/documentation/FileManagement/Conceptual/On_Demand_Resources_Guide/index.html`.

In the previous two chapters, we discussed questions of model acceleration and compression in more detail.

It is good to make sure in advance that your model is easily portable for mobile platforms. For example, suppose you've decided to train a model with one of the frameworks and convert it to a Core ML format for iOS deployment. Before training a complex neural network for a week on a GPU server, verify that untrained network with this architecture can be converted by `coremltools`. In this way, you will avoid disappointment later when you figure out that `coremltools` doesn't support one of the layers in your super-cool architecture. Actually, Core ML now supports custom layers, but do you really want to write one if you can replace it with something more traditional? You can call your solution portable only if porting costs much less than rewriting from scratch.

Production

Some machine learning models require regular updates due to the changing nature of their environment; others do not. For example, language changes faster than human appearance, but fashions change even faster. In fraud detection systems, a constant arms race between defenders and attackers goes on, and both sides try to be creative. The problem of a changing environment is known as concept drift. The wrong word problem of the model getting irrelevant over time is known as model decay.

How can you tackle these problems? There are several possible ways:

- Periodically retrain your model
- Use online learning algorithms to incorporate new data and drop the old one: an example algorithm is KNN
- Use algorithms that allow you to weigh the importance of your data and assign highest importance to recent data

Best practices

In this section, we've collected some general ideas worth keeping in mind during the whole development process.

> It's impossible to collect all important thoughts in one place, so here is a list of some really insightful guides from seasoned machine learning engineers on the best practices they recommend:
>
>
>
> - *A Few Useful Things to Know about Machine Learning* by Pedro Domingos,
>   at: https://homes.cs.washington.edu/~pedrod/papers/cacm12.pdf
> - *Best Practices for Applying Deep Learning to Novel Applications* by Leslie N. Smith, at: https://arxiv.org/abs/1704.01568
> - *Rules of Machine Learning: Best Practices for ML Engineering* by Martin Zinkevich,
>   at: http://martin.zinkevich.org/rules_of_ml/rules_of_ml.pdf
> - *Best Practices for Machine Learning Applications* by Brett Wujek, Patrick Hall, and Funda Güneş,
>   at: https://support.sas.com/resources/papers/proceedings16/SAS2360-2016.pdf

Benchmarking

When you are creating a model for solving a popular machine learning task, how do you know it is any better than anything else that has been invented by your predecessors? The answer is one word: benchmarks.

There are some well-known datasets that serve to compare accuracy across different models. For instance, for the task of large-scale visual object classification, a benchmark is the ImageNet dataset.

Privacy and differential privacy

Surprisingly, in the last few years, most scientific papers where mobile devices and machine learning were mentioned together were not about computer vision or natural language processing. The topics discussed the most were information security and privacy. These two fields intersect in several scenarios:

- The attacker employs offensive machine learning as a part of his/her toolkit. It can be used for discovery and analysis of vulnerabilities or for the attack itself. Examples are face or voice recognition for surveillance and finding data leaks in an improperly anonymized data.
- Defensive machine learning is used to protect against cyber attacks. It can be utilized for both threat detection and analysis. An example is fraud detection algorithms in banks and antivirus software.
- Adversarial machine learning is a setting when algorithm itself is under attack. Examples are search engine optimization (SEO) – tricking search engines and conversion rate optimization (CRO) – tricking spam filters.

Now, if machine learning is used to maximize the spam emails open rate, it is clearly an adversarial setting; but both the offender and defender are armed with machine learning, so all three scenarios meet in one place.

In the context of mobile security, machine learning has been used for:

- User authentication based on different features: voice, face, gait, signature, and so on
- Side-channel attacks: speech recognition, key logging, and stealing passwords using only motion sensor data
- Manipulating with voice assistants using noises unintelligible for humans
- Tricking image classification algorithms into mislabeling one object as another
- Extracting all kinds of personal information from a user's photo library: documents, bar codes, NSFW photos, credit card info, and so on

The last example is especially troubling because in iOS, any app that has access to the photo library has an access to all of the user's photos, including those in the hidden folder. They can analyze it in any way without limitations. All this leads to the conclusion that at the moment, offensive machine learning on mobile devices prevails over defensive learning and it is restricted only by the attacker's imagination and battery consumption.

Outside of the mobile development domain, machine learning is routinely used for surveillance, obtrusive targeted advertising, mining social media for personal information, and other ethically questionable practices. This is a problem that doesn't have technical solution. Like almost any other powerful tool, machine learning comes with responsibility. The computer can only optimize the objective function; the human is the one who chooses the function to optimize. Are you optimizing the revenue and number of items sold, or the quality of your products and well-being of your users?

At WWDC 2016, Apple officials brought up the topic of differential privacy in the context of machine learning. According to them, differential privacy is a major research topic and Apple is in the process of introducing differential privacy throughout the company's services. The idea here is to collect users' data but to add noise to it and aggregate it in such a way that information about any individual cannot be extracted.

 For more information on Apple's approach, check out the differential privacy overview document at: `https://images.apple.com/privacy/docs/Differential_Privacy_Overview.pdf` and the WWDC presentation at: `http://devstreaming.apple.com/videos/wwdc/2016/709tvxadw201avg5v7n/709/709_engineering_privacy_for_your_users.pdf`.

According to Apple, iOS has a 200 MB dynamic cache of personal information to train models right on the iPhone. That personal information includes app usage data, interactions with other people, and keyboard and speech input; it never leaves the device. Because the data does not have to travel over the network in this case, this is a good example of how mobile machine learning can decrease the potential cyber attack surface area and improve a user's security.

Researchers from Google also proposed a secure data aggregation protocol for machine learning. This was needed to implement the decentralized learning system—small local models are being trained on mobile devices and then they send an update to the big central model, which aggregates the experience of all the small models.

 This approach is known as federated learning. To learn more about it, check out the paper *Communication-Efficient Learning of Deep Networks from Decentralized Data*. H. Brendan McMahan et al, at: `https://arxiv.org/abs/1602.05629`.
Also visit the Google research blog: `https://research.googleblog.com/2017/04/federated-learning-collaborative.html`.

Debugging and visualization

When our usual code has a bug, it either doesn't work or works in the wrong way. When ML code has a bug, it often continues working but just degrades in quality. Because machine learning algorithms can be extremely complex, good debugging and visualization tools are of extreme value. For TensorFlow for example, such a tool is TensorBoard, which allows exploring model graphs, weight distributions, loss charts, and so on.

For now, humanity has not invented a better way to understand data than to visualize it. Often, 10 minutes of writing code for visualization lead to more insights than hours of debugging on a console. As Prof. Ben Shneiderman from the University of Maryland once noted in his talk:

> *"Statistics without visualization should be illegal."*

Documentation

Surely, it's better when your tool is so simple; it doesn't require a manual. And we all know the deeply rooted tradition of self-documenting code in the Objective-C community. But in the machine learning domain, code without documentation is often useless. Even when there is a documentation, results often cannot be easily reproduced because some exact values of hyperparameters or other seemingly small details are not known.

So, what exactly should be documented in your machine learning-related code? Most importantly:

- Data sources
- Preprocessing steps
- Combinations of features
- Model hyperparameters
- All tricks of the trade
- Error messages
- Loss functions
- Experiments
- Model checkpoints
- Random number seeds
- Quality metrics

Do not forget to put references to original research papers wherever appropriate. Try to avoid calling variables a, b, c, x, y, z, w, α, β, ρ, θ and so on in your code if those names come only from some formula that is directly referenced in the comments nearby.

Machine learning gremlins

Ben Hamner, a data scientist at Kaggle, referred to common machine learning gotchas as ML gremlins.

 You can watch Ben's original talk at: `https://www.youtube.com/watch?v=tleeC-KlsKA`.

I like the metaphor because it makes my brain think about evil characters rather than some vague, abstract concepts. In addition to the original gremlins presented by Ben, I want to add several of my own and also present a taxonomy of gremlins (see the following diagram). I employed this metaphor throughout this chapter to avoid boring issues and problems when discussing how to identify and neutralize those pests:

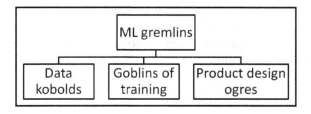

Figure 13.3: The simplified taxonomy of machine learning problems

Data kobolds

Dealing with data is hard; that's why we call it data science and data mining! Many different things can go wrong at different stages. Ben mentions data insufficiency, data leakage, non-stationary distributions, poor data sampling and splitting, data quality, and poorly anonymized data. Let's add a few more.

Tough data

Your data can be tough in a lot of ways: it can be sparse (in features or in target variable), it can contain outliers or missed values, or it can be high-dimensional or high-cardinal (for categorical features). Numerical features can be (and usually are) of different magnitude or suffer from multicollinearity. There is no bulletproof solution. Use force. Tidy your data up. The common techniques here are dimensionality reduction, missing values imputation, outlier detection, and statistical data normalization. Textbooks on statistics and data science will help you learn more on this topic.

Biased data

The Word2Vec algorithm (discussed in, `Chapter 10`, *Natural Language Processing*) is a good example of how easily cultural stereotypes and prejudices leak into machine learning models. For instance, vectors trained on the Google news corpus tell us that:

USA - Pizza + Russia = Vodka

While this may sound very funny for some people, this sounds equally offensive for many more. Is the algorithm biased? No, it is all in the dataset.

Another example of badly biased data was a web service based on a neural network that assessed a face's beauty by the photo. Apparently, all of the training data contained white faces, so the model was giving the lowest scores to all non-white faces. I truly believe that the developers had no bad intentions in training their model. They just did not pay enough attention to the variety of input data.

Batch effects

Usually, if you have to label a big dataset manually, you split it into manageable batches. Several people can then work in parallel on different portions. The problem here is that each of those people will introduce a different amount of variability in his/her batch. This is especially the case when subjective opinions are involved, such as "Is this movie review slightly positive or rather neutral?"

Batch effect is also a common problem for datasets that were compiled from several different sources. In many cases, batch effects become apparent when you plot the data obtained from different sources separately.

Goblins of training

In addition to overfitting, in this category fall problems with resource consumption, model interpretability, hyperparameter tuning, and so on. Most of them we have already discussed elsewhere in this chapter and other chapters.

Product design ogres

In his talk, Ben mentions only one of this kind: solving the wrong business problem. But there are so many more!

Magical thinking

I want to tell a story to illustrate the point. A friend of mine asked me to build a machine learning system for his startup because he believed it would solve some problem in his mobile app. I asked what data he has and he answered that they are planning to collect a lot of data from their users. They wanted to make highly personalized predictions for each of their users and right in time (precision, within minutes). "Okay," I said, "Imagine you have this kind of data about yourself, your wife, and your dog. Will it be useful to make correct predictions about me?" "No," he shook his head. "Now imagine you've just started collecting information about me. How much time would it take to start making reasonable predictions?" He looked disappointed. "So is it just a statistic? I thought it would figure out somehow on its own." Fortunately or not, machine learning has nothing supernatural in it. It will not create a solution for you in a miraculous way out of nothing. What it can do for you is to get more value from less data. These basic facts are sometimes not obvious to non-technical people.

Cargo cult

Somehow, it has happened that we live in a culture where technologies are a matter of fashion and objects of almost religious worship (think about tech evangelism, "changing the world," and tabs versus space wars). AI is on the peak of its popularity now. We often say, "Everybody does machine learning, so let us also build a neural network into our product and advertise it as artificial intelligence!" Undoubtedly, machine learning is an excellent hammer, but not all things around are nails. As you probably know, any product gets better if you add Bluetooth to it. However, this rule does not hold true for machine learning. The author of this book believes that there were too many great services that became inconvenient and unpredictable when machine learning was added to them. Rephrasing the famous quote by Jamie Zawinski about regular expressions:

> *"Some people, when confronted with a problem, think "I know, I'll use AI". Now they have two problems."*

Feedback loops

At a conference, a speaker talked about a new product that his company was developing. Airline sites, explained the speaker, change their ticket prices in a hardly predictable way depending on various indicators and using models known only to them. So the speaker and his colleagues collected the data on price trends from some airline sites and built a regression model. This would predict changes in ticket prices and provide users with advice on whether to buy a ticket for a flight at that time or wait to save money. One of the listeners (it wasn't me) raised a hand and asked: "What will happen when the airlines learn about your site and update their models to take into account your forecast?" The question took the speaker by surprise because this scenario was completely unforeseen by him. Setting aside the question of whether the airlines would actually take into account such a site, this is a good example of what is known in machine learning as a feedback loop. When your model's prediction affects the actual outcome, this can lead to one of two unwanted scenarios: self-fulfilling prophecy or self-negating prophecy.

A simple example: your system predicts what news will be of interest to the user. The user reads them, and the system remembers that the user is interested in such information. In fact, the user opened it not so much because he is engaged but because you showed it to him (self-fulfilling prophecy). So he had no other choice except to read what was presented or to close an app. As a result, after a few cycles, the recommendations become monotonous and so dull that the user stops using your application. The problem here is that the training data gets polluted by the model's predictions and the model gradually degrades.

How to deal with feedback loops? There's no way. Just do not create them.

Uncanny valley effect

The term uncanny valley initially appeared in the context of robotics and described the feelings people experience from interacting with humanoid robots. Starting from 1970, Japanese and Korean companies have been producing androids, copying an appearance of a person up to the slightest detail. The androids usually were the copies of some visually attractive models. However, it was observed that such robots seem to cause rejection because they induce associations with corpses or mentally-impaired people. At the same time, robots that did not try to imitate a person's appearance evoked sympathy from observers. Later the concept was extended to the area of 3D animation and video games, where uncanny valley was successfully employed to create scary characters:

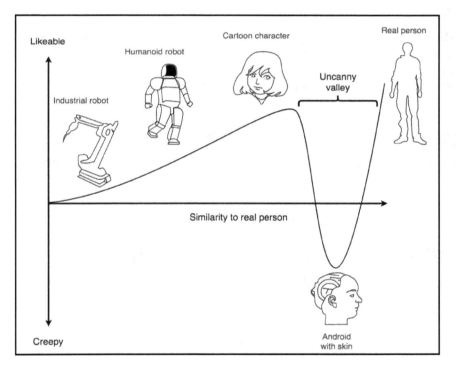

Figure 13.4: Uncanny valley effect. Picture by Mykola Sosnovshchenko.

Some authors apply the concept of uncanny valley in the context of AI systems, such as recommender systems and voice assistants. Systems simulating human behavior that are not believable enough can induce emotional rejection by users. Why? Let's try to figure it out.

Interactions between people are based on the ability to understand and predict each other's behavior. There are even specialized neurons in the brain (mirror neurons) that are responsible for this. You are greeting a person and hear the greetings in response, or you are telling a joke expecting that the listener will smile. If your companion does not respond to your greetings or reacts strangely to your jokes, you feel that something is wrong. Machine learning systems often behave insufficiently in this way. They are not predictable enough for human observers, which can cause a feeling of wrongness. For example, a news feed that is sorted by date or topic is similar to a room in which you know precisely where things are located. But if your news feed is sorted according to an unknown AI algorithm, it becomes similar to a mirage in the desert. There was a piece of news you were interested in, but now it has disappeared somewhere and you cannot find it, however hard you try.

Predictability is the basis of good user experience. There can be predictable randomness and then users are aware that something happens by pure chance. But even then, our brain is trying to find some patterns in those random events. If you call it AI, the creepy concurrences become even creepier: "Facebook AI algorithms recommend me the community "Books on shamanism," because I am in the AI community." My favorite example of uncanny NLP in action is a blog named *Weird Duolingo Phrases* that collects weird things that the app asks its user to translate.

Along the same lines, make sure that your personalized models do not produce a spooky user experience. If your app knows too much about the user, that may be a good reason to uninstall it.

Recommended learning resources

In this book, we've only scratched the surface of the immense body of knowledge behind the term machine learning. If you want to learn more, we highly recommend the following resources.

The main criteria for choosing the courses and books were clarity of presentation and a CS-oriented approach. Other criteria for the books were free online availability and open source code samples. All courses mentioned in this list are free (as of May 2017) and of introductory level.

Mathematical background

The handwritten comic-style lectures on Calculus by Robert Ghrist from the University of Pennsylvania can be found on YouTube or Coursera. This teaches single-variable calculus: Taylor series, Newton method. This should be your choice if you don't know how to take a derivative of a sigmoid function or which functions are differentiable. For more information refer to: `https://www.math.upenn.edu/~ghrist/`.

Coding The Matrix: Linear Algebra Through Computer Science Applications course and book by Philip N. Klein. Teaches linear algebra via Python examples and assignments: eigenvectors, eigenvalues, SVD, convolution, wavelet, and Fourier transform. For more information refer to: `http://codingthematrix.com/`.

Immersive Linear Algebra by J. Ström, K. Åström, and T. Akenine-Möller is an interactive online textbook found at: `http://immersivemath.com/ila/index.html`.

Open source textbooks, video lectures, and exercises on probability and statistics from OpenIntro. Also available as a Coursera course by Mine Çetinkaya-Rundel. Probability, Bayesian statistics, probability distributions, conditional probability, inference, confidence level, chi-square, ANOVA, regression, coding assignments in R. For more information refer to: `https://www.openintro.org/stat/`.

Machine learning

The Analytics Edge course from MIT at edX. Teaches applied data analysis in the R programming language, including classification, clustering, and data visualization through a set of real-world cases. Model quality evaluation, sentiment analysis. For more information refer to: `https://www.edx.org/course/analytics-edge-mitx-15-071x-3`.

Neural networks class—Université de Sherbrooke by Hugo Larochelle. Everything you want and don't want to know about neural networks. For more information refer to: `http://info.usherbrooke.ca/hlarochelle/neural_networks/content.html`.

Deep Learning by Ian Goodfellow, Yoshua Bengio and Aaron Courville: This is a deep learning book. Available online for free at the book's site at `http://www.deeplearningbook.org/`.

Programming Collective Intelligence by Toby Segaran. Code samples: `https://github.com/ferronrsmith/programming-collective-intelligence-code`.

Computer vision

CS 6476: *Introduction to Computer Vision* by Georgia Institute of Technology. Mathematically-light intro to computer vision with the coding assignment in MATLAB/Octave. For more information refer to: `https://www.udacity.com/course/introduction-to-computer-vision--ud810`.

CAP 5415: *Computer Vision* course by University of Central Florida. For more information refer to: `http://crcv.ucf.edu/courses/CAP5415/Fall2014/index.php`.

A classic textbook by Richard Szeliski, *Computer Vision: Algorithms and Application*, is freely available online: `http://szeliski.org/Book/drafts/SzeliskiBook_20100903_draft.pdf`.

CS231n: Convolutional Neural Networks for Visual Recognition course from Stanford University. Introductory course on convolutional neural networks with coding assignments in Python. For more information refer to: `http://cs231n.stanford.edu/index.html`.

NLP

CS224n: *Natural Language Processing with Deep Learning*. Coding assignments in TensorFlow. Word vector representations, LSTM, GRU, neural machine translation. For more information refer to: `http://web.stanford.edu/class/cs224n/`.

Summary

This was the final chapter of the book; so we discussed a machine learning app's life cycle, and common problems in AI projects and how to solve them. We also provided a list of good study material for further progress of our readers. We hope that you were not disappointed and wish you many successes in your own AI experiments!

Index

www.ingramcontent.com/pod-product-compliance
Lightning Source LLC
Chambersburg PA
CBHW080612060326
40690CB00021B/4670

* 9 7 8 1 7 8 7 1 2 1 5 1 5 *